DATE DUE

DATE DUE	
NOV 2 2 1991	
JAN 2 1 1992	
OCT 2 7 1993	
FEB - 5 1996	
FEB 1 9 1996	
APR - 9 1996	
BRODART, INC.	Cat. No. 23-221

CHRONICLE
OF
A REVOLUTION

CHRONICLE OF A REVOLUTION

A Western-Soviet Inquiry into Perestroika

ABRAHAM BRUMBERG
EDITOR

PANTHEON BOOKS

NEW YORK

Library of Congress Cataloging-in-Publication Data

Chronicle of a revolution : a western-Soviet inquiry into perestroika.
    Abraham Brumberg, editor.
        p.   cm.
    ISBN 0-394-57706-X
    1. Soviet Union—Politics and government—1985–   2. Perestroĭka.
    I. Brumberg, Abraham.
    DK286.5.C48   1990
    947.085′4—dc20   89-43242

Book Design by Robert Bull Design
Manufactured in the United States of America
First Edition

★

C O N T E N T S

CONTENTS
★

CHRONICLE
OF
A REVOLUTION

★

INTRODUCTION: LEAP INTO THE UNKNOWN

★

ABRAHAM BRUMBERG

CHRONICLE OF A REVOLUTION REPRESENTS a joint Western-Soviet effort to examine the wellsprings, direction, and implications of a momentous period in the history of the USSR. In late 1988, a prominent Soviet historian characterized perestroika as a "revolution from above."[1] The words seemed appropriate for a process that began as a series of bold reforms and gradually turned into an assault on some of the fundamental features of the Soviet system, but one still inspired and directed by a group of men at the top of the political pyramid. By now, with the assault rapidly escalating and embracing an increasing number of people from all walks of life, it has become at least as much a revolution from below as from above. Like any major upheaval, its course is uneven and its outcome unclear. But after nearly five years it is possible to identify its generative forces and those that urge it forward, which is precisely what the contributors to this volume set out to do.

Any analysis of an ongoing social and political process must be predicated on a set of assumptions that in turn proceed from a reasoned assessment of the past. Few if any Western students of Soviet affairs can claim to have foreseen the events of the last few years, from the revolt

3

against hallowed dogmas and the ruthless exposure of the country's history, to the explosion of ethnic and working-class unrest. The same is true for their Soviet colleagues. Many of them, including several contributors to these pages, have helped to lay the groundwork for perestroika and glasnost, but none had expected their efforts to yield such dramatic results.

On both sides of the divide, but above all in the West, where the study of the Soviet Union and other Communist countries and movements had acquired the status of a distinctive discipline, analysis and projection were based, broadly speaking, on either of two assumptions— one that in effect ruled out the prospect of significant changes in the structure of Soviet society and the Soviet system, and one that, on the contrary, postulated development and transformation. Since the principal essays in this book were written by Western scholars, it may be useful to begin with a review of these contrasting assumptions, if only to provide a framework for the many surprises that still await us in the future.

I

To speak of two groups of scholars invites the charge of oversimplification. While allowing for internal nuances and differences, it is nevertheless possible to draw a line between scholars subscribing to the "totalitarian" model and those to what might be called the "evolutionary" model of Soviet society. The first group regarded the Soviet state as a fixed entity, shaped both by Russian history and the imperatives of Marxist-Leninist dogma solely into an instrument of power and oppression. In this reading, the ruling apparat exercised unlimited control over every facet of public life. There was no room in it for autonomous social forces; any attempt to engage in unsanctioned activities was bound to be crushed by terror or bureaucratic fiat, or by a combination of both. The apparat justified its rule in the name of a presumably "scientific" doctrine that promised the end of history ("full communism") at whatever cost and regardless of the means used to attain it; its real objective was to maximize and perpetuate its power.

The totalitarian model long dominated official thinking, policy, and public opinion alike. It spawned a number of complementary theories (or if you will, "mini-models")—for instance, that Soviet communism

4

was rooted in the Russian "psyche," or in the country's "Asiatic mode of production," or in the "patrimonial" character of Russian political culture—or, to take a rather contrary notion, favored among others by Alexander Solzhenitsyn—that communism was a particularly noxious offspring of Western Enlightenment.[2] Each of these mini-models has had its own adherents; some flourished for a while and some have remained to this day, but one became, as it were, an integral part of the totalitarian model at large—namely, that the USSR (and by extension every other Communist regime) was innately expansionist, seeking world domination either through outright territorial aggrandizement or through "friendly" governments and pliable Communist parties. Since world domination was not altogether compatible with world revolution (another popular perception of Moscow's ultimate goal), the latter gradually came to be seen as little more than a subterfuge disguising Moscow's manipulation of revolutionary movements in its own geopolitical interests.

The idea that Moscow had no use for world revolution and little but contempt for its "brotherly allies" was grounded in irrefutable evidence.[3] To the critics of the totalitarian model, however, this was not tantamount to seeking world domination. No less intense in their abhorrence of Stalinism, they nevertheless regarded the totalitarian model as being, as a whole, starkly at odds with reality. The view of a society entirely at the mercy of a despotic regime and bound by a rigid ideology failed to take into account important social changes that had taken place even under the reign of Stalin. It led to a disproportionate emphasis on the techniques of rule and control, on the mechanics of terror, or on the content of ideological pronouncements, and to the neglect of topics such as the social effects of urbanization and industrialization, the implications of the spread of literacy, and the relations among various ethnic groups—quite apart from the clash between Moscow's policies of russification and centralization and the aspirations of Soviet national minorities.

Similarly, the totalitarian model nurtured a view of international relations at once Manichean and conspiratorial: on the one hand, a power armed to the teeth and bent on subverting if not conquering other countries, on the other the "Free World" gallantly fighting for its survival. Much as the view of the Soviet internal system tended to gloss over features specific to different phases of Soviet history as well as the complex nature of the country's social fabric, so too did the perception of Soviet foreign policy tend to lump all non-Communist countries into one distinct group (the "Free World")—presumably characterized by a common commitment to "democracy," yet in fact embracing despotic states such as, say, South Africa and the murderous regimes in Guatemala and Salvador.

Moreover, since the Soviet system was both fundamentally immutable and evil, it followed that other Communist parties, Communist-ruled states, or for that matter any "left-wing" regimes should be combatted no less robustly than the USSR, whatever the indigenous circumstances such as economic misery and foreign or local oppression that had brought them into being. It followed, too, that any changes in the Soviet Union were either ephemeral, superficial, or—most likely— elaborate deceptions.

Hence the widespread conviction following Stalin's death in 1953 that he would soon be succeeded by another bloodthirsty tyrant. Hence, too, the dismissive attitude toward Khrushchev's "thaw," the turmoil within international communism, or the first signs of a Soviet-China rift. None of them—so it was claimed—was important; none would alter the basic, that is to say totalitarian, nature and policies of the USSR.

II

The criticisms of the totalitarian model emanated, of course, from the adherents of the evolutionary school of thought. Less numerous than the "totalitarians," their impact on public opinion and Western policy was correspondingly smaller. The central contention of this school of thought was that the Soviet Union, despite its authoritarian traditions and consummate structure of social, political, and cultural controls, was no less subject to change—however slow—than any other society. It rejected the view of Soviet society as rigid and changeless. Its practitioners—historians, political scientists, economists, and others—produced works of lasting scholarly significance, many of them aimed at depicting the processes that were stirring and reshaping a seemingly ossified society. However, their impact on popular perceptions was, to repeat, limited.

The situation began to change after Stalin's death. Once the "thaw" began to reveal contradictions and fissures in Soviet society, in the East European countries, and within the international Communist movement, the static image of the Soviet system had to be revised, however circumspectly. In the USSR, intellectuals split into warring "liberal" and "conservative" camps. Social unrest beset Poland, East Germany, Hungary, and Czechoslovakia; less conspicuously, it even affected workers in the Soviet Union itself.[4] Fierce ideological quarrels led to the breakup of the international Communist movement, once blindly loyal to the USSR, and to the collapse of the Sino-Soviet alliance. With the emergence of wildly different Communist regimes, from Albania and Cambodia at one end of the spectrum to countries such as Poland and Hungary at the other, and with even Castro's Cuba challenging Moscow's hegemony over the "national liberation struggle," the concept of a "Soviet" or "Communist" bloc, too, seemed tenable no longer.

What to some were palpable signs of continuous ferment was dismissed by the "totalitarianists" as cosmetic or, at best, "within-system changes." To invest them with any significance was not only fallacious but positively dangerous, for it led to a grave underestimation of the inherent stability and malevolence of communism.[5] Nowhere was this attitude more pronounced than in foreign policy (see the essays by David Holloway, Yuri Davydov, and Sergo Mikoyan). The US involvement in Vietnam, with its espousal of the domino theory and relentless preoccupation with credibility, illustrated the popular notion of the Soviet "drive for world domination." (Only toward the end of the war was China, ostensibly North Vietnam's mentor and ally, cast in the role of the principal culprit.)

Similarly with the widespread US perception of left-wing movements in Latin America: fear that Allende's victory in Chile threatened the stability of the entire Western hemisphere, or that the Sandinista army in Nicaragua was about to establish a Soviet beachhead on the doorstep of the United States testified to the strength of the belief in the "Soviet peril." Just as Stalinist theory regarded social democracy as a "tool of Western imperialism," so has much Western opinion tended to see every upheaval in the Third World as a product of Moscow's machinations—indeed, as little more than a tool of Soviet imperialism.

Various developments in the late 1960s and 1970s helped to feed this somber vision. In the Soviet Union, the Khrushchev reforms were followed by the Brezhnev counter-reforms. True, there was no return to Stalinism. In fact the future contours of perestroika were adumbrated during the Brezhnev era (see the chapter by S. Frederick Starr). But since these efforts were not always visible to the naked eye, they earned less attention than the tangible departures from the policies initiated under Khrushchev, at the same time lending more credibility to the contention that those policies had been insignificant in the first place. A closer examination of the twenty-year interregnum between Khrushchev and Gorbachev (and some did in fact examine it) would have revealed not only the reversals, but the cumulative effects of the advances scored in freedom of expression, in legality (see the chapter by William Butler), in economic experimentation (see Alec Nove's essay), or in the argument among party intellectuals over basic political concepts (see the chapter by Archie Brown).

Furthermore, the proponents of the evolutionary model pointed out that the various repressive acts implemented by Brezhnev and his immediate successors were in effect a measure of the growing assertiveness within Soviet society. Thus the writers who were jailed or exiled for "defaming" the Soviet Union would not have dared to send their works abroad, even under the cover of a pseudonym, a mere ten years earlier. Dissidents were persecuted under Brezhnev; but before Brezhnev, neither samizdat nor a dissident movement had even existed.

For all that, the post-Khrushchev era seemed one of reaction, retrenchment, and decay. In the Soviet Union, corruption reached the highest circles of power, with party apparatchiks living high off the hog, striking deals with criminal mafias, and keeping their subjects in near-bondage (see essay by Ronald Suny and commentaries by Leonid Batkin and Otto Latsis). In Eastern Europe, successive revolts were crushed either by Soviet troops (as in 1968 in Czechoslovakia) or by local Communist armies (as in Poland in 1970 and again in 1981). Soviet policy towards the West was guided by confrontation, "ideological struggle," and obstinate attempts to expand Soviet influence. The general impression, then, was of a system tenaciously and on the whole effectively resistant to change.

This not only reinforced the appeal of the totalitarian model; it also helped to erect something of a bridge between its disciples and the evolutionists. The first called attention to the elements of continuity in Soviet history while the others stressed the elements of change. The first pointed to the durability of institutions such as the secret police and the one-party state, to the resistance to any proposals aiming at decentralizing the command-administrative economic system, or to Moscow's relentless attempts to fish in foreign waters. The others took a more agnostic view of Soviet power, foreign-policy objectives, and military capability (see chapter by David Holloway).

8

Nonetheless, the evolutionists generally accepted as a truism that there are built-in limits to change in Communist-ruled societies. They insisted that any attempt to define these limits must take into account distinctions between one Communist country and another. Poland was palpably an example of Communist tolerance *in extremis*. No other Communist regime allowed the existence of so powerful a rival as the Catholic Church, no other Communist country boasted so much intellectual and cultural freedom, and no Communist government acquiesced to so large a private agricultural sector as did Poland under Communist rule. Latitudinarianism was obviously broader and more flexible in Poland than, say, in Czechoslovakia, whose post-1968 leadership was clinging fiercely to its power and *modus operandi*, or in Rumania, where Balkan nepotism was flourishing cheek by jowl with a particularly doctrinaire brand of "Marxist-Leninist" orthodoxy. But all these societies, irrespective of the differences between them, could tolerate only so much modification and freedom—and no more.

It is here that the followers of both schools of thought met on common ground. No Communist regime, everybody agreed, would tolerate a challenge to the "leading role of the party," which in plain language meant the monopoly of power and control exercised by the ruling elite. No Communist government could countenance a free and open press that would inevitably disseminate potentially dangerous doctrines and no less dangerous facts. No ruling Communist party would permit the formation of groups or associations likely to become nuclei of organized political opposition. To the proponents of the totalitarian model, virtually any political pluralism in a Communist state was unthinkable. To the evolutionists, the gradual growth of pluralism was a distinct possibility, but not the kind of pluralism that might offer alternatives to the principle of a one-party state. These were what Lenin had called the "commanding heights" which no Communist government could ever be expected to cede.

III

Which brings me to the present—and to this volume.

Barely two years before the onset of perestroika, Indiana University Press published a collection of essays under the title of *After Brezhnev: Sources of Soviet Conduct in the 1980s*.[6] The contributors, all distinguished experts, trained their sights on the impending "succession crisis" in the USSR; and all agreed, in the words of its editor, that the new younger leadership that would come to power after the eclipse of the Brezhnev oligarchy would opt for little more than "muddling through and muddling down." The "immobile" and "stubborn" nature of the system, said the editor (speaking for all the contributors), precluded any "fundamental changes," at least "until the 1990s," much as the ultimate survival of the Soviet Union depended on them.[7]

It is instructive, after nearly five years of perestroika and glasnost, to peruse this most comprehensive and thus most representative compendium of American Sovietological scholarship produced at a time when the question of whether and how the Soviet Union would evolve had become a matter of urgent concern, and to find that none of its contributors had been willing to consider the possibility that a new leadership would embark on a radically new course.[8] And it is legitimate to raise the question of why. Why had so many of our foremost specialists been so confident—and in a book "aimed at helping American policy respond effectively to . . . Soviet conduct in the 1980" at that—in forecasting simply more of the same?[9]

The answer, it seems to me, lies not only in the totalitarian model as such, but also in the methodology, in the analytical tools, and in the kind of questions it fostered. Old habits die hard, and even the staunchest critics of the totalitarian model sometimes lose sight of the fact that some of the conventional questions and categories are no longer pertinent to an unprecedented situation, which is to say to one for which there are no "models." Now that the Soviet Union is being propelled into altogether uncharted and once unthinkable terrain, those who had long maintained that the country was bound to alter and evolve (which includes, as the reader may have gathered, the contributors to these pages) may feel justifiably vindicated. Yet even the latter had not expected a steadily moving current to be transformed, within a few years, into a torrent toppling established verities no less than, to paraphrase Brezhnev's definition of Soviet socialism, "actually existing" institutions.

Can it be halted? How far can this revolution be allowed to go on? These are some of the questions that have been asked, and like so many other questions about the future, they must remain unanswered. More to the point, they stem from a traditional assumption that social and political processes in the USSR are subject to ultimate control from above, when in fact there is no longer any single ultimate authority that decides "how far" anything may go. As of this writing, some of the control mechanisms are still intact—for instance, a censorship apparatus that dictates the extent of foreign and domestic news coverage. But how much longer? The controls may be tightened—but not because "the authorities" decide one day that the media have gone too far, but because of what in Communist parlance is called "a shift in the correlation of forces," which is to say the ascendance of a particular group within the party or government apparat. But this, too, is not written in stone, recent events having demonstrated on more than one occasion how a defiant parliament can triumph over entrenched bureaucracies.[10]

In the meantime, the area of forbidden subjects is shrinking, and the barrier of fear is gradually crumbling. Indeed, a genuine civil society is on the rise in the USSR, a society in which conflicting interests, ideas, and institutions vie for influence and power. The reader will find this amply documented in this volume. In economics and in politics, in history, in foreign policy, in jurisprudence, and in literature, once sacrosanct notions are being replaced by a search for alternatives to traditional structures and official ideology.

What, for that matter, is today's "official ideology" and what constitutes heresy? These questions must haunt a party that had staked its legitimacy on a received doctrine, and they will have to be confronted sooner or later. On the other hand, the escalating revolution—or what Soviet writers had been fond of calling "life itself"—may render such exercise null and void. In 1989, a Soviet political scientist can advocate a vision of society more in common with social democracy than with Leninism (see Boris Kurashvili's commentary). By the time this book goes to press, more revolutionary ideas will have been proclaimed, to be superseded by even more extraordinary developments when it reaches the readers.

Nothing should surprise us any more. In her essay "History Reclaimed," Jutta Scherrer demonstrates how an initial reluctance to challenge the "founding fathers" has turned into a full-scale reappraisal if not revision of their basic texts. In his chapter on political changes, Archie Brown describes how genuinely independent political organizations have already taken root in the USSR and in the Baltic republics.[11] In the absence of scriptural or temporal authority, "official doctrine" has become merely one of the many clamoring for public support. All of which renders the term "heresy" no longer viable.

At a time of flow and flux, the once-popular tendency of Western observers to invest official statements with momentous significance has

11

become obsolete, no less than the once-popular "Kremlinological" approach, which sought to divine changes in Soviet policy by tracing the backgrounds of Soviet leaders, and the intricate web of personal loyalties and internecine quarrels. The method has its uses, but today, when political differences are no longer swept under a rug, and when public passions and openly voiced public opinion are apt to be more decisive than Byzantine intrigues, it can no longer play as important (or, in the eyes of its onetime practitioners, so crucial) a part as it did. Personal ties are still of analytical value—as they are in non-Communist systems. But to scan Soviet newspapers for hidden meanings or official photographs for clues as to "who stands where" or "who is against whom" (*kto kovo?*) is of little value at a time when party-approved candidates for high office are turned down by parliament members no longer subject to *diktat* and keen on asserting their prerogatives as freely elected representatives of the people.

Yet another tendency of some Western observers is to focus on demonstrable failures or shortcomings and overlook equally demonstrable achievements. This tendency is rooted in the assumption that nothing good can be expected of a basically irremediable system.[12] Like its opposite—uncritical admiration and praise—the propensity for worst-case scenarios is dictated more by ideology than dispassionate observation. Neither of these tendencies is of much help in assessing so complex and dynamic a process as the one proceeding apace in the USSR.[13]

What about Gorbachev's role in this process? When the final chronicle of the current chapter in Soviet history comes to be written, Gorbachev's achievement as its principal architect will no doubt be fully acknowledged. Without the active participation and support of thousands of people, of course, Gorbachev would not have been able to preside over perestroika and glasnost; but it is difficult to think of any other Soviet leader equal to this task. He can hardly be faulted for not having foreseen the elemental fury of the forces he had unleashed. History may well forgive him for his blunders and misjudgments, too, despite the dismay and even anger they have generated even among his once most loyal supporters (see the commentaries by Gavriil Popov and Leonid Batkin).

The "outer" or "built-in" limits are rapidly eroding, and the erosion is likely to affect Gorbachev, too. Not in the sense that he will be swept from power—though this, too, cannot be ruled out—but rather that he

INTRODUCTION: LEAP INTO THE UNKNOWN
★
ABRAHAM BRUMBERG

may eventually find himself unable to remain abreast or ahead of what he himself has come to call "revolutionary processes." The eclipse of the one-party system in Eastern Europe has resulted from indigenous factors such as economic decay, the ideological and political crises within the ruling parties, and last but not least the collapse of the "Brezhnev doctrine." But some of these factors, plus others (e.g., outright secessionist movements within various republics, and massive disorders engendered by the catastrophic decline in living standards and in the availability of the most elementary consumer goods) may produce similar results in the Soviet Union.

Gorbachev, in his understandable desire both to overhaul and to save the system may find that the two tasks are irreconcilable, and that in the end restructuring—perestroika—has left few of the original structures intact. Or he may yet come to play a role similar to the one played in the 1970s by King Juan Carlos of Spain, who successfully led his country through the transition from dictatorship to democracy. His personal fate is as unpredictable as is the denouément of all the remarkable processes traced in the pages ahead.

I V

A few remarks about the structure of this book.

Part One consists of eight essays by Western writers. Each examines the origins and character of a given area of Soviet society and policy affected by perestroika and glasnost. The authors address themselves to the following questions: What impelled Gorbachev and his allies to launch radically new policies? How do they differ from previous attempts to rectify the Soviet system (primarily the Khrushchev "thaw")? What do they seek to achieve? How have they changed in the course of the past few years? What are they likely to bode for the future? Of the eight chapters, "The Road to Reform," by Frederick S. Starr, deals only with the immediate prehistory of perestroika and glasnost, and Vera Dunham's "Lyrics: The Pain of Discovery" explores only one facet of the cultural scene—contemporary Russian poetry.

Part Two, "From the Other Shore" consists of ten commentaries by eminent Soviet scholars and journalists. Each of the authors takes one of the Western essays as a point of departure for his or her own reflections. Boris Kurashvili offers his views on the evolution of the Soviet political system and on what he considers the most desirable form of a socialist society. Alec Nove's essay on the Soviet economy is the subject of the commentaries by Otto Latsis and Gavriil Popov. Arkadi Vaksberg comments on the Soviet legal system and Roy Medvedev on the contemporary state of Soviet historiography, as well as on his own role in it. Julian Bromlei and Leonid Batkin provide different perspectives on the nationalities problem in the USSR, and Natalya Ivanova offers a survey of contemporary Russian poetry. Finally, Yuri Davydov and Sergo Mikoyan examine the implications of David Holloway's topic— the "new thinking" and new directions of Soviet foreign policy. The commentaries are not "typical" of Soviet views, if only because (to repeat) there is no single view in the Soviet Union today, official or unofficial. Rather, they reflect a range of opinions, approaches, and beliefs that illustrates the richness of contemporary intellectual discourse in the USSR. The book, then, is something of a dialogue between Western and Soviet scholars. As such, I should like to think of it as one more page in the chronicle of the current revolution—and one of many that may come to be seen as part of the natural order of things.

I should like to express my thanks to my wife, Josephine Woll, for her generous editorial advice and assistance in translating some of the Russian manuscripts, especially Natalya Ivanova's commentary, to Antonina Bouis for her translation of Leonid Batkin's commentary and for keeping my lines to Moscow open, and to all my contributors, in the United States, Great Britain, France, and the USSR, for so valiantly putting up with the demands of the subject and of the editor.

—October–December 1989

PART ONE

THE LAY
OF
THE LAND

★

★

THE ROAD
TO REFORM

★

S. FREDERICK STARR

THE SOVIET REFORMS OF THE LATE 1980S
were prompted by a general crisis in the Soviet bloc and in Moscow's
relations with the outside world. The protracted and increasingly feckless
war in Afghanistan; plummeting world prices of oil, the USSR's chief
export; Soviet blunders in arms-control negotiations with the United
States; the effect of the Chernobyl disaster on public opinion in the West;
abortive attempts to expand Soviet influence in Africa and Latin America—these and other developments contributed to the steady erosion of
Soviet power and prestige in the international arena. At home, there was
a growing mood of doom and gloom caused, among other things, by
poor grain harvests, sagging industrial productivity, massive corruption
in the party and state apparats, and a pervasive sense of alienation within
the intelligentsia. Never since the death of Stalin had the USSR experienced so much strain, and never since 1953 had it been more ripe for
reform.

The "reform package" introduced in 1985 is of course linked with
the new leadership that came into power in that year. But the specific
policies contained in the package did not spring full-blown from Gorbachev's mind, though it is under his skillful leadership that they are

17

being promoted. In fact, many of the principal elements of perestroika had already been adumbrated and discussed first under Khrushchev, and even more so, odd as it may seem, during Brezhnev's "period of stagnation." Indeed, it was precisely under Brezhnev that the discussions expanded to embrace a growing number of topics and participants. The latter can be broken into two groups: at one end, government officials, prominent economists, political scientists, and foreign affairs experts; and at the other independent individuals and informal groups of dissidents writing for samizdat. While the unofficial and dissident voices were more outspoken in their views and prescriptions, their concerns were essentially the same as those of the first group.

Only part of this reformist dialogue was carried out in the mass media. The most radical proposals were aired in esoteric publications enjoying little or no general readership.[1] Hence, it is no wonder that reform never constituted the main theme of policy or discourse under the Brezhnev oligarchy. It was, rather, a kind of countermelody that wove in and around official policy throughout the 1970s and emerged fully only under the impact of crises in the 1980s. Yet it was this reformist dialogue that largely defined Gorbachev's agenda.

A simple example will illustrate the relationship between the current reforms and the period of the 1970s. During his first two years in office, Gorbachev mounted a fierce campaign for greater sobriety and discipline as a key solution to the ills plaguing Soviet society. Much debated in journalistic articles in the early 1980s,[2] the idea of such a campaign had preoccupied KGB head Yuri Andropov since his elevation to the Politburo in 1973. Gorbachev encountered this notion in the press and among members of Andropov's entourage in Moscow. After being named general secretary, he made it a key element of his own initial reform program. When this campaign eventually failed, Gorbachev replaced it with other policies that were similarly drawn from the debate of the 1970s.

THROUGH THE GLASS, DARKLY

The reformist dialogue embraced many contradictory positions and was more a grab bag of ideas than a coherent program. Such consistency as it possessed lay not in its conclusions but in the seriousness with which all parties to the dialogue took cognizance of the grim realities of the 1970s. When the Club of Rome issued its 1972 study, *The Limits to*

Growth,[3] official Moscow claimed that the problem of diminishing resources pertained only to capitalism, not socialism. Soviet spokesmen repeated this view a half decade later when the Club of Rome issued a further study.[4]

Yet in 1976, when Soviet scholars carried out a socioeconomic analysis of the country's work force, they reached thoroughly gloomy conclusions about the country's labor pool.[5] Others recognized that capital for investment, too, had grown increasingly scarce, due both to low industrial productivity and to the shifting of resources into the military.[6] In addition, economists perceived for the first time the limits on the USSR's natural resources, despite those Moscow officials who so airily dismissed the Club of Rome report. Oil production sagged, but natural gas reserves proved difficult to exploit. Mounting environmental concerns raised the price of tapping other energy and mineral resources. Siberian specialists warned of the danger of diverting water to Central Asia, and *Izvestia* editorialized against the reckless exploitation of arable land.[7]

In short, Soviet realists acknowledged that all three of the essential inputs to the economy—labor, capital, and natural resources—were severely limited. The only recourse was to make more efficient use of existing inputs. And so "intensification," scarcely mentioned before the 1970s, became the catchword of writings on development during that decade and thereafter.

How was intensification to be achieved? Optimists in the Soviet Union hoped that the implementation of Andropov's proposals to tighten labor discipline would save capital and resources. Under Brezhnev's freewheeling oligarchy, however, such reforms were out of the question. More realistic was the plan to shift the emphasis from quantity to quality through the application of new technologies and techniques of management. Under the slogan of "high quality and effectiveness," Brezhnev embraced this appealingly conservative line. Building on foundations laid earlier by Aleksei Kosygin and the group of pragmatic managers who surrounded him, researchers sought rational and occasionally innovative solutions to current problems. While few such proposals were implemented, they nonetheless changed the way in which Soviet economists viewed their system.

For example, most economic decision-making had long been guided by Marxist formulae. Now rigorous cost-benefit analyses were brought to bear on at least a few economic issues, including decisions regarding the integration of the economies of the East European countries. Computer-generated models of the economy gave rise to proposals for new ways of measuring performance. An effort by economist Nikolai Petrakov to apply cybernetics to the Soviet economy was roundly criticized in the press, yet his emphasis on net profits—the bottom line— cut through reams of dogma.[8] In the same spirit, economists debated policy on prices, calling for greater flexibility and mobility.[9] No less fundamental in its implications was the fact that several experts called for basic changes in the incentive formulae governing firms and whole industries.[10]

The thrust of all these discussions was to cast serious doubt upon the existing system of centralized planning and control. Criticism of ministerial bungling became commonplace. The Siberian economist Abel Aganbegyan proposed reforms that would create large superministries, while others found more direct means of attacking centralization by stressing the need to be responsive to managers at the enterprise level.[11] Virtually every participant in the reformist dialogue assumed the path to improvement lay through administrative decentralization, although few were so bold as to advocate a market economy.

Tsar Nicholas I (1825–55) is remembered as an archreactionary, yet experiments at reform undertaken during his reign paved the way for the abolition of serfdom after his death. Brezhnev, too, though firmly clinging to the "command-administrative" system, nevertheless countenanced an important series of organizational "experiments" that dramatically anticipated Gorbachev's perestroika. The American economist Gertrude E. Schroeder has reviewed these experiments—the so-called Shchekino Plan, the Orel system, and others—and concluded they were "unprecedented in scope and intensity, in [their] effort to improve efficiency in the economy's use of resources and the quality of its products."[12] Most of these experiments followed the chemical factory at Shchekino near Tula in decentralizing decision-making within the ministries. Others went further and actually devolved managerial control to local elective bodies. The ideal of local self-government thus came to the fore as an alternative both to centralized ministerial rule and to bureaucratic decentralization.

The beneficiaries of plans for devolution were to be the long-moribund elective councils, or soviets, which would gain influence over the management of the local economies. Scholars called for the revitalization of the soviets and their protection from administrative caprice.[13] This debate culminated in the promulgation in 1980 of a new law on the "Basic Powers of the Territorial and Provincial Soviets." While scarcely adequate, this law (and also the Brezhnev constitution of 1977, discussed below) reflected renewed interest in the notion that officials should be accountable to elected councils, and that such bodies should play a central role in economic development. Both ideas became central elements of Gorbachev's perestroika.

It was inevitable that reformers in the national republics should also take up ideas of self-government. Advocates of this concept stressed the contribution soviets could make to economic development at the republic level and claimed that only firms shaped by such bodies could satisfy the demand for products suited to regional conditions. Such were the tentative first steps that led to the 1987 "Declaration of Sovereignty" in Estonia.

Cautious reformers in Brezhnev's entourage favored administrative centralization; moderates spoke for greater devolution or self-government in economic affairs; and some bolder spirits embraced the goal of partial privatization. Indeed, Brezhnev's administration restlessly toyed with this idea and even translated it into a series of limited experiments in agriculture. A 1977 law protected household plots, while measures instituted in 1980–82 enhanced other aspects of the private sector in agriculture.[14] Much of this legislation pertained to the "brigade" system championed by sociologist Tatyana Zaslavskaya and others. Initially a means of enabling collective farms to contract with independent work crews, brigade labor was soon extended to shipyards and other industries. Many who stopped short of advocating private control of the land nonetheless believed that the brigade system of private labor held promise of becoming the USSR's "main unit of work."[15]

A skeptic might fairly argue that all these reformist ideas together were in reality merely a bureaucratic means of co-opting a system of privatized farm labor that had already arisen autonomously. There is some truth in this. Yet at the same time, other reformers were calling for an expanded private sector in such diverse areas as handicrafts, photography, cosmetic production, automobile and appliance repair, and home construction. The government in effect encouraged this debate, which was entered into the provisions of Article 17 of the draft constitution of 1977.[16] This article elicited thousands of approving letters from the public and gave rise to the creation of home industries and family-run cafes—nominally cooperatives—in both the Baltic states and the trans-Caucasian republics.[17]

The roots of the Gorbachev program on cooperatives can be traced

21

to this debate over Brezhnev's new constitution. However, economists and publicists alike quickly realized that the economy would derive little benefit from private initiative unless it opened greater possibilities to the consumer. Moreover, many Soviet citizens were accumulating savings far larger than they could ever expect to spend legally in the existing marketplace, and thousands of illegal enterprises sprang up, dedicated to the satisfaction of consumer needs. These contributed directly to speculation and corruption, and to the formation of mafia-like criminal bands. Yet the burgeoning "second economy" also led to a burgeoning discussion of consumer problems. Academic sociologists rushed to carry out market studies and journalists eagerly published the results.

In time, the economic debate spread to the normally closed world of foreign policy discourse. In various scholarly journals, specialists began to acknowledge that the economic future of the USSR was bound up with the economies of other countries. Stalinist autarky gradually gave place to ideas of global integration; Western writings on "interdependence," once rejected out of hand, were quietly assimilated; and a sizable literature defended the proposition that the so-called international division of labor was an acceptable "socialist" concept. By these means the reformist dialogue rationalized the importation of grain, technology, and investment capital from abroad.[18]

THE HEART OF THE MATTER?

The dialogue on means of intensifying the Soviet economy through decentralization, self-management, and privatization was rich in implications for the political order. Anyone promoting the role of the soviets, for example, was in effect criticizing not only Brezhnev's restoration of the ministerial system that had been partially dismantled by Khrushchev, but also the party elite (*nomenklatura*). That many members of Brezhnev's entourage took part in this debate confirms the accuracy of Robert V. Daniels's characterization of the prevailing form of government as a "participatory bureaucracy."[19]

For Brezhnev to permit his senior officials to engage in this dialogue was not without risk. To minimize danger to the system, the language of discussion had to be purged of ideological rhetoric. The fact that the dialogue arose from practical economic concerns made this easier, for it placed a premium on pragmatism. All this tended to weaken the role of Marxist-Leninist ideology as such. When Andrei Sakharov in 1974 attacked those limited by the "dogma of the [Marxist-Leninist] faith" he gave expression to a bold new attitude that had already gained wide currency under the protection of Brezhnev's own bland pragmatism.[20]

The Brezhnev years were marked by the hounding and arrest of dissidents, sordid courtroom dramas (such as the trial of the writers Yuli Daniel and Andrei Sinyavsky shortly after Brezhnev assumed power), the promulgation of punitive laws dealing with freedom of expression and assembly, and the expulsion of some of the leading figures of Soviet arts and letters, notably Aleksandr Solzhenitsyn. Paradoxically, however, those years also saw efforts to protect individual rights and the rule of law. For instance, the government instituted measures to protect the bureaucracy's critics from reprisals, to further expand the role of counsels for the defense, and to secure the confidentiality of citizens' medical records. Granted that such initiatives failed to address the institutional problems thwarting the implementation of new laws, and granted, too, that the bureaucracy's own rule-making remained intact, such legislation nonetheless marked an important change. Issues of civil rights figured conspicuously in the public dialogue at the time of the Helsinki Agreements in 1977, but officials were giving voice to similar concerns both before and after that date, thanks to public interest in such issues.[21]

The single event that did most to stimulate fresh thinking on the rule of law and on more participatory forms of political life was the debate over the draft of the so-called Brezhnev constitution in 1977. True to Russian practice dating back to the tsars, the drafters of this document in the Ministry of Justice examined the practices of other countries on each relevant issue. To be sure, they eventually rejected most of the concepts and practices culled from foreign experience, among them the Hungarian system allowing multiple candidates to stand for local elections. However, such ideas were actually debated within the government and among the intelligentsia, with the result that even though they were excluded from the new constitution they gained a solid place on the reformist agenda. Brezhnev admitted as much, saying that "the discussion of the draft constitution has ranged beyond the analysis of the text itself. It has developed into a candid and genuinely nationwide discussion of the most urgent questions of our life."[22]

This debate eventually embraced a large segment of the public, thus sensitizing it both to the mounting violations of law, and to the possibility of changing the system so as to correct such practices. When in 1979 the Institute of State and Law surveyed the public's attitude on social issues, Moscow residents ranked "the observance of the USSR's constitution by state organizations and officials" second in importance only to the struggle against crime.[23]

Nor did such concerns fade with the ratification of the constitution, since that step set in motion official and public discussion of various other legislative acts needed to translate the new constitutional norms into law. The powers of the soviets, the role of voluntary associations, the expansion of the private sector in agriculture, the development of cooperative or private businesses, the confirmation of the freedom of emigration and of movement generally, the limitation of the powers of ministries, and even the role of the *nomenklatura* figured in the ongoing dialogue spawned or encouraged by the new constitution.[24] All in all, then, we shouldn't be surprised at the vigorous interest that so many Soviet citizens now take in human rights, in the privileges and power of the country's bureaucracy, and in political and legal matters in general. The seeds of such interest had been sown long ago.

Much the same is true for yet another remarkable aspect of today's political climate in the Soviet Union: the explosion of glasnost, and more specifically the increasing boldness of literary works, as well as of the press and other mass media. Khrushchev's "thaw" had opened the gates to an outpouring of novels, plays, poems, and literary debates that challenged the hitherto sacrosanct principles of "socialist realism," although without openly advocating alternative aesthetic or political models. And although Brezhnev tried with increasing success to bring this process to a halt, it nevertheless went on, and in fact assumed an explicitly political character.

Central to all these concerns was the role of public opinion in the Soviet Union. Just as the debate on the economy led to the recognition of the role of consumers, so did the debate on corruption and the abuse of political power lead to a greater awareness of the importance of public opinion. A required seminar held at the Institute for Advanced Training of Party and Soviet Executive Cadres informed party ideologists that they must be aware of the views of Soviet citizens and learn how to respond positively to them.[25] Terms such as "democracy" or "democratization"—now an essential part of the glasnost vocabulary—were not yet in vogue. Yet the widening discussion suggested a gradual shift from the emphasis on change "from above" to that of greater participation "from below."

THE ROAD TO REFORM
★
S. FREDERICK STARR

Gradually, too, the locus of public discourse switched from art to journalism, from literary magazines to the daily and weekly press. The conventionally bland and predictable Soviet press began to take up many sensitive and heretofore taboo topics. Journalists decried the existence of unheated rural schools, bribery, speculation, and medical malpractice. Articles on such timely ecological issues as the gradual disappearance of the Aral Sea, the salinization of groundwater in Kazakhstan, and the pollution of rivers went beyond general expressions of concern to the lodging of detailed charges against specific ministries. Television, too, began the process leading to glasnost when reporters produced candid documentaries on environmental issues. Nor were such concerns confined to the central media: TV and print journalists from Lithuania to Siberia broadened their range of coverage.[26]

During the Brezhnev years, censorship of literature, films, and the arts was tightened, and some of the cultural figures who had come into prominence during the Khrushchev "thaw" were forced into retreat or obscurity. Yet even as this was taking place, official publishers issued works that revealed the poverty, aimlessness, and spiritual alienation pervading large parts of the Soviet population, especially in the countryside. The publication of highly critical works by Valentin Rasputin and other writers of the "village prose" school bears the same relation to official censorship as the Shchekino experiment does to reigning principles of ministerial oligarchy. Both encouraged public dialogue on reform.

Many Soviet citizens were disappointed by the failure of the media to be bolder and more outspoken. This attitude was echoed even in some official writings. Thus an article in the journalists' professional magazine noted that a third of all headlines consisted of outright commands, while others embodied shallow and primitive stereotypes.[27] And a senior editor of *Pravda* spoke a few bitter truths about his profession, even though he couched them in language typical of Stalinist exercises in "criticism and self-criticism": "We journalists indulge in sloganizing, empty descriptions, and writings in which the ponderous repetition of elementary truisms merely hides the banality of what the writer is saying. The times require journalism of a higher order."[28]

Ten years later, the "higher order" came into being.

OTHER VOICES, OTHER ROOMS

Many reforms in the Brezhnev era were championed by officials or articulated in the open—or semi-open—press. However, all this occurred against the background of a spontaneous movement for change involving many members both of the intelligentsia and the public at large who stood outside the world of officialdom. Whether they were acting within the law, on its edge, or well beyond the limits of legality, members of this diverse group of independent activists raised themes that paralleled many of the themes in the open dialogue.

Several developments fed this common stream of public initiative. The rapid growth of the so-called second economy represented the extreme application of notions of self-government and privatization. A nascent free labor-union movement attracted more attention than actual members, but a growing number of wildcat strikes attested to the willingness of Soviet labor by the 1970s to act independently of its official unions.[29]

Meanwhile, the government's efforts to shape cultural values from above proved difficult to sustain. And so the task of shaping public views was gradually taken over by nonparty organizations, unofficial bodies, and private citizens in virtually every field of endeavor. The doctrine of socialist realism having lost any standing among serious writers and artists, new genres and aesthetic currents began to flourish, many of them championed and put into effect by consumer- or audience-based groups that were fully democratic and even populist in character.

A crucial role in this process was played by many informal associations and independent networks that grew up outside the law. Numerous unofficial youth groups came into being during the late 1960s, many of them in the area of popular culture and jazz.[30] Petitions and group letters became a common means of expression by the early 1970s, often attracting five hundred or more prominent and independent citizens to such causes as legal rights, religious liberty, or creative freedom in the arts. The Helsinki Watch groups organized in Moscow, Vilnius, Kiev, Tbilisi, Yerevan, and Tallinn after 1976 gave more formal expression to such sentiment, and often included international links. Private (and hence illegal) presses produced an impressive number of works in a kind of spontaneous "glasnost from below."

As with the officially tolerated reformism, the independent currents spread to the non-Russian republics. And no sooner did this occur than they became enmeshed in the various independent national movements. When raised in Russia proper, calls for greater self-government meant a stronger voice for elective organs at the city and oblast (district) level. Translated into the non-Russian republics, these same calls meant greater autonomy not only in economic affairs, but also in politics, education, and cultural policies.

Thus, the very policies that defined reform in Moscow were often cause for anxiety among ethnic Russians living in non-Russian republics. The 1970s saw the rapid development of ethnic forces in virtually every republic where extreme tensions later flowered under Gorbachev. They also saw the emergence of groups of Russians eager to reassert their imperial claims over the "fraternal" non-Russian republics, or to maintain that it is the national and religious aspirations of the Russian people—and not of other ethnic or religious groups—that have been ignored and suppressed by Stalin and his successors. This blend of chauvinist, anti-Western, and anti-"alien" (that is to say, mainly anti-Semitic) attitudes eventually spawned associations such as *Pamyat* (Memory), which have taken advantage of the policies of glasnost and perestroika to become, in effect, a political movement opposed to the framers and to the essence of those policies.

While the Soviet government tolerated—and occasionally tacitly approved of—the reformist dialogue, it did its best to contain it and prevent it from posing any real threat to the status quo. Hence, even the large "second economy," the massive demonstrations in Georgia in favor of greater cultural autonomy in 1979, or Sakharov's verbal assaults on bureaucratic centralism did not pose a grave challenge to the wielders of power.

Yet this is not to say that those who championed independent social initiatives (whether within the law or outside its bounds) left no imprint on the reformist dialogue. Samizdat, burgeoning national and human rights movements, the spread of unofficial groups all constituted a vital strain in Soviet public life, and thus contributed to a sense that Stalinism was on the defensive. To borrow from the Soviet military-political vocabulary, the civil society that was fitfully coming into being implied by its existence that the "correlation of forces" had shifted against the diluted forms of Stalinism that ruled the country from 1953 to 1985.

THE LEGACY OF AN ERA

The search for keys to the past and alternatives for the future began more than thirty years ago, shortly after the death of Stalin. Much to the astonishment of those who had assumed—not unreasonably—that years of fear and terror had extinguished all independence of thought and action in the USSR, the search for alternatives accelerated under Khrushchev, and—astonishingly—during the so-called period of stagnation. Indeed, it was precisely under Brezhnev that the "reformist dialogue" became an essential part of the Soviet political discourse *in toto*.

Yet what of its impact? Unfortunately, the rich diversity of thought displayed both in the open, or official, writings and in samizdat were exceptions, bright spots against a gray background of ideological dogma, bland formulae, and stubborn refusals to reckon with changes that had already occurred in Soviet society. No wonder that leading Western economists, reviewing the reformist literature and various concrete experiments, concluded that the USSR under Brezhnev was on a "treadmill of reform."[31] Few ideas from either the official or unofficial side of the reformist dialogue were acted upon, and those that were implemented were so carefully circumscribed that they exerted only a minimal influence on the system as a whole. Nonetheless, the importance of this dialogue cannot be gainsaid. Specifically, it had a profound impact on long-term developments in four significant areas:

- First, by drawing public attention to problems that had long gone unacknowledged, the reformist dialogue undermined the status quo. The gap between rhetoric and reality became more conspicuous, and turned many moderates into confirmed proponents of change.
- Second, because the various reformist experiments were designed so as not to disturb the essential nature of Soviet rule, they produced a growing disenchantment with the practice of merely tinkering with the system. The disenchantment affected not only intellectuals, economists, and foreign-affairs experts, but important Communist party officials, such as Gorbachev, who were determined to climb off Brezhnev's "treadmill of reform" and launch a forward march.
- Third, a number of gifted men and women joined in the search for alternatives, thus leaving a lasting imprint on the newly emerging public agendas. They included such people as Tatyana Zaslavskaya, Abel Agenbegyan, Aleksandr Yakovlev, and scores of others who now

play a prominent role in the processes of perestroika, glasnost, and *demokratizatsia*.

- Fourth, the expanding dialogue made many opponents of change aware of the looming threat to their interests. Brezhnev's penchant for toying with limited experiments that would not affect the fundamental nature of the system helped to prevent open confrontations between the reformers and their adversaries. But it also helped to galvanize the latter—who, like the reformers, entered the Gorbachev era fully armed for battle.

For all its strength, the reform movement remained isolated from the mainstream of Soviet politics until Brezhnev's death and for several years thereafter. Only when the various crises enumerated at the beginning of this essay became so acute that a new leadership could not ignore them did reform move to center stage. And it did so with the force of an explosion.

★

RECONSTRUCTING
THE SOVIET
POLITICAL SYSTEM

✮

ARCHIE BROWN

IT IS IMPORTANT TO PUT INTO CONTEXT the remarkably bold attempts of the Gorbachev era to reform the Soviet political system. That means considering both the extent to which the Soviet system had already changed over time and the nature of the system Gorbachev inherited. In this way it should become clearer how the concept of political reform and actual political change under Gorbachev differ from past chapters of Soviet history.

THE HERITAGE OF POWER

The Soviet political system has undergone several changes, inasmuch as the powers of particular institutions have varied from one period to another. Thus, from approximately 1934 until his death in 1953, Stalin was probably more powerful than the rest of the Politburo put together. That was not the case in the 1920s, nor has any one of Stalin's successors wielded such absolute power. Khrushchev did on occasion make policy without adequate consultation with his colleagues, and sometimes acted as if the first secretary of the Central Committee (as the general secre-

30

tary's post was known then) was not bound by any norms of collective responsibility. However, this style of rule—as well as the combination of the post of first secretary with the chairmanship of the Council of Ministers of the USSR—was part of his undoing. He became the first, and thus far the only, leader of the Soviet Communist party whose political demise preceded his earthly one.

Just as the relative powers of the general secretary and of the Politburo have varied over time, so have the powers of party organs and of the ministries. During Stalin's ascendancy, and perhaps especially in the postwar Stalin years, a great deal of power was vested in the ministries. Their authority was also reflected in the fact that a majority of Politburo members in the late Stalin years belonged to the ministerial network. Under Khrushchev the abolition of most of the industrial ministries in 1957—and the creation of the regional economic councils (*sovnarkhozy*)—constituted a substantial change in political structures and one which was part of a reassertion of the authority of party organs vis-à-vis the organs of the state. That reform, however, was hardly a great success, with the "departmentalism" which had been the besetting sin of the centralized ministries replaced by the "localism" of economic regions that hoarded materials and took no broader a view of the needs of the country as a whole than the ministries had done. It was no surprise, therefore, when resuscitated ministries and state committees replaced the regional economic councils within a year of Khrushchev's removal from office.

A constant feature in party-ministerial relations until the most recent past has been the existence of party economic departments supervising the work of state bodies. At the Central Committee level, there have generally been at least twenty departments of the apparatus, of which approximately half were made up of economic departments, responsible for the major branches of the economy and supervising one or several ministries. These have included, for example, the Agriculture Department, the Heavy Industry Department, and the Chemical Industry Department. This is an area where structural change has now been quite drastic, as we shall see.

There had, of course, been some changes in the institutional distribution of power in the post-Stalin period. Thus, for example, the development of "socialist legality" under Khrushchev greatly reduced the element of arbitrariness in the Soviet legal system, although neither then nor in the Brezhnev years did it safeguard such basic liberties as freedom of assembly and of association or the rights of authors and journalists to publish the truth as they saw it concerning past and present social and political injustices.

One of the more important institutional aspects of the new "socialist legality" under Khrushchev was the removal of the relative autonomy of the security forces which had previously been responsible to Stalin personally and to virtually no one else. In Khrushchev's time, as at least some of Stalin's crimes were exposed, the KGB—already symbolically downgraded from ministerial (MGB) status—was somewhat on the defensive and was firmly subordinated to the collective party leadership. Under Brezhnev the subordination of the KGB to the Politburo and Secretariat of the Central Committee (rather than one top leader) continued; but, with the prohibition of public attacks on Stalin and the Stalin period, the security forces were able to shed some of the odium bequeathed to them by their NKVD predecessors, and were encouraged to play a substantial role in combatting organized dissent in Soviet society.

Other reforms, such as the enhancing of the powers of soviets or the introduction of competitive elections, were sometimes discussed in print during the Khrushchev and Brezhnev periods.[1] This showed that even within the parameters of the system there were alternative ways of thinking, but it led to few practical results. Behind the monolithic facade of the post-Stalin but pre-perestroika political system, there were in fact groupings within the party and society advocating a variety of different views, but these differences could not at that time be given institutional form. The formation of any organized group other than those endorsed and supervised by the party was regarded as potentially subversive, and considerable resources were devoted to the surveillance and harassment of numerically small groups. People who tried to work for change from within the system could only continue to do so by making substantial compromises. Those who began as within-system reformers, but were of a more uncompromising disposition, such as Andrei Sakharov, were often turned into dissidents by the rigid policies of the Brezhnev leadership.

Thus, the political system Gorbachev inherited—and the one in which he had, of course, worked his way upwards—was palpably antipluralistic. It was also one in which the highest authority was vested in party organs but a great deal of day-to-day decision-making power was lodged in the ministries and, within their own special spheres of activity, in the KGB and the military. On the eve of Gorbachev's accession to power in 1985, discussion was already freer on a number of issues than it had been in Brezhnev's—or indeed Khrushchev's—time. Most political debate, however, remained at a rather esoteric level, lacking both theoretical legitimacy and political institutionalization.

A majority of Western political scientists realized that it was much more misleading than helpful to continue to call this post-Stalin system "totalitarian." Yet there was no denying that it remained highly authoritarian. Attempts to characterize it as an example of "institutional pluralism" or as "corporatist" involved excessive conceptual stretching, though the granting of considerable discretionary powers to a variety of bureaucratic agencies under Brezhnev did contain some quasi-corporatist elements.[2]

What this system did not contain was much sign of democracy or democratization. In that respect, although not in all, the Brezhnev era represented a step back from Khrushchev's, where some of the reforms, in a naïvely populist way, were at least intended to serve the cause of democratization.[3] While the manner in which Soviet political institutions operated had changed greatly by the middle of the 1980s as compared with the Stalin years, the basic structures displayed considerable continuity with those established in the 1920s and 1930s. Moreover, at a conceptual level they were deemed to be the very embodiment of socialism. Soviet leaders were prepared to allow that there might be different *roads* to socialism but denied that there could be different *models* of socialism. Socialism meant "actually existing socialism," a term coined under Brezhnev—what was on display in the Soviet Union and in the systems of its orthodox allies in Eastern Europe.

THE MEANINGS OF PERESTROIKA

The changes being discussed and, to some extent, introduced in the Soviet Union today under the rubric of perestroika mark a qualitative advance over previous reform efforts. They are not, of course, devoid of ambiguity. The very term, perestroika, is translated into Western languages in various ways and accorded somewhat different meanings. Increasingly, it is not translated at all, which allows Western readers to impart to it whatever meaning they wish. In that respect, they are not unlike their Soviet counterparts. Practically everyone who makes a public utterance on perestroika in the Soviet Union is, on the surface, in favor of it, but for some the term means only economic modernization, for others a bureaucratic restructuring, for yet others no more than the correct catchword of the epoch, while for its most serious proponents it signifies a fundamental reconstruction of the Soviet political and economic system.

Even among those who belong to that last category, there are important differences of principle. The reformist Communists wish to establish a "socialist pluralism" in which the Communist party itself becomes substantially democratized, and its "leading role" redefined. The reform wing of the party leadership is undoubtedly serious about political and economic reforms that are dramatic by the standards of anything seen over the past seven decades. The New Economic Policy (NEP), which was introduced by Lenin in 1921 and which is held up by many reformers as the model for perestroika, may have been just as radical an economic shift as that now being envisaged. But the political reform presently being pursued is more far-reaching than anything seen in the 1920s or subsequently. Yet the reform from above that has been launched in the Gorbachev era has helped to stimulate pressures from below that threaten to go beyond anything the Communist party leadership has hitherto been prepared to accept, including demands for a multi-party system.[4]

When the Russian word *perestroika* is translated into English, the word used most often is *restructuring*. This, however, is adequate only for one part of perestroika—that element in the political and economic reform process which is concerned with rationalizing the economy and reorganizing political institutions. The more radical connotation of the concept is better captured by "reconstruction." That term, too, is not an unambiguous one. It may mean rebuilding something which once existed and has been destroyed—NEP, for instance—or it may mean constructing a quite different edifice from the foundations up.

The prominent Soviet historian Yuri Afanasev noted (in a conversation with this author in 1987) that "We talk about reconstruction, but first of all we need to know what it is that we wish to reconstruct." This, in turn, presupposes serious research on the whole of Soviet history, the search for foundations worth building on, and a differentiation between structures that may be suitable for renovation and others that are strong candidates for demolition. To a Western observer, it may well appear that no one period of Soviet history offers anything approaching ideal foundations on which to build a new edifice. But history is not architecture, nor is it a blank sheet on which well-meaning (and some ill-meaning) Westerners can prescribe the future of Soviet people who are rooted in their historical experience and their own traditions. Fortunately, that experience is more contradictory, and the traditions much more diverse, than is often assumed—fortunately, because if those who wish to reconstruct the Soviet system find no indigenous foundation on which to build, they will probably fail.

IDEAS—NEW AND OLD

In politics four elements are of preeminent importance: ideas, institutions, interests, and culture. I shall consider each of them briefly in the contemporary Soviet context.

The idea of socialism has by now a long Russian tradition as well as powerful institutional supports, and most (though by no means all) Soviet reformers wish to reconcile whatever new ideas they espouse with socialist principles as they understand them. But the former Soviet orthodoxy, noted in the introduction to this essay, that there were no such things as different models of socialism (though there could be different paths to it) has been explicitly rejected by senior party intellectuals and by some leading officials. Among the former are such prominent reformers as the director of the Institute of Economics of the World Socialist System, Oleg Bogomolov, and Fyodor Burlatsky.[5] The latter include, significantly, the Central Committee secretary responsible for ideology, Vadim Medvedev, and more recently—and more explicitly and importantly—Mikhail Gorbachev.[6] They and many other Soviet Communist reformers now publicly acknowledge that a variety of models of socialism does, in fact, exist and that this is not something to be deplored.

The scope and flexibility of socialism as a body of doctrine has been enormously expanded, to the extent that the formerly sharp dividing line between Soviet Communist and social democratic traditions of socialism is becoming blurred. Soviet reformers have argued that a fundamental mistake was made when state ownership was deemed to be the highest form of socialist ownership, and many of them now emphasize the need for a multiplicity of forms of ownership, such as individual ownership, cooperatives, joint ventures (with foreign companies), and even joint stock capital investment (whereby "working people use their savings to participate in stimulating the kinds of products they are crying out for"[7]), as fully compatible with socialism.

Yevgeni Ambartsumov, one of the most erudite and reform-minded political analysts in the Soviet Union, has explicitly argued that socialization of the means of production should not be regarded as the main criterion of socialism, but rather that the criteria adopted should be those which follow from the celebrated remark of Marx and Engels in the *Communist Manifesto* on the replacement of "bourgeois society" by one "in which the free development of each is the condition for the free development of all." For Ambartsumov, this means "the all-around free development of the individual and social justice."[8]

The aspect of Soviet "new thinking" that has received most publicity in the West is that which has a direct relationship with foreign policy, such as the new priority given to universal values as against class values.[9] But other ideas that are new in the Soviet context, though far from novel in a broader one, have a more direct impact on the reform of the Soviet political system.

For years any idea of convergence between the Soviet and Western systems (which at one time had a certain popularity in Western circles) had been vehemently condemned by Soviet theorists. But Ambartsumov has suggested that it was a mistake to reject this concept completely, pointing out at the same time that Marx's prognosis that socialism would be a postcapitalist system has turned out to be wrong, since "today we exist simultaneously with capitalist society and will exist simultaneously also in the foreseeable future."[10]

The need to learn from other political systems has been phrased more cautiously, though interestingly, by Georgi Shakhnazarov, who is not only president of the Soviet Association of Political Sciences but also (since early 1988) one of Gorbachev's full-time personal assistants. Writing in *Pravda*, Shakhnazarov criticizes as "antihistorical" the former Soviet view that after the rise of socialism, any further progress in the evolution of democratic institutions in the West was impossible. It is fully understandable, he goes on, that "now, when a profound reform of the political system of our country is unfolding, the experience in this sphere not only of socialist but of all other countries merits attention and study, with the possibility of putting it to creative use."[11]

Three ideas which have been taken up by Soviet party reformers in recent years, and which have received the personal endorsement of Gorbachev, deserve special mention. They are the concepts of pluralism (usually qualified, in Gorbachev's use of the term, by the adjective "socialist"), the law-governed state (*pravovoye gosudarstvo*, or state based on the rule of law), and "checks and balances."[12]

Gorbachev has made a distinction between "political pluralism" (with its connotations of a competitive party system that he has not thus far accepted) and "socialist pluralism" or a "pluralism of opinion," which he has endorsed and advocated. Other Soviet writers, however, have taken up the notion of pluralism, and many of the pressure groups outside the party (the "informal groups," in Soviet parlance) champion a more fully fledged version of pluralism. Though Gorbachev's "socialist pluralism" stops short of legitimizing the activities of independent organizations which are deemed to be "antisocialist," and has not yet made room for competing parties, his acceptance of that term (which dates only from 1987) was an important breakthrough, inasmuch as it provided authoritative support for diversity of opinion and for political debate. The boundaries of the permissible have been pushed ever wider in the subsequent discussions in the pages of officially published Soviet newspapers, journals, and books, not to speak of unofficial publications.

The second idea that is being actively promoted is that of the state based on the rule of law. Many Soviet jurists and others have been pressing for some years for more precisely defined laws and for truly independent advocates and judges. Even in the Gorbachev era, they are some way off from attaining that goal, but the acceptance in principle of the supremacy of law is a considerable advance, as is the acknowledgment by its most active advocates within the party and outside it that a state ruled by law is still in the process of construction.

A third, and in part at least associated, idea of great importance (as well as novelty) in the Soviet context is the concept of "checks and balances." It was broached at a meeting of the Soviet Association of Political Sciences in early 1987 and first endorsed by Gorbachev in late 1988. It is a recognition of the need not only for goodwill or of a return to so-called Leninist norms, but of the necessity of actual institutions that will introduce accountability into the Soviet political system and prevent "the concentration of all political power in the hands of one organ (or individual)."[13]

INSTITUTIONAL REFORM

The institutional reform now being implemented in the Soviet Union is likely to be—unless perestroika suffers a serious reversal—only the first stage in the reconstruction of the Soviet political system. The most significant changes thus far have been the creation of competitive elections and the formation of an elected assembly that has become a forum for genuine debate and, to some degree, a check on executive power.

It is hardly surprising that the Soviet Union did not move in one fell swoop from completely manipulated, single-candidate elections to fully democratic ones. The one-third of deputies to the Congress of People's Deputies chosen by public organizations—of such varying size and significance as the Communist party, the Academy of Sciences, the Union of Writers, and the Cultural Foundation—were selected by varying means. In some cases, the choice was made through preliminary soundings, and the elected representatives of the public organization were left to vote for a slate of candidates no longer than the number of seats allocated to their association.

This was notably the case with the one hundred candidates allocated to the Communist party. However, it was only after the March 1989 elections that Gorbachev was able to persuade a large number of elderly members of the Central Committee to sign a collective letter of resignation. Until then the composition of the Central Committee clearly lagged behind the pace of events and of personnel changes throughout the country. Left to itself, it might have elected a more conservative slate of deputies to the Congress of People's Deputies. (In fact, only when the party rules are altered at the next Party Congress—to enable Central Committee membership to be renewed, from a pool broader than the ranks of candidate members, between the five-yearly Congresses—will that body become a more appropriate electoral college during a time of rapid political change.) The Central Committee at the time of the election of members of the Congress of People's Deputies contained many members whose place on it derived from positions they no longer held, and it was elected when Gorbachev had been Soviet leader for less than a year and had much less power than he had acquired by 1989.

In the new Soviet climate, however, too little responsiveness to members of the various "public organizations" could have its dangers, as the Presidium of the Academy of Sciences discovered during the 1989 elections when its initial slate excluded the names of some of the Soviet Union's most outstanding and most outspoken natural and social scientists, including Andrei Sakharov (later to compete and win in a rerun election). The imperfections of the electoral system, but its possibilities as well, were also revealed in the contests for territorial constituencies.

ARCHIE BROWN

In about a quarter of the seats the electorate was presented with only a single candidate. But since the new law provided for voting in absolute secrecy (as confirmed by various local and international observers), and for the defeat of any candidate who had not obtained more than fifty percent of the votes, many party apparatchiks lost simply by virtue of having their names crossed out by the voters. A change of procedure since past elections to the Supreme Soviet was that all electors had to enter the voting booth even if they were endorsing the single candidate; in the past, to vote *for* the single candidate meant simply dropping the ballot in the box without marking it. A procedural reform of this kind may seem minor on the surface, but in reality, it was of some significance, especially in the new political climate. It had been proposed by reform-minded Soviet scholars as long ago as the late 1960s, though of course it was not adopted at that time.

The defeat of leading members of the party establishment (such as the Leningrad regional party secretary and candidate member of the Politburo, Yuri Solovyov) was a major consequence of perestroika, if in part an unintended one. So was the overwhelming victory of Boris Yeltsin in Moscow in the face of overt hostility from the highest party organs. Together they signified the fact that the Soviet people—as distinct from the general secretary, the Politburo, or the Secretariat of the Central Committee—had changed the balance of forces within the Soviet political system. This step along the road of democratization would make it hard, even for a leadership so minded, to persuade the Soviet electorate to act like automatons again. In addition, the fact that the Congress of People's Deputies and the new-style Supreme Soviet constitute something more like a parliament than the Soviet Union has ever seen has introduced an important new check on the Soviet political executive, though it is still a long way from balancing it.

There is certainly no denying that the new Soviet legislature is already a significant political institution. Both its larger outer body, the 2,250-strong Congress of People's Deputies, and its inner body, the 542-member bicameral Supreme Soviet, have become forums for sometimes searing criticism and for passionate debate. It would be difficult to think of an acute problem of contemporary Soviet society that did not receive an airing at either the First Congress of People's Deputies (which convened in late May 1989 and lasted for thirteen days) or at the Supreme Soviet sessions that followed. By lifting the lid off these burning issues, the new assemblies allowed some of the built-up pressure to escape.

They also, moreover, proved themselves capable of calling senior officials to account. Important leaders, including Gorbachev himself, were criticized, although Gorbachev in his guidance of the Congress went out of his way to ensure that prominent critics (especially on the liberal wing of the assembly) were given rather more time at the podium than their numerical weight within the legislature strictly warranted.

When the Supreme Soviet was elected by the deputies to the Congress and finally met, it formed a series of committees (with members drawn from both chambers) and commissions (of each chamber, the Soviet of the Union and the Soviet of Nationalities, separately). These provided a new experience for everyone—not least for the chairman of the Council of Ministers. Nikolai Ryzhkov, who had been confirmed in that role, himself announced fairly sweeping changes in the Soviet ministerial team, including the actual abolition of a number of economic ministries and the important appointment of Leonid Abalkin, the former director of the Institute of Economics, to head a new State Commission on Economic Reform with the rank of a deputy chairman of the Council of Ministers.

But the changes were even greater than Ryzhkov and the leadership as a whole had bargained for. The various nominees were cross-questioned by deputies, in some cases quite rigorously. The committees of the Supreme Soviet actually rejected six of Ryzhkov's proposed members of the government, and other nominations were either rejected by the Supreme Soviet as a whole or withdrawn in the face of strong opposition. In the end as many as eleven out of Ryzhkov's seventy-two nominees for the Council of Ministers failed to get through the confirmation process. Those who failed to secure endorsement included Vasili Zakharov, who had been minister of culture since 1986, as well as the new nominees for such important economic posts as the chairmanship of the State Committee on Prices, the chairmanship of the State Bank (*Gosbank*) and the minister of the oil and gas industry.

It is perhaps of special interest—and in accordance with the demands of a number of deputies who spoke at the Congress of People's Deputies and the Supreme Soviet—that among the new committees was one on defense and state security. At least a minority of members of that committee, and of the Supreme Soviet as a whole, have shown a desire to ensure that the defense establishment and the security forces are in future held accountable to some degree for their activities and expenditures. Previously they had been virtually immune from accountability other than to the Administrative Organs Department of the Central Committee and the Politburo—in other words, to party organs at the highest level rather than to representatives of the people as a whole.[14]

The combination of the general secretary's post with the new-style presidency—the office of chairman of the Supreme Soviet—has been a controversial change even within the ranks of Soviet reformers. The chairman is vested with greater powers (including that of commander-in-chief of the armed forces and the right to appoint the chairman of the Council of Ministers) than were attached to the former chairmanship of the Presidium of the Supreme Soviet. On the one hand, there are those who welcome the strengthening of the position of a reformist leader, Gorbachev, in the face of all the remaining institutional obstacles to perestroika. On the other hand, there are those who think that the highest political echelons of party and state hierarchies should reflect the new awareness of the value of "separation of powers" and "checks and balances."

One of the most biting critiques of the institutional framework of the Soviet system, including the reforms adopted thus far, is the article by Sergei Andreyev in the Leningrad journal *Neva*.[15] Andreyev argues that there is still no guarantee against the emergence of another Brezhnev, and that the key political office in the country remains that of party general secretary rather than the presidency. "But the general secretary of the Central Committee," he goes on, "is elected by a narrow circle of people, by a few hundred votes."[16] A change of general secretary is obviously of great consequence for the population as a whole, but neither the rank-and-file party members nor, still more, the approximately ninety percent of Soviet adult citizens who do not belong to the party have any say in the matter.

A strong presidency need not necessarily, however, be inconsistent with the further reconstruction of the Soviet political system. Indeed, to the extent that its incumbent wields power by virtue of his state, rather than party, office, the strong presidency can actually be a significant part of the reconstruction. There has already been progress in cutting down the size of the party apparatus: in 1988 the number of Central Committee departments was reduced from twenty to nine, and in the process all of the branch economic departments except the one responsible for agriculture were abolished.[17] Lip service has long been paid to the need for a clearer differentiation of functions between party and state bodies. The latest restructuring and reduction in the size of the party apparatus is an indication that this time, Gorbachev and his like-minded colleagues in the leadership are serious about it.

Whether a powerful presidency will be compatible with the democratization or even liberalization of the Soviet political system depends essentially on three factors: the further strengthening of the competitive principle in Soviet elections, the extent to which the Supreme Soviet further develops its independence as a representative assembly, and the spirit and letter of the laws being framed to institutionalize freedom of speech and of association. Progress in these areas is still opposed by many within the official structures. Given the reformist disposition of the particular incumbent of the highest party and state offices at the present time, it is far from evident that stronger curbs imposed on him *within* the executive would further the reformist cause. What matters more is that there should be *checks on*, and *political accountability of*, the executive as a whole.

In this respect, nothing is more important than the institutionalization of freedom of speech and of the press. These freedoms must go beyond glasnost, which can still be interpreted, in the words of writer Vladimir Lakshin, as "only a temporary certificate issued to the public and the press."[18] Lakshin advocates legal guarantees for a "real freedom of the press" that will ensure that "neither a man, nor a good cause, nor a bright idea can be silently trampled upon to the great loss of society." In the same article Lakshin uses the adjective "socialist" not as a way of restricting a particular right—as has so often been the case in the Soviet Union—but as an argument for broadening it:

> Not long ago we shamed and ridiculed the words "freedom of speech" a thousand times, usually by adding the word "bourgeois." Now we agree to recognize that "bourgeois freedom of the press," contrary to the banal cliché, means the rather wide freedom to criticize your own society and discuss the most varied problems, if they are of interest to the reader. But why shouldn't we wish for a fuller, socialist freedom of the press, where the press does not depend on newspaper monopolists or owners of publishing houses, like [Axel] Springer, and is only under the control of public opinion? The concept of "socialist" should be combined with a greater level of freedom rather than with a hypocritical reduction of it.[19]

Finally, in any discussion of contemporary Soviet political institutions, mention must be made of one of the most important elements of pluralism, which has in reality, and not only in theory, emerged within a system only partly free of the bonds of authoritarianism: that is, the emergence of genuinely independent political organizations—the "informal groups," as they are known in the Soviet Union—referred to briefly above. These vary enormously in size and political weight, as well as in political orientation. Thus a huge political gulf separates, for instance, the adherents of Memory (*Pamyat*) from those of Memorial, the similarity of their names in English notwithstanding. The former is a Russian nationalist movement with strongly anti-Semitic overtones; the latter is a reformist, anti-Stalinist association whose aim is to throw more light on the past persecution of citizens for political reasons, and to prevent any repetition of this dark side of Soviet history.

In the Baltic republics, National Fronts have mobilized huge popular support to promote the interests of the titular nationalities of Estonia, Latvia, and Lithuania. In turn this has led to the formation of organizations stressing "internationalism" within the republics and the interests of Russians and others who have made their home there. Indeed, one of the responses to the ethnic assertiveness of the Baltic peoples has been the rise of Russian nationalism in the Baltic republics and elsewhere.[20]

It must be stressed that up to the present, these manifestations of political pluralism are more *de facto* than *de jure*. Some of the groups go beyond the limits of "socialist" in "socialist pluralism," as that term is understood by either wing of the party leadership. But the groups are sufficiently widespread and influential to make the present scale of political group activity qualitatively different from the days of the tiny and persecuted dissident groups of the Brezhnev era.

INTERESTS AND NEW CONSTITUENCIES

Interests are by no means only economic interests, although they are often treated as if that were so. Given the extent, however, to which economic interests bulk large in political and social life, those who wish to reconstruct the Soviet system are hampered by the fact that, in the short run, change does not appear to be in the material interest of a majority of citizens. Only a few social groups are better off materially as a result of perestroika, chiefly members of the new cooperatives. They have consequently become the object of envy and sometimes of vandalism.

Moreover, there are groups such as unskilled workers for whom the economic reform does not offer much comfort even in the medium term, since it envisages a widening of pay differentials to reward the acquisition of skills and qualifications. In addition, if even the economic reform already endorsed in principle is fully implemented, it will open up the possibility of job insecurity. Hitherto, Soviet workers in most parts of the country have had a guarantee not only of employment but of employment in the same enterprise. (One result of glasnost has, however, been the revelation of quite high unemployment rates in Soviet Central Asia.) The prospect of forced occupational mobility, which has not been a feature of Soviet life in the post-Stalin period, and the possibility of at least short-term unemployment, seem to be stripping workers of rights they already possessed.[21]

In contrast, the political reforms involve an extension of the rights of workers as well as of other Soviet citizens. Competitive elections (and even, as we have seen, noncompetitive ones) have granted them a right to deny local party bosses a seat in the legislature. This so undermined a number of these officials' authority that it has come close to providing citizens with a veto on the incumbency of local party officials as well. This is very clearly in the interests of the great majority of Soviet people, just as it is a curtailment of the privileges of party officials and other local dignitaries. The latter have always been called to account by those above them, but it is a new experience to be accountable to those below. Thus the political reform—especially the move to competitive elections—is in the interests of far more people than those on whose interests it impinges, though the latter still constitute a powerful and increasingly disgruntled group.

Officials who have wielded an irresponsible power have grown used to not being held accountable to the great majority of people whom they nominally serve. Even when they cannot directly oppose policies now emanating from the center, they can water them down or simply fail to implement them. This, in turn, can promote popular loss of confidence in the success of reform and lead at least a significant minority of Soviet citizens to conclude that Gorbachev is all talk and perestroika just another slogan. As the eminent sociologist Tatyana Zaslavskaya has put it, "The tendency towards emasculation of the principal ideas of perestroika by the organs of executive power negatively influences social consciousness, undermining people's faith in its success."[22]

There are several problems for reformers wishing to retain and broaden the appeal of perestroika. One is the interlinkage between economic and political reform. So far as economic reform is concerned, it has produced little if any rise in the standard of living, and the money supply has increased faster than the supply of goods, so that shortages are worse and queues longer. But there are more fundamental difficulties: some essential ingredients of the economic reform, such as a shift to market pricing, are being postponed for fear that the price rises will provoke popular discontent and strengthen the conservative rather than reformist forces.

This is a Catch-22 for the reformers. They cannot afford to move to market prices until there is a much better supply of goods, but they cannot greatly increase supplies until they can offer adequate incentives to producers. Even a successful reform will not benefit broad social classes equally. As suggested above, unskilled workers have less to gain even in the medium-term future than skilled workers, and greater intra-class differentiation is likely, as are differing perceptions by diverse social groups of their own interests. Moreover, political reform and also the political climate vary greatly in different parts of the Soviet Union. Many provincial Russian towns have remained relatively immune to perestroika, as has almost the whole of Soviet Central Asia.

One aspect of political change that is clearly in the interests of the majority of workers, as well as intellectuals, is glasnost (not to speak of that freedom of the press advocated by Lakshin). It is in the most direct interest—in terms of work satisfaction—of the creative intelligentsia, though not necessarily of all of them. For the writer of little or no talent, the old ideological guidelines were as much a help as a hindrance, especially since they eliminated some of the potential competition for a place in the literary journals. Thus, there has been a backlash not only from cultural bureaucrats but also from writers who have found it harder to be published in large editions in the face of the newly publishable backlog of works previously taboo. The authors of the latter embrace both dead and living Soviet authors, including some now abroad, as well as foreign authors of books previously as welcome as time bombs and regarded as their ideological equivalent.[23] In the former category the most remarkable name is that of Aleksandr Solzhenitsyn, whose Soviet publications now include even *Gulag Archipelago*. In the latter category, among the most striking works to be published are Orwell's *Nineteen Eighty-Four* and *Animal Farm* and Koestler's *Darkness at Noon*. All this is welcomed by a majority within the intelligentsia, as the substantially larger rise in the circulations of liberal than of conservative Soviet literary journals indicates.

In one sense, however, glasnost is even more in the interests of workers than intellectuals. In the past, workers were more dependent on the domestic mass media for information on their own country and the outside world than were intellectuals, who had more contacts with foreigners and in many cases could listen to foreign-language radio broadcasts (which, unlike broadcasts to the Soviet Union in Russian and other Soviet languages, were not jammed). The end of jamming of Russian-language foreign broadcasts by 1988 is a significant extension of the right to information, though the much greater frankness of the Soviet mass media themselves is still more important.

One of the most difficult tasks facing Soviet reformers is to make perestroika in the near-term economic as well as the political interest of a majority of Soviet citizens and of a wider range of social groups. It is not easy to commend *economic* reform merely on the basis of promises of future prosperity, for such promises must be seen in the context of too long a history of people being asked to sacrifice the present for a future that did not turn out as they had been led to believe. Yet at the same time, Soviet workers, contrary to the view of many Soviet intellectuals and Western observers, have already made it clear—not least through their voting behavior—that they have a strong interest, in both senses of the term, in *political* reform.

OLD CULTURE AND NEW VISTAS

The cultural context in which perestroika is taking place is often regarded as one of the main obstacles to the success of reform. Just as distrust of economic entrepreneurship and attachment to egalitarianism is part of an economic culture not notably supportive of the principal tenets of the economic reform, so the authoritarian political tradition of the Soviet Union and of prerevolutionary Russia has produced a political culture in which democratic and libertarian values and aspirations have been relatively weak.

In a fascinating discussion published in *Literaturnaya gazeta* between Soviet Deputy Foreign Minister Anatoli Adamishin and Fyodor Burlatsky, the newspaper's political commentator and the chairman of the Public Commission for Humanitarian Cooperation and Human Rights (an official Soviet body), one of the issues touched upon was that of Russian political culture. Burlatsky observed that "it was the great misfortune of our country's history that Russia did not have a liberal tradition—in other words, individual human rights." Commenting on the Soviet period, Burlatsky said:

> We longed to find forms of democracy that did not continue the old forms but refuted them by demonstrating their bankruptcy. In the process we not infrequently threw out the baby—the common contents of democracy—along with the bourgeois bathwater. The worst of the traditions of old Russia filtered through into the new society via hundreds of different channels—psychological, political, and moral—and made themselves at home here.[24]

While not directly contradicting Burlatsky, Adamishin chose a quite different emphasis in his interpretation of Russian history. He stressed the common roots of Russia and the West, observing that "Christianity alone . . . had a powerful and in many ways similar influence on the political culture of Russia and Western countries. . . . Ideas of personal freedoms," he argued, "and of the limitation of state power in favor of the individual and society were not alien to the Russian people." It was not such a long time "in historical terms (half a millennium)" that separated the Soviet Union from the medieval traditions of Pskov and the Novgorod republic and the traditions of the popular assembly (*veche*).[25]

Addressing the "fashionable" view that "we are not ready for democracy and that we have no appropriate tradition," Adamishin suggested that this was "both true and not true." What Lenin called "Asian barbarism" had put severe pressure on "the principles of freedom," but no one had ever succeeded in "eradicating the Russian democratic impulse," so prominent, he added, in "such pillars of Russian culture" as Tolstoy and Dostoevsky. Burlatsky, in turn, did not disagree with such an assessment, but drew attention to the "enormous gulf" between the leading lights of Russian culture, on the one hand, and the mass political culture on the other.[26]

Both contributors to the discussion made valid points. There *is* a sense in which reconstruction of the Soviet political system comes up against greater cultural obstacles than similar attempts in some East European Communist states. Five hundred years may not be such a long time "in historical terms," but it is a long time in politics. We should, however, guard against the misleading view, to be found so often in the West and also in certain East-Central European countries (for instance, Poland and Hungary) that interprets the Russian and Soviet mixture of autocracy and oligarchy as the product of an irredeemably authoritarian Russian national character.

People's values, fundamental political beliefs, and expectations—key components of a political culture—do change, and at some times more quickly than at others, for they are the product of concrete historical experience. There are good reasons why such change should have been under way in the post-Stalin USSR, and at an accelerated rate in recent years.

Political cultures are a product of direct experience of political institutions as well as of the ideas disseminated within a society. Glasnost cannot fail to make an impact on Soviet political culture, above all on the values, beliefs, and expectations of the younger generation. Among the institutional changes, the reformed electoral system is particularly significant. The act of voting according to one's individual judgment rather than along the lines laid down from above is the kind of autonomous behavior likely to lead to political cultural change. There is a large body of evidence from social psychology which suggests that attitudes are reinforced by direct personal experience. Heterodox political views can be strengthened by heterodox political action.

This point applies all the more strongly to those who participated in the dissident movement of the Brezhnev era, but while that movement comprised only a few thousand people, today's nonconformist voters number millions. In the political climate of the Gorbachev era, to vote against the district or even city party secretary is not an act requiring the boldness of a pre-perestroika overt dissident. Indeed, the very fact that it does not require any special courage to do this may be regarded as one of the greatest achievements of perestroika.

If the repoliticization of millions of formerly apolitical Russians can, on the whole, be seen as a positive contribution to the reconstruction of the Soviet political system, the revitalization of national aspirations in other republics is likely to have a much more ambiguous impact. This subject is treated elsewhere in this volume, so suffice it to say that only a move towards a much more meaningful federal system that allows for the flourishing of a wide variety of national cultures, including those of peoples not enjoying republican status, can provide the necessary prerequisite for the further democratization—indeed, for the very survival—of the USSR. The process will require continuous and skillful political adaptation. Given the extent to which expectations have been aroused, probably the only alternatives to the symbiosis between perestroika and national cultural diversity are either a return to a higher level of centralization, authoritarianism, and naked force than prevailed during the Brezhnev era, or the disintegration of the Soviet state.

The destabilization of a nuclear superpower would be to the advantage neither of the Soviet population nor of the rest of the world. The road to political pluralism is a much more obstacle-strewn one in the multinational Soviet state than in the East European countries where dramatic, yet peaceful, transitions are now under way. "The worse the better" has always been an absurdly short-sighted Western sentiment in relation to the Soviet Union. The interest of both West and East lies in the continuing progress of fundamental reform, or reconstruction, of the Soviet political system—not in its descent into chaos or extreme coercion.

★

AN ECONOMY
IN TRANSITION

✷

ALEC NOVE

THIS ESSAY EXAMINES THREE BROAD
questions: First, what part—and how much—of the Soviet economy is
in need of reform? Second, what kind of reforms have been proposed?
Third, are the projected reforms viable, and will they work when (and
if) they are implemented? In addition, I shall examine previous attempts
to restructure the Soviet economic system, and also—especially in the
light of past experience—the problems and difficulties the reformers must
contend with.

ANATOMY OF A CRISIS

That the Soviet economy is in a deplorable state has now been fully
acknowledged by Soviet economists and Soviet political leaders alike.
Perennial shortages, declining growth, staggering waste, imbalances,
stagnation, and corruption have brought it—in the words of Gorbachev
himself—into "a precrisis situation." The distinguished economist Nikolai Shmelev put it bluntly:

AN ECONOMY IN TRANSITION
★
ALEC NOVE

It is essential to realize that the cause of our difficulties is not only
due to the heavy burden of military expenditures and to the highly expensive global responsibilities assumed by our country. . . . Persistent,
long-term efforts to defy the objective laws of economic life and to suppress
the age-long natural incentives to work have led to results directly opposite
to those we had anticipated. We now have an economy that is out of
balance and plagued with shortages, an economy that rejects scientific
and technical progress, one that is unplanned and—if we want to be totally
honest—unplannable. . . .
Massive apathy, indifference, theft, and disrespect for honest labor,
together with aggressive envy toward those who earn more—even by
honest methods—have led to the virtual physical degradation of a significant part of the people as a result of alcoholism and idleness. There is a
lack of belief in the officially announced objectives and purposes, in the
very possibility of a more rational organization of social and economic
life. . . .
Clearly all this cannot be swiftly overcome—that will take years,
perhaps several generations.[1]

Since the publication of Shmelev's article, even more serious indict-
ments have appeared in the Soviet press. According to many writers,
the country's economy is now in a state of full-fledged "crisis." Indeed,
the situation has deteriorated, as can be seen in the alarm expressed by
E. Gaidar in his analysis of the economic year 1988[2] and in numerous
articles by Leonid Abalkin, the influential director of the Institute of
Economics who became vice-premier in 1989.

Even these few examples should suffice to illustrate why the new
Soviet leadership embarked on a process of change. But why at that
time? After all, none of the problems that have come to be aired in the
Soviet press and in the speeches of the leaders is exactly new. Many had
been plainly visible even prior to World War II, and had in fact been
subject to criticism before. The answers to this question must be divided
into two parts: those relating to the long-term evolution of the Soviet
economic system, and those arising from specific malfunctions, some of
fairly recent origin.

The fundamental cause of the malaise lies in the very nature of the
centralized command-economy model, which Gavriil Popov, recently
appointed editor-in-chief of the monthly *Voprosy ekonomiki* (Problems
of Economics) called, in a seminal article, "The Administrative System."[3]
The system had come into being under Stalin, and its overriding purpose
was to mobilize all material and human resources for the political prior-

ities set by the state. Since the priorities were few in number, since they were all in effect determined by the supreme despot, and since, furthermore, they relied (in Popov's words) on a "subsystem of fear" (that is, terror) and on devoted agents to carry out the policies, the system produced results, at least in the short run. Thus, Stalin did succeed—at a hideous cost—in industrializing the country, and in creating a military-industrial complex.

However, as Popov emphasizes, even those early successes were seriously marred by losses and inefficiencies, caused by the stifling of initiative and overcentralization. As the economy continued to grow, as the tasks set by the planners became ever more numerous and complex, the losses and inefficiencies multiplied, eventually overwhelming the planning and control apparatus. The assumption that the central authorities knew what was best for society proved a sham. Moreover, the power of the authorities to issue instructions ("plan-orders") to hundreds of thousands of enterprise managements throughout the country no longer worked. The planning apparatus was forced to splinter, many of its parts working at cross-purposes.

Instead of centralized and coordinated control, the system yielded gradually to what became known as "departmentalism" and "localism." The millions of bureaucrats employed by the central planning agencies still continued to determine everything from the number of nails made to the distribution of women's shoes, but more often than not the results bore little relation to the plans. Neither the quantity nor the quality of the goods (especially in the consumer sector) conformed to market demands and to the growing aspirations of the Soviet public.

Popov makes another crucial point: The supreme despot is gone. Terror is no more. Advances in technology require increasingly complex and variegated solutions. The old breed of faithful servants degenerated and corruption spread.

The problem of the magnitude of the new tasks may be illustrated by a quip made some time ago by Nikolai Fedorenko, to the effect that a fully balanced, fully checked and detailed plan for the year ahead would be ready, with the help of computers, in roughly 30,000 years' time. There are millions of product variants. There are hundreds of thousands of enterprises in industry, agriculture, construction, transport, and distribution. It is necessary to make thousands of millions of decisions in the area of supply alone. The plans must also relate to labor, wages, costs, profits, investments, and economy of materials. They emerge from different parts of the planning hierarchy. They are all too often inconsistent with each other, as for instance when supplies do not match the output plan. Because next year's plan must be ready by next year, and not in 29,999 years, it is inevitably neither balanced, checked, or disaggregated. It is, in effect, not a plan in any meaningful sense of the term.

Fedorenko's is more than a quip: it rests on a massive literature available to anyone within and outside of the USSR. Plans in rubles of turnover encourage the use of expensive inputs and discourage the production of cheaper models. Plans in tons penalize economy of metals, and reward heavy products. In road transport, plans in ton-kilometers reward those who succeed in transporting the heaviest goods for the longest distances. Until recently, construction enterprises had been working to fulfill plans expressed in rubles *spent*, and their wage bills are still calculated as a percentage of this, so that more economical construction actually penalized both management and labor.

Furthermore, under those conditions technical progress is in effect discouraged, partly because there is no reward for risk-taking, and partly because the material means and investment financing are tightly controlled from above, thus allowing for no initiative from below. Finally, with fulfillment of the plan the primary criterion for success, managers—anxious above all else to have their plans fulfilled—have regularly understated their production possibilities to keep some capacity in reserve for contingencies. In turn, the constant worry about supplies caused not only the overapplication for materials, but also large-scale hoarding. Within such a system, the needs of the customer had little or no influence on what was being produced.

Some Soviet critics have also pointed out the misleading nature of the output statistics: for instance, the USSR produces eight times more combine-harvesters than does the United States, but a large proportion of these harvesters are always out of action for lack of spare parts and proper maintenance. In this and other cases it would make economic sense to produce less, but what with the relevant ministry chasing growth targets, production stays high, regardless of need and quality.

This growth for growth's sake, says Shmelev in another article,[4] makes no sense. Other economists have said much the same thing. Shortages, they assert, coexist with overproduction of what is not needed. The completion of investments is often delayed by too many projects, simultaneously pursued: as many as 350,000 "production investment projects" are already in hand.[5]

It may be objected that this picture is too negative or one-sided.

Even if each of these defects can be illustrated by literally dozens of quotations from Soviet sources, a critic might say, the economy still continued to grow, the wheels kept turning. There are several explanations. Planning worked in those sectors to which the state gave priority and whose needs could be easily quantified. This applied first and foremost to armaments, but also to electrical energy, where the product is homogeneous and thus readily "plannable." It also applied to production of oil and gas, and to the construction of a network of pipelines: In each of these fields, the Soviet system had scored impressive achievements.

Second, plans are not made on a blank sheet of paper. Those involved in the process know what they did the year before, and assume (usually correctly) that they will draw supplies from the same sources and will be asked to produce more or less the same things, probably a little more this time around. This "planning from the achieved level," as it has come to be called, is now being criticized for its manifest flaws, but it helps to explain why the wheels did turn. To this must be added a complex network of unofficial relations between the parts of the economy; some of these relations are purely corrupt, while others take the form of mutual aid. For example, a manager who has succeeded in hoarding excess stocks of metal sheets might arrange to barter them, in exchange for caustic soda or wooden logs or whatever he happens to need, outside of the formal allocation network.

The basic criticism to be leveled against this system is that it has come into contradiction with the requirements of a modern industrial economy and of a society with rising living standards and even more sharply rising expectations. To take two examples: Few Soviet citizens had been concerned about repair facilities for consumer durables until these become widely available, as they are now. And many Soviet citizens had learned to accept the appalling lack of decent housing until the mid-1950s, when Khrushchev began to turn his attention to this problem. Housing construction accelerated in the 1960s, but slowed under Brezhnev. Gorbachev has promised a separate house or apartment for every family by the year 2000, and housing as well as schools and the seriously neglected hospitals are receiving higher priority today. The new goals are clearly a response to popular demand, voiced with increased stridency in the press and at public gatherings.

THE PLOT THICKENS

These, then, are the long-term and fundamental reasons for a change of the system. What about the short-term causes of the "crisis"? One was demographic: the extremely slow rise in the numbers of the working population meant that growth now depended almost wholly on increases in labor productivity. Another cause was related to agriculture: especially in the 1970s, huge investments and subsidies had been poured into the countryside, with very little effect. In fact, it proved necessary to mobilize additional millions of workers, students, and soldiers to help with the harvesting. It would take me too far afield to analyze the causes of the agricultural imbroglio, but suffice it to say that its burden on the rest of the economy contributed to the overstrain and slowdown of the entire economic system.[6]

Yet another factor is the arms burden. Its actual magnitude was concealed until 1989, when the figure of 77.3 billion rubles was published. Clearly the effort to achieve and maintain parity with the much richer United States has been very costly, with scarce skills and equipment having been diverted into these unproductive channels.

The gradual exhaustion of readily accessible raw materials and fuels, necessitating larger investments in remote areas, especially in Siberia, has been one more factor contributing to the relentless decline of the economy. The decision to invest in energy in remote areas was rational, but enormously expensive. However, the Baikal-Amur railroad project is now seen as wasteful.

Nor did the policies pursued by the Brezhnev regime bring any succor. In fact, it was precisely under his reign that corruption spread into the party and state regime, to a degree unparalleled in the history of the USSR. Brezhnev and his colleagues duly acknowledged that the economy was not functioning well and even introduced some reforms. However, the latter were always described as "the further perfecting" of the existing system (though it's hard to see how anything "perfect" can be made even "more perfect"); its major features were left intact. And so the measures failed to make any significant impact.

All told, then, the economy on the eve of Gorbachev's assumption of power was full of the most alarming defects and shortcomings. There was a clear need for decisive measures to increase efficiency and accelerate the diffusion of technology, eliminate waste, and bring about higher labor productivity and a closer adjustment of output to the needs of the economy and of the consumer.

For reasons set out above, the system had proved incapable of meeting these needs. Only a "radical reform" could turn the situation around. And in view of the widespread passivity and indifference, the problem was not only economic. The three concepts proclaimed by the new leadership—glasnost, perestroika, and *demokratizatsia*—were emblematic of the profound changes that were to be introduced in all areas of Soviet life, political, social, and cultural. All three were interlinked, each one of them important by itself and each essential to the other. There was to be no more talk about "perfecting the existing system." The system itself would have to be changed.

THE PAST: TINKERING WITH THE SYSTEM

Before turning to the proposed reform program, let us take a look at past attempts to cure some of the enduring ills of the Soviet economic system. Some of them had been diagnosed already in the 1950s. One of my own first articles on this subject was filled with examples, culled from the Soviet press, of waste and distortions due to plans expressed in gross value rubles and tons, and other such practices.[7] Measures to reform Stalinist agricultural policies were adopted as early as September 1953, and industrial planning was the subject of a decree in 1955.

Indeed, the Khrushchev era (1956–1964) saw a number of bold attempts to tackle the afflictions of the "administrative system."[8] Under the protective wing of V. Nemchinov, an economist in good standing with the party leadership, the reformist economist Yevsei Liberman published several critical articles, and during this period, too, Viktor Novozhilov and Leonid Kantorovich were allowed to publish ideas on optimal planning, involving mathematical methods, which had been hitherto proscribed. In fact, Nemchinov, Novozhilov, and Kantorovich shared the Lenin prize in 1964, and the 1965 reform measures reflected some of Liberman's ideas—this, even though Khrushchev had already fallen.

However, while greater freedom of expression gave several reforming economists an opportunity to advocate new ideas, the centralized planning system remained impervious to authentically radical change. The reform decree of 1965 also reconstituted economic ministries, which

Khrushchev had abolished in 1957. These ministries were now made responsible for the performance of "their" enterprises, and, despite references in the decree to managerial autonomy and to a reduction in the number of compulsory plan indicators, plan-orders from above continued to rule the system. In 1967, the price "reform" still left prices based almost exclusively on cost-plus (though the "plus" now included a capital charge), and neither in theory nor in practice did they incorporate supply-and-demand conditions or value-in-use.

To be sure, there were some attempts not only to "perfect" but to change certain features of the system. But all of them were little more than variations on a centralizing theme, and did nothing to alter the planning mechanism. For example, an attempt was made to introduce "normed value-added" as an indicator alongside gross value of output. This was to measure the net value the given product should have. It failed. In fact, plan-indicators increased in number and the role of profit, stressed in the 1965 decree, was actually downgraded in 1979.

As stagnation set in, reform-minded economists tried to advocate more radical ideas. At the Siberian headquarters of the Academy of Sciences in Novosibirsk, Abel Aganbegyan and Tatyana Zaslavskaya, who subsequently became leading exponents of perestroika, proposed a variety of strategies. Their unpublished memoranda were leaked to the West, for which they were strongly reprimanded. In the meantime, the older generation of doctrinaire economists was passing from the scene, and with it the dogged resistance to innovation. The concept of "market socialism" was still taboo, but gradually the words "socialist market" crept into the published literature.

From available fragments, it finally became possible to reconstruct a reform program not unlike the one that saw the light under Gorbachev.[9] True, for many years the program remained a consummation devoutly to be wished. Hopes were raised when Andropov succeeded the ailing Brezhnev in 1982, but they were dashed when he was succeeded by the colorless Chernenko.[10]

Gorbachev's speeches, therefore, as well as the measures proposed by his closest advisors, did not come exactly "out of the blue." They had a long prehistory, albeit one marked far more by failure than by success. At first, Gorbachev moved slowly and cautiously, leading some observers to conclude that he was proposing essentially yet another set of measures designed to "perfect" an unperfectable system.

Whether his ideas underwent a change when he realized the full measure of the crisis, or whether he found it politic to unveil his reform program gradually, waiting for the moment when he was strong enough to implement it, we do not know. At first his emphasis seemed to be on accelerating growth (*uskoreniye*), and tighter discipline. In any case, there was no discernible blueprint; as Zaslavskaya has said, it had been no one's task to draft one. Gorbachev turned for help to a number of prominent reform-minded economists, but even today it cannot be said that a wholly coherent package has been presented, much less adopted.

In fact—as will be seen below—there is as of this writing no consensus on many important elements of the reform process. Moreover, though Gorbachev tended in his speeches to align himself with the most radical critics, his actual measures, such as the Law on State Enterprises, showed signs of compromise and were criticized by the radicals as halfhearted and contradictory. Numerous articles and letters by managers have pointed out that the "law" in no way protects them from arbitrary interference from ministries, which continue to impose obligatory plans upon them.

PROJECTS AND AGENDAS

Let me, then, turn to the reform program as it has emerged from legislation (some of it still on the drawing board), from resolutions, and from speeches by Soviet leaders. What follows is less a description of the actual situation than one of what the reformers hope *will* take place when the measures spelled out below are implemented.

Though hundreds of details and legislative acts are still to be worked out, one thing seems clear: the reform "package" is intended to remedy those "systemic" deficiencies set out in the earlier part of this essay, and not merely to patch up the old and discredited model. Here are its basic ingredients:

First, the vast majority of enterprises are to be free to determine the bulk of their output and their product mix, in negotiation with their customers or trading intermediaries. There are to be no more plans imposed in rubles, tons, meters, and so on. The exceptions will be top-priority "state orders," which will be compulsory, but these too are to generate profit for the enterprise. The success criteria and bonuses for management and workforce are to depend decisively on profits. Enterprises are to stand on their own financial feet and will no longer be able to get subsidies and soft credits. The emphasis is clearly on the role of the market.

Second—and this flows from the first principle—management is to be free to choose its own suppliers, and the administered "rationing" of material inputs is to be phased out. (The traditional centralized system embodied a complex linked network of production and allocation plans.) Not being tied to a specific supplier by the plan means, and is intended to mean, competition between suppliers, with effective customer pressure to improve quality.

Third, a major price reform is plainly essential, so that it would be profitable to produce necessities. Prices are to reflect not just costs but also use-value. In the more radical versions of the reform (still under discussion), most prices are to be negotiable between supplier and customer, with supply and demand playing a major role.

Fourth, a major modification in the conduct of foreign trade is under way. Until 1987, virtually all trade was channeled through the Ministry of Foreign Trade and its specialized corporations. There was virtually no connection between domestic and foreign-trade prices, and the difference, positive or negative, resulted in a profit for or a subsidy from the state budget. Soviet management was cut off from foreign markets and had neither the opportunity nor the knowledge, nor yet the material interest, to produce for export. This was one reason for the poor performance of Soviet manufactures in world markets (the bulk of Soviet exports to the West still consists of fuel and raw materials). Now economic ministries and large enterprises are allowed to deal directly with foreign countries, and are allowed to keep a proportion of the foreign currency they earn.

Another decree, published in 1987, provides for joint ventures with foreign, especially capitalist, companies, and in its latest version allows foreign capital to play a dominant role. Also under discussion is the creation of "enterprise zones," possibly in some of the Baltic republics, which are in the process of claiming a high degree of economic autonomy. Important measures affecting the labor force are also in preparation. To combat widespread apathy, there are new steps to secure workers' participation in decision-making, and management at various levels is to be elected by the workforce. Wages are to be more closely tied to the financial performance of the enterprise and to productivity. The trade unions are to play a more active protective role (in practice, strikes have been called by unofficial workers' committees).

A further important measure concerns cooperatives. Soviet leaders now freely admit what has long been known—namely, that collective farms (kolkhozes) and the cooperative trading network are cooperatives in name only. Both are integral parts of the state planning system, and both have been subject to detailed orders from above. The new cooperatives, as envisioned by the Law on Cooperatives passed in 1988 and the speeches by Gorbachev and premier Nikolai Ryzhkov, are different creatures altogether. They are projected as voluntary, genuine, free from official tutelage and control, and engaged in a wide variety of activities in competition with each other and with state enterprises— e.g., in small-scale manufacture, services, trade, construction, even banking. By 1989, over four million people were already organized in such cooperatives.

In agriculture, the new plans call for many of the large state and collective farms to become federations of small cooperative units, with cooperative service agencies operating as subcontractors to farms. They will thus replace the monopolist (and inefficient) state-run organizations responsible, among other things, for repairs, supplies, "chemicalization," drainage, and the like. A new law allows families to lease land and livestock; the period of the lease, at first only up to five years, has now been raised to fifty years, or even for life, with right to inherit.

Less satisfactory is the legal position of private enterprises. There are restrictions on full-time private activities of persons of working age, and (unlike in China, Hungary, and Poland, and even East Germany) no one is allowed to employ anyone outside of the narrowly defined family. Yet there is, at least on paper, a way out: a cooperative can be set up with a minimum of three persons, and it may also employ outsiders (provided it pays them at the official rate). Still, the restrictions are onerous and a serious obstacle (rooted both in ideology and vested interests) to the rational development of the Soviet economy.

SLOW PACE AND DOGGED RESISTANCE

On the whole, the projected reforms can certainly be characterized as radical. If and when implemented, they would not merely "perfect" the old system, but overhaul it.

But will they? Thus far, the record is a mixed one. Some reforms are yet to be enacted, some have been implemented, but only partially.

Gorbachev admitted as much in his speech to the Nineteenth Party Conference in June 1988, and others have been saying much the same thing, if not more. To quote the economist and director of the Institute of Economics of the USSR Academy of Sciences, Leonid Abalkin:

> If we were to speak of real economic successes, of the indicators of development, of the situation in the market and the shops, then, unfortunately, very little has been achieved. Is this really unexpected? In my view, it is logical. Why should things have suddenly gotten better? Have we in fact started operating all the levers and factors (of reform)? We have adopted one or two laws, taken decisions, approved various documents. But it is naïve to hope that real life can be changed by decrees and regulations.[11]

So far, key elements of the proposed changes have not been put into effect. A new pricing system is to be introduced in 1991, with some of its provisions coming into effect only two or three years later. The practice of allocating the means of production from the top is yet to be replaced by trade and free choice of supplier. The current five-year plan runs through 1990 and remains in force. To ensure its fulfillment and to ensure the production of items that are not profitable at the old prices, the compulsory "state orders" (*goszakazy*), which were to have been confined only to a few super-priority items, are still applied to the bulk of industrial production. In other words, most Soviet enterprises still receive orders from above as to what to produce and for whom.

Worse still, because of the official commitment to speeding up the growth rates, the economic ministries impose targets in rubles, tons, and so on, since that is how growth is measured, rather than by orienting management to satisfy user demands. The Soviet press has been full of complaints that a multitude of obsolete and often contradictory regulations stands in the way of genuine enterprise autonomy and innovation. Similarly, despite official policy statements, including those by Gorbachev, that officials must stop interfering with the management of state and collective farms, the old practices endure. There have even been reports of local officials actually destroying private greenhouses for early vegetables.[12] As one Soviet economist told me: "Unfortunately, there are millions of people in our country who prefer not to have any early vegetables rather than see their neighbors make money by growing them."

Clearly, a major reason why progress in implementing the reforms has been so disappointingly slow is that many people oppose and resent them. This has several aspects. One is a visceral dislike of the inequalities that flow from payment by results, from the freedom to set up cooperatives and to charge higher prices. Under conditions of chronic shortage, it is all too easy to make high profits which cause cooperatives and private activities to be seen as "speculation."

The dislike is not confined to bureaucrats; ordinary citizens are unhappy too. For instance, the long-overdue efforts to bring prices into line with supply-and-demand, thus eliminating the onerous and wasteful practice of state subsidies, has met with massive resistance, even though Gorbachev promised to compensate for the proposed price increases with commensurate wage hikes. This reform has been postponed to avoid trouble. By the same token, the emphasis on efficiency and financial discipline, which may result in the closing of many enterprises and in redeployment of labor from overstaffed to understaffed industrial sectors, has frightened millions of workers. Gorbachev has sought support "from below" for his measures, but it has not been easy. Restrictions imposed in early 1989 on cooperatives reflect not only bureaucratic prejudice but also popular resentment.

Party and state functionaries have a special reason for resisting the reforms—namely, because they regard them as a challenge to their power and privileges, and in many cases a threat to their jobs. Glasnost has opened the door to spirited discussions not only about the excessive number of parasitic bureaucrats, but also about their privileges—their special shops in which goods unavailable to ordinary citizens are sold at modest prices, their own hospitals, country villas, and transport. Their salaries, now published, are not high; hence the value they set on the privileges.

In a revealing interview, the economist Abel Aganbegyan, one of Gorbachev's closest advisers, cited a "high Soviet official" who had visited Hungary and found, to his horror, that in Hungary anyone can get anything in the shops. "Is this socialism?" the official exclaimed.[13] Clearly, commented Aganbegyan, for this as well as for many other officials, "socialism" is equated with privileged access to goods and services. No wonder radical reform does not sit well with such people.

Of course, blatant self-interest, however tenacious, can hardly be used as an argument against reform. But ideology can. This is not to say that the appeal to ideology is necessarily sophistry, even though in the Soviet Union ideological principles have been adapted time and again to suit the political needs of the time. Some beliefs are genuinely held. One of them is the tenet that socialism and the market are incompatible, and that production for sale is gradually to be replaced by conscious planning. Since the Soviet reforms—and even more so those already adopted in Hungary and China—point in the opposite direction, the sayings of Marx and Engels can always be cited against them.

Egalitarianism is yet another principle that the anti-reformers can rely on for their defense. This may seem contradictory, because privileges for officials are scarcely what Marx and Lenin meant by equality. But such privileges are out of the public eye, and what's more important, they go with rank—that is to say, they are a reward for "public service." Market-based inequalities, however, such as those arising from the sale of early vegetables, are seen as part and parcel of the capitalist mentality, the sordid chase after "profit," and thus a violation of the "socialist" ethos.

It would be an oversimplification to regard all bureaucrats as opponents of reforms. Tatyana Zaslavskaya is right to remind us, as she did in a paper presented in Vienna in 1987, that much depends both on the effect of the proposed changes on the career prospects and functions of given officials, and indeed also on the confidence in their abilities to work under new conditions. Similarly, she points out, younger and more skilled workers are likely to see advantages and opportunities in the proposed changes, whereas the older and less skilled are apt to resent them. Some managers welcome new responsibilities, others fear and shun them. The essential point is that, taken together, human attitudes, particularly those of officials who are expected to implement the new policies, present serious obstacles to reform.

PRACTICAL DIFFICULTIES AND UNANSWERED QUESTIONS

The reformers are also faced with purely practical difficulties. One of them is what might be called the inevitability and impossibility of gradualness. For instance, to be effective, the reforms require a new set of prices, and the abandonment of administered material allocation. But how can this be done swiftly in view of the horrendous shortages, excess demand, and material imbalances?

To the latter difficulty must also be added financial imbalances. As

Gorbachev confirmed in his speech to the Nineteenth Party Conference in July 1988, the budget is in deficit, and credit discipline is poor.[14] During 1989 numerous sources have referred to the vast scale of the budget deficit, excessive wage rises, rising money supply, and serious shortages of many goods. One cannot rely on the price mechanism if the monetary system is in disorder. One reason for imbalance between supply and demand for consumer goods has been the reduction in the supply of vodka, introduced in 1986. The policy has been largely a failure not only because it led to the virtual disappearance of sugar from stores (bought out for the purpose of making *samogon*—moonshine), but also because it has proved impossible to cover the gap by a sufficient supply of other goods, and because the loss of revenue from vodka only exacerbated the budget deficit. On top of this, the fall in oil prices has adversely affected the balance of payments and led to a reduction in imports of consumer goods and in budget revenue from foreign trade.

There are powerful reasons, then, for the inability to implement the whole reform package at once. However, gradualness also creates contradictions, with two "logics" existing at one and the same time. Thus enterprise autonomy requires a radical reform of prices and the abandonment of allocation of materials and the stress on plan fulfillment. All this requires the elimination of shortage (excess demand). Each element of the reform depends on the others. In an economy beset by shortages, anything that does not figure in the central production or allocation plan is deemed to be low-priority, and therefore liable to suffer from nondelivery of some of the needed inputs. To cite one example, according to the reform plans, enterprises are to have more resources for investment. However, if machinery, equipment, or building materials are in short supply and "rationed," the resources will not be available, and investment will suffer.

The chronic shortages are now openly discussed in the press and on television, and Gorbachev himself has blamed them on the present allocation system. To wait for the end of the shortages before abolishing the system, he said, would mean waiting forever. Perhaps the emphasis on financial discipline, a balanced budget, and payment of wages strictly in relation to performance will eliminate excess demand for both consumer and producer goods and facilitate the introduction of new prices, together with much greater freedom to vary or fix prices by negotiations. As of now, however, these measures have not been put into effect.

Yet another difficulty is the habits and relationships formed during the long reign of the "administrative system." Managers have not had to bother about finding customers, since they were designated by their superiors in the planning hierarchy. And with guaranteed sales came sloth, incompetence, and almost total lack of initiative. Under the reforms, managers would have to learn the arts of competitive marketing, to which they are not accustomed and for which they were never trained. No wonder many of them seek out state orders, so that they may continue to work within the familiar procedures.

The same is true for bank managers with little or no experience in assessing the soundness of investment projects. Under the old system, their functions have been mainly to channel funds in accordance with instructions from above, and to check on the enterprises' use or misuse of funds. Now, with a much larger segment of investment to be decentralized and to be financed partly out of retained profits and partly out of bank credits, their functions will be markedly different. And so, a period of training is mandatory. But is there time for it?

Another problem concerns the new role of the Communist party and its full-time officials, as well as of the economic ministries. According to Gorbachev, party functionaries are not to meddle in the managerial decision-making process. In fact, many party functionaries are to play the role of government officials, thus combining the two roles. A city party secretary, for example, would be at the same time the chairman of that city's soviet. The Central Committee's industrial department has been abolished, with some of its staff (for instance that dealing with the chemical industry) transferred to the appropriate industries.

Aside from the questionable logic of this new arrangement—i.e., how do you reconcile the fusion of two roles with the stated principle of "separation of powers"?—it also raises some vexing problems of a practical nature. For instance, what precisely are to be the functions of the party apparat on the one hand, and of the economic ministry on the other? What are to be the relations between the ministry of chemical industry and the chemical industry enterprises and between those enterprises and the local soviet? How can the party's role in making all key appointments (the *nomenklatura* system) be reconciled with free elections of managers (also stipulated in the reforms)? Again, these questions—though continually discussed in the Soviet press—remain unanswered and unresolved. (Elections of managers seem to have ended.)

The "reform package" is open to other criticisms, too. For instance, it pays little attention to externalities—that is, to situations in which micro-profitability may be a misleading guide to efficiency. For example, in America and elsewhere public transport does not "pay," but this would not be a reason for closing the subway in New York. Pollution is an external *dis*economy (it is usually profitable to pollute, it costs more money to clean up). The Soviets do now pay much more attention to ecology: For the past few years, both the press and high Soviet officials have been painting a shocking picture of ecological blight and of its effect on the health of millions of people. Already in June 1986, so many speakers at the Writers' Congress concentrated on this issue that the meeting came to be known as the "Ecological Congress." And at the Nineteenth Party Conference exactly two years later, Fyodor Morgun, the chairman of the recently formed USSR State Committee for Environmental Protection, said—among other things—that some fifty million Soviet citizens live in 102 cities where the pollution level exceeds permissible norms by ten times or more.[15] By now, numerous ecological groups have been formed, with ever more people participating in them. However, antipollution measures add to costs and reduce profits, and so conflict with the aim of improving the financial results of enterprises.

Another problem area is that of investment. Aside from the problem of ensuring the availability of needed machinery and equipment, the decentralization of investment decisions raises the need for a capital market, or of some other way of enabling enterprises with financial reserves to invest in other enterprises. There is also a dearth of information about future costs and needs that in no economy can be conveyed by current prices, however reformed: To invest in the future, one must be able to estimate future prices and costs, and to have access to information about the investment plans of one's potential competitors and/or suppliers of complementary inputs.

Then there is the problem of risk: Who is to bear it? Who is either to be rewarded in the event of success or penalized in the event of failure? The reform now contains an explicit provision for bankruptcy, but available evidence suggests that it is very seldom applied because of the pressure to maintain full employment. (The same, incidentally, is true for Hungary.) Other questions too are legitimate, and urgent: Should workers suffer wage cuts if an enterprise proves unprofitable, especially if they had no voice in making the original investment decision? For that matter, would this not still be the case even if the decision is taken by a manager elected by workers? The press has cited many instances of election of enterprise managers—and has also shown concern in cases where the "winner" tolerated slack discipline.

Another vexing question is that of the powers of republics and local soviets. There has been much criticism in the Soviet press of the fact that overcentralization has meant that the vast bulk of the republics' output is allocated by and from Moscow, and that local soviets are powerless, inasmuch as they neither dispose of their own financial source nor have any control over material resources. With the revived slogan of "all power to the soviets" and the new constitutional provision for local tax revenues, local soviets have been encouraged to set up their own small-scale enterprises, alongside those controlled by all-union and/ or republican ministries. In addition, republican powers have also been enhanced.

Yet all these praiseworthy moves have raised new issues. Some republics—in the first place the Baltic republics—have demanded and received "economic independence"—that is, control by each republic of enterprises within its borders. Yet might such a step not prove disruptive of interrepublican and interregional links? Surely the disastrous effects of loosening centrifugal forces in Yugoslavia should serve as an object lesson for Soviet planners. It is understandable that Lithuania, for example, resents the fact that eighty-five percent of its industrial output is controlled by Moscow. But is the answer to give that power to Vilnius? Would it not be better—and more in tandem with the reform model— to vest this power in management, leaving it free to negotiate with customers all over the USSR, and also, for that matter, with foreign firms? In fact, this is how the radical reformers see the way forward.[16] Much less potentially disruptive is the power of republics to experiment freely with reforms, notably in agriculture. In this instance Estonia is blazing a trail, with encouragement of family farming on long or even indefinite leases. In the Baltic republics there still survives an authentic peasant spirit that could take advantage of these new opportunities, but progress is slow. It will not be helped by the decisions of the Central Committee plenum held in March 1989, which envisaged the granting of leases by state and collective farms and not (as the reformers proposed) by the local authorities. (The farms are much more likely to retain control over what happens on what they still regard as "their" land.)

GROPING TOWARDS THE FUTURE

It should be clear, then, that the Soviet leadership is indeed trying to introduce radical reforms in the economy, and equally it should be clear that progress has been slow and uneven. There are, to repeat, three basic reasons for it: first, *opposition*, much (but not all) of it due to vested interests and privileges; second, the sheer *practical difficulties* of implementing the desired changes; and third, the *gaps and ambiguities* in the reform model itself.

Perhaps the most acute dilemma embedded in this process is that of plan versus market: In what form can the two be effectively combined? Where lies the boundary between them?

Thus far, the dilemma remains unresolved. In an article written jointly by two reformist economists, Gavriil Popov and Nikolai Shmelev, the authors address this very issue. How does it happen, they ask, that a rigid centralized system, based on an indissoluble link between production and supply-of-inputs plans, generates a chronic supply deficit? "The answer," they write, "is trivially simple. . . . One cannot foresee everything," especially indirect requirements, as for instance of wire for electric motors required for oil pumps that pump oil required by the petrochemical industry, which makes dyestuffs that are needed for the cloth that in turn is needed for the clothing industry. The planners' traditional "material balance" approach tends to underestimate the magnitude of the indirect requirements.

Popov and Shmelev go on to discuss the importance of rational and flexible prices and the dangers of monopolistic abuses if price controls were eliminated. They quite rightly call attention to the dangers inherent in the pure "free-market" solutions, especially in long-term decisions that affect structural change, ecology, and the quality of life in general. Each system, they say, is bound to have both advantages and disadvantages. And then they offer their own solution: planning and price controls limited "to a few hundred of the most important products, that is, those which under favorable circumstances can be counted in physical units at the present level of knowledge and techniques for processing data." The remaining output should not be planned at all, either directively or indicatively.[17]

The authors' solution seems eminently sensible. But it must be stressed that it is only one of the various proposals now being discussed, and that it is difficult to predict exactly how this crucial problem will be settled.

Yet whatever the eventual "mix" between plan and market, the direction in which the reformers are groping is clear, and so is their basic aim—namely, to create a more democratic socialist society in which there is a sizeable cooperative and private sector and in which the bulk of state enterprises produce for the market. To reach this goal, the reformers had to agree from the very outset that what has existed in the USSR heretofore was a "deformation" of socialism—indeed, as many authors have openly stated, no socialism at all. Thus the economist A. Rakitsky rejects the Brezhnev view that the Soviet Union had "real (mature) socialism," and continues: "We live under a barrackslike deformation of socialism; our society is not yet socialist. Our society is so organized that the means of production are owned not by a society but by a caste that governs in the name of society."[18] Others have put it in even starker terms. Indeed, some writers have even questioned the wisdom of the Founding Fathers. Thus the economist A. Sergeyev:

> Marx and Engels held that socialism and commodity production were not only contradictory but also incompatible. Lenin held the same view. Even today no one would have the theoretical effrontery to claim that Lenin was the founder of the theory of commodity production under socialism. Was the theory of Marx, Engels, and Lenin, then, incorrect?[19]

This essay has outlined the numerous problems, difficulties, obstacles, and inconsistencies in the reform process now taking place in the USSR. It has also called attention to the formidable opposition to this process from various strata of society. Does this mean that failure is inevitable? I do not think so. Every reformer, including Gorbachev, is painfully aware of these problems, and of the urgent need for resolute measures.

The problem of food and consumer goods is a case in point. Over the past few years, shortages in this critical area, always a problem in the Soviet Union, have become acute, so much so that they have come to threaten (as Soviet writers openly admit) the very legitimacy of perestroika. Thus the *Izvestia* columnist Aleksandr Bovin:

> It is clear to everyone that if the country is not supplied in the next few years with foodstuffs, with clothing, shoes, furniture, electric appliances and so on, if at least some kind of order is not brought into the services industry, if millions, tens of millions are not delivered from the exhausting senselessness of queues and of systematic humiliation by anyone dispensing such "services," all faith in perestroika will evaporate. . . .[20]

The reason why this situation has deteriorated is not a decline in supply but a rapid rise in incomes. There is now much more money chasing the same (or almost the same) volume of goods. The budget deficit and "soft" credits are part of the cause, and so is a slackening of control over wages. Inflation is recognized as a growing problem. There is a collapse of confidence in the ruble, since it is increasingly difficult to buy what one wants. The practical problems of transition, the process of learning to work in new ways, is one cause of what is now seen as an acute crisis. But it is also true that inflationary pressure and worsening shortages make the transition even more difficult, if not impossible.

Some economists, such as Nikolai Shmelev, have advocated large loans to buy consumer goods from the West. Another idea that has been floated is to buy machinery in the West in order to expand the production of consumer goods. Yet another is to expand rapidly joint ventures with Western firms, and to open up the internal market to them. In fact, this last suggestion has already been adopted. None of these variants is ideal—e.g., the last one is a drain on the supply of *valyuta* (foreign currency), while some economists object to "quick fixes" because they perpetuate the country's dependence on the West and fail to address systemic defects. Most economists reject the Shmelev proposals. Even without them, the Soviet debt to the West has doubled between 1986 and 1989. Many advocate the dropping of expensive investment projects, allowing a shift in Soviet imports from machinery to consumer goods. However, the ministers have been strongly defending their investment projects.

Be that as it may, Gorbachev and his allies are alert to these problems and are seeking solutions to them. Above all, they are aware, as Gorbachev himself has put it, that "there is no other way" except reform. Continued stagnation would threaten the security of the regime, internally and externally. Whatever the magnitude of opposition within the ranks of the apparatchiks, it is the party leadership that is pressing forward, conscious as it is of the fact that economic failure translates into political failure as well.

It must be stressed that it would be unreasonable to expect any rapid improvement either in productivity or living standards; and that there may even be temporary regress, unless the radical measures adopted in agriculture (such as family leases, transfers of land into private hands, and so on) prove to have a quick and decisive effect on food supplies, but as of now this seems unlikely.

AN ECONOMY IN TRANSITION
★
ALEC NOVE

By the same token, it is unreasonable—in fact, unconscionable—not to welcome the changes now going on in the Soviet Union. Some people in the West, still mired in their anti-Communist obsessions, take the view that the West should do everything to ensure the failure of the Gorbachev reforms, on the ground that a more efficient USSR would be a more dangerous USSR. This view stands logic on its head. In point of fact, a USSR concentrating its efforts on setting its own house in order, on forging closer economic and cultural relations with the West, and on cooperating rather than engaging in protracted conflict with Western powers—as Gorbachev is patently trying to do—will be a country infinitely more pleasant to live in—and with.

Unfortunately, the situation, political as well as economic, is deteriorating as these lines are written. Far from moving towards a market-based equilibrium, what we now have is a rapid spread of consumer rationing (meat, milk, sugar, soap, and many other items are no longer freely on sale in many parts of the country), and delays in completing investment projects are longer than ever. Economic malfunctions exacerbate the already dangerous tensions between the nationalities. There are fewer grounds for optimism, and many observers (in the Soviet Union and outside it) express alarm as to possible outcomes.

Should Gorbachev fail—and failure is by no means to be ruled out—the outcome would be a misfortune, perhaps even a calamity, for everyone concerned. The outcome depends first and foremost on internal factors. However, there is every reason for the West to extend a welcome to the reform process, to help as much as it can to speed it along—and every reason not to obstruct it.

★

TOWARDS THE
RULE OF LAW?

✱

WILLIAM E. BUTLER

FEW ELEMENTS OF PERESTROIKA AND glasnost have aroused greater hopes in the West than the discussions about the formation of a *sotsialisticheskoye pravovoye gosudarstvo*. How to translate this term is perplexing, for it depends on the meaning assigned to it by the architects and proponents of perestroika. Different people have various understandings of what a *pravovoye gosudarstvo* should or might be; an insensitive choice of the English equivalent may distort a legal, philosophical, and political issue of the greatest moment.

Four equivalents are widely employed in English-language writings. One draws upon classical Anglo-American terminology: the "rule-of-law state." Another attempts a more literal rendering: "law-governing state." Occasionally one comes across the expression "legal state," and on the assumption that "pravovoye gosudarstvo" is a caulk from the German "Rechtsstaat," the last term also is used in English-language translations. The dilemma is compounded by the failure of the English tongue to distinguish sharply between two meanings of law: *jus* and *lex* (Latin); *Recht* and *Gesetz* (German); *droit* and *loi* (French); *pravo* and *zakon* (Russian), and so on in countless other languages. Consequently, many finer points of the Soviet dialogue about the rule-of-law state

TOWARDS THE RULE OF LAW?

★

WILLIAM E. BUTLER

(which is the translation I believe most apt for the present) are lost to the Anglo-American reader unless he is aware of the distinctions made by the author.

Where did the idea of a rule-of-law state originate? As one pre-revolutionary Russian legal philosopher wrote:

> The idea of a rule-of-law state in the history of European political thought has a significantly longer past than its underlying plans and programs for state transformation; to trace its roots is to review virtually the entire heritage of theoretical work explaining law and state.[1]

To many people in Tsarist Russia the concept of a rule-of-law state held out the hope of introducing genuine democracy into the country at the expense of the absolute autocratic power claimed—though in later years not actually possessed—by the Russian Imperial throne.

So meager is the indigenous literature on this subject, and so abruptly has it now been introduced and endorsed in party documents, that Soviet jurists have had difficulty dealing with it in rigorous fashion. They are groping for conceptual consensus at a moment when the policy requirements of perestroika demand action with little time for theoretical reflection.

SOURCES AND ORIGINS

Although there are some Soviet scholars who suggest that a socialist rule-of-law state came into being immediately after the 1917 October Revolution only to be eliminated by the Stalin "personality cult," most acknowledge that such a view is a travesty of history. Even committed Leninists would balk at the notion that the dictatorship of the proletariat could be regarded as the "rule of law." As for Stalinism, the less said of it the better. Rather, the current consensus holds that the Soviet origins of a rule-of-law state date from the late 1950s and early 1960s, the era of N. S. Khrushchev, when the USSR was declared to have become an "all-people's state" or a "state of the whole people." The period of "stagnation," which roughly speaking spans the twenty years immediately prior to Gorbachev, prevented the rule-of-law state from maturing. Hence, in the word of one legal expert, the "socialist rule-of-law state . . . is being formed by perestroika."[2]

Another legal historian offers a somewhat different periodization and rationale. Until the late 1950s the predominant view was that until communism was achieved, the state would exist solely in the form of the dictatorship of the proletariat, which would ultimately wither away. This belief obstructed the development of more sophisticated intermediate forms of state and law. Moreover, until the mid-1930s it was widely accepted that only "bourgeois law" could exist temporarily under socialism; the concept of a "socialist law" was denied, which further retarded the emergence of a socialist political system. And when the "Vyshinsky school" took the contrary view—that is, that a socialist state and socialist law must be introduced in order to strengthen and secure the gains of the revolution—the result was a state operating on an "administrative-command" system in which power was vested in the state apparatus and law was viewed as a system of orders or commands from top to bottom.[3] But the author concurs that the substitution in the 1960s of the all-people's state for the dictatorship of the proletariat laid the basis for the rule-of-law state, and that this was reinforced by the legal principles for state and social life set out in the 1977 USSR Constitution, now in force as amended in December 1989 to reflect the Gorbachev reforms.[4]

Soviet jurists, encouraged by the Twenty-Fifth Party Congress (1976) and by the constitution, began "for the first time"—as one Soviet writer put it—to broach the subject of a socialist rule-of-law state. Unfortunately, he adds, efforts "to substantiate the need for creating a rule-of-law state gave rise to resistance"[5] and the discussions proceeded no further. One legal scholar recalled that an article written in late 1976, following the Party Congress, on the socialist rule-of-law state was rejected by the publisher on the grounds that he was "using bourgeois conceptions."[6]

There is in fact no doubt among Soviet jurists that the socialist rule-of-law state, whatever its precise meaning, is deeply indebted to Western legal and political philosophy. The term, they acknowledge, dates back to at least the seventeenth century and originated as a reaction against unrestrained absolute monarchies. The concept was influential in the English, American, and French revolutions and progressive Russian nineteenth-century legal thought. Although "bourgeois" in origin, however, it is no longer to be rejected, in keeping with Lenin's behest to "seize with both hands the best from abroad" irrespective of where it originated. The "rule-of-law state" as a counterpoise to a repressive bureaucracy is essential; so what, asks one writer, "if it is similar" to the rule of law in the American system or the Rechtsstaat in the West German constitution? The task, he says, is to develop a "rule-of-law state of a socialist type."[7]

Opinions differ as to what the rule-of-law state may or should mean, and in those differences lies a range of views about the nature and pace of perestroika and the political and constitutional alterations enacted by the USSR Supreme Soviet in 1988 and 1989. Most legal scholars agree that the rule of law means the "supremacy of law [zakon] in all spheres of the life of society," the "subordination of authority [vlast] to law".[8] Or, as another legal scholar expressed it, the "very idea of a rule-of-law state consisted of restricting the arbitrariness of the authorities, endeavoring to subordinate its activities to law [pravo] standing above it."[9] As another scholar put it, logically the rule-of-law state is called upon to perform those very same functions "in a socialist society" as it did in other societies and regardless of the historical conditions in which it had been born. Its aim, put bluntly, is "to counterbalance the disproportionate concentration of authority in a few hands and to guarantee the rights and freedom of citizens."[10]

Why specifically should the Soviet Union introduce this term as well as institutions that would bring it to life? Have there not been efforts on behalf of strengthening legality, developing democracy, enlarging the involvement of citizens in state administration, and the like? What has been missing? The answer, suggests Professor Baglai, is the "acknowledgement of human freedom as the highest value—freedom, and not merely well-being, however important the latter may be." Consequently, the formation of a rule-of-law state presupposes "new in principle state-law institutes having the character of democratic guarantees."[11]

These are powerful sentiments, quite unlike what we in the West have been accustomed to hearing. They conceal an important philosophical conundrum, raised recently by the various uses of the term pravo and zakon. Is the state subordinate to pravo, or law writ large, and if so whence does that law originate? Or is the state subject merely to zakon, statutory law created by the highest parliamentary authority, the constitution being the basic law [osnovnoi zakon]? The former connotes eternal values of right and justice embodied in pravo which no state or official may transgress; the latter implies conformity to orders or commands of the state in the form of zakon, a view of law in the positivist tradition. It may therefore make a considerable difference as to whether the rule-of-law state is expected to conform to one or the other.

However defined, the rule-of-law state cannot subsist purely as an abstract proposition. It requires institutionalization in a myriad of forms, and for the moment the forms must engage the attention of Soviet jurists, because the 1988–89 constitutional amendments and collateral legislation represent the rule-of-law state in action. Let us examine some of these forms.

PARLIAMENTARY SUPREMACY

To Anglo-American eyes the Soviet system represents an amalgam of British parliamentary supremacy and the American written constitution. The rule of law in the United States originates in the fundamental character of the constitution, which no branch of government may transgress. An elaborate set of checks and balances has been introduced to prevent, however imperfectly, the legislative, executive, or judicial branches from arrogating excessive power. The law, in this view, is always above the state in the ultimate sense. In Britain the unwritten constitution sits uneasily with the doctrine of parliamentary supremacy. The absence of a written document reduces drastically the incidence of constitutional confrontation, and in its extreme form the principle of parliamentary supremacy could allow any parliament to undo what its predecessors may have done. The principle of popular sovereignty expressed through representative organs, in other words, gives greater regard to the majority of the day under parliamentary supremacy, whereas the American approach gives greater formal deference to individual and minority rights vis-à-vis the majority view.

Soviet jurists are aware that they are seeking to bridge the two approaches, and that the task is not an easy one. The attempt to secure the "rule of law," while essential, is viewed by some Soviet scholars as insufficient, or "limited." It is necessary, they maintain, to proceed from the "broader principle of parliamentary supremacy." Rule of law in this view is possible only if the law [zakon] is enacted by a representative organ elected by the people; the court applies the law, and a violation of the law—even if by the head of state—must be subject to punishment. Parliamentary supremacy is the *grundnorm* of a constitutional regime capable of overruling the powers of the executive branch and party apparatus.

This is the approach embodied in the 1988–89 constitutional amendments. The newly established Congress of People's Deputies becomes the ultimate repository of popular will—except in those rare instances when an issue might be put forth for decision directly to the general public by a referendum (all Soviet constitutions have provided for a referendum, but no implementing legislation has ever been enacted). The Congress elects its own permanently functioning organ, the USSR Supreme Soviet, from among its members; and the Supreme Soviet, as measured by the duration and frequency of its sessions and the importance of the issues it decides, becomes the principal *de facto* repository of popular sovereignty. The chairman of the USSR Council of Ministers (head of government), the Constitutional Supervision Committee, the chairman of the USSR Supreme Court, the USSR procurator general, the head of state (chairman of the USSR Supreme Soviet), and the heads of the principal supervisory body (People's Control Committee) and bodies charged with adjudicating economic disputes (state *Arbitrazh*) are all chosen or confirmed by the Congress. The Supreme Soviet appoints the chairman of the USSR Council of Ministers, confirms his recommendations for ministerial appointments, forms the USSR Defense Council, elects the USSR People's Control Committee and the USSR Supreme Court, appoints the USSR procurator general and the chief state arbitrator of the USSR, and forms or abolishes ministries and state committees.

Moreover, the Congress of People's Deputies has the exclusive power to amend (or, theoretically, to repeal) the constitution. The constitution is virtually silent on the question of separation of powers and it contains no ultimate restraint upon the abuse of power by the Congress of People's Deputies. In what sense, then, can the state be required to abide by its own law [*zakon*] and to act consistently with law [*pravo*] writ large? The answer, apparently, is—as in all parliamentary systems—self-restraint and a willingness to balance deeply held community values with present exigencies. This is especially so in the absence of a social ethos which venerates the rule of law as an end in itself, for Marxism-Leninism has always stressed the role of law as an instrument of class warfare.

Under Soviet conditions "separation of powers" has an added dimension: the demarcation of powers (thus far there has been almost no discussion of a checks-and-balances relationship between the state and the Communist party). "Unless this problem is resolved," commented one jurist, "all dialogue relating to a rule-of-law state and strengthening the power of the soviets is simply empty words."[12]

The argument at this stage is not the single-party system as such, but interference in and overlapping of state and party functions. The constitutional reforms contain no specific provision with respect to the party except to affirm on the constitutional level the party's right to be represented as such in the Congress of People's Deputies. (The course of party reforms vis-à-vis the relationship with the state is a separate issue considered elsewhere in this volume.)

The principle of parliamentary supremacy is not being newly introduced by the current reforms; rather, it is being reinforced and enlarged by a variety of innovations, but most especially by the transformation of the USSR Supreme Soviet into a large representative organ more or less permanently in session. Which brings me to the next question—to wit: Who is the ideal deputy?

PARLIAMENTARY REPRESENTATION

Apart from age, citizenship, and affiliation with a territorial or ethnic entity or with a social organization, and the usual moral qualities, Soviet law imposes no requirements as to who may be elected a people's deputy. In the past, announcements of election results have been accompanied by a breakdown of the social origin, sex, age, party membership, educational level, and other characteristics of those elected. The emphasis has been upon breadth of representation, rather than the parliamentary skills or expertise of candidates, and this in turn has led to the selection of candidates whose commitment to legislative affairs was passive and amateurish. Counterbalanced against this tradition of choosing legislators is the view widely shared in Soviet legal circles that legislation and legislating are, or ought to be, scientific and thoroughly professional. A parliamentary body truly capable of exercising its responsibilities in permanent session should, Soviet scholars argue, "reflect a certain legislative professionalism in its membership." Draft laws ought to be prepared by the deputies themselves rather than from "without"—clearly a reference to ministries and departments and/or the party apparatus. (Legal scholars claim that they have been excluded from the legislative process, a claim only partially true by Western standards.) The implication is that the Soviet deputy has essentially "confirmed" draft enactments prepared by others with minimal, if any, contributions at the committee stage. The corrective proposed by some is that deputies be nominated to a much greater extent from the ranks of "jurists and professional politicians" capable of taking part in the legislative process by reason of their knowledge and expertise.

Whether or not legally trained individuals by inclination or design come to play a larger role in Soviet public affairs, the view that legislation is part of "legal science" and that legislating ought to follow "scientific principles" is becoming more prominent in the rule-of-law debates. Proposals have been made to introduce a law on normative acts; such a law would elaborate not merely the stages of the legislative process but perhaps regulate the canons and even the terminology of legislative drafting in an effort to raise the standard of lawmaking. Many jurists are in favor of introducing legislation over a long period of time, from five to fifteen years. The specialist lawyer's view on legislation has been expressed as follows:

> Specialists write [laws], and then for some unknown reason someone else rewrites them completely. . . . The [1987] Law on the State Enterprise was written by economists, who could insert nothing but economic categories. As a result there is the question of whether a new law is needed. Jurists discussed the Law on the Labor Collective and made many suggestions. What for? Who listened to our view? . . . If a physicist creates an atomic bomb, for example, [no high official interferes by telling him] "put a screw here, and one there." Why do nonspecialists interfere in the legislative process? Laws are no less complex than the atomic bomb, perhaps more so. Half of the Soviet Union could be destroyed by an atomic bomb, but the entire Soviet Union might be destroyed by using [an improper] law.[13]

PARLIAMENTARY DEMOCRACY AND THE APPARAT

The Soviet bureaucracy is under siege by reason of its grotesque size and inefficiency, but these are incidental concerns to proponents of the rule-of-law state. The latter dwell especially upon two problems relating to the bureaucracy. The first rests upon a distinction between law (*zakon*), the highest positive law enacted by the plenary parliamentary authority, and legislation (*zakonodatelstvo*), a looser expression that can refer to all positive enactments of whatever level or to all enactments of a subordinate (*podzakonnoye*) character created by bodies other than parliament. A great number of Soviet enactments, says one Soviet critic, are classed as legislation, and acting "on the basis of and in execution of" laws, the ministries and departments regularly distort or defeat the intention of the legislator:

> A law must not be too detailed or turned into a set of official instructions. Life itself, it is argued, will provide the details. But the details are filled in not by life, but by the departments [i.e., by various governmental bodies], which employ a multitude of legally binding acts to nullify the very idea of the law and render it inoperative.[14]

In one sense the jurists' unhappiness springs from the fact (as noted above) that legislation is all too often drafted to reflect departmental interests rather than the requirements of law. But there is a more subtle and compelling point here related to another principle of perestroika—namely, that "everything not expressly prohibited by law is permitted." Widely proclaimed to be at the heart of economic restructuring and individual freedom, this principle undertakes to reverse the Stalinist postulate "everything not expressly permitted by law is prohibited."

The latter doctrine has been exaggerated in some Western models of "totalitarianism," but there is no denying its pernicious and pervasive influence in the legal regulation of the national economy prior to 1985 and its psychological legacy in the criminal law. The key question is, however, what is meant by "law?" Is it *zakon* or *zakonodatelstvo*? The better view is that "law" in its constitutional meaning of *zakon* must be correct, for otherwise if—"as frequently happens in everyday life and in the press—the word 'law' is taken to mean any normative act, then as a result of the orgy of prohibitions" the formula would become meaningless.[15]

The formula, however, as Soviet jurists also point out, may extend only to individuals in their personal capacity. Were administrative agencies or officials allowed to live by the formula, the result would be arbitrariness and chaos; a superior administrative body would interfere at will in the affairs of its subordinate enterprise—and defeat the object of the economic reforms.[16]

The second "check" on the bureaucracy is a rather imperfect piece of legislation enacted on June 30, 1987 after many years of dilatory delay.[17] Entitled the "Law on the Procedure for Appealing to a Court the Unlawful Actions of Officials Which Impinge on the Rights of Citizens," it was enacted pursuant to Article 52, para. 2, of the USSR Constitution *ten* years after provision originally was made for the possibility of suing bureaucrats for acting unlawfully. The enactment of the law itself was one of the earliest manifestations of parliamentary glasnost; the Supreme Soviet deputies declined to accept the text submitted for "confirmation" and insisted upon amendments which were ultimately inserted. But the crucial battle, in the view of many, was lost. The final text of the law makes officials susceptible to judicial redress only for decisions taken *individually* and not collegially.

The 1987 law was a dead letter from the outset, and very few cases were filed and even fewer accepted by the courts for consideration. On 2 November 1989 that law was replaced by a new one, to take effect on 1 July 1990, which makes both officials and executive agencies subject to judicial review for unlawful actions that impinge upon the rights of citizens.

PARLIAMENTARY SUPREMACY AND THE PUBLIC WILL

The supremacy of the highest, directly elected legislative authority in a democratic society is founded normally on the premise that the people govern through their duly elected representatives. If the people grow disenchanted with those who represent them, they may decline to reelect them. Where the legislature seeks reassurance that a measure of fundamental importance or great controversy enjoys public support, or declines to enact legislation which the majority wish to be enacted, many political entities allow for what in theory is regarded as the ultimate in true democracy: referral of the issue directly to the electorate at large in the form of a referendum. Article 5 of the USSR Constitution authorizes this procedure in two respects, one taking the form of "discussion by the whole people," in which the text of a draft law is published widely and the submission of written comments and observations invited. The 1988 amendments to the USSR Constitution were discussed precisely under this procedure, but criticized by many Soviet citizens on the ground that the deliberations of the drafting commission were secret.

The second procedure is a referendum, and although authorized by the constitution, the USSR Supreme Soviet has never introduced the machinery for holding referendums, perhaps entertaining second thoughts as to how feasible they are. The practical difficulties with referendums are well known. Often basic issues of law cannot be simplified or isolated adequately to admit a yes-or-no response. They are expensive to operate unless held simultaneously with general elections, in which case the referendum issue may be overshadowed by others. On the other hand, proponents see the referendum as a way of enhancing the prestige of law generally,[18] and imply that the constitution is undermined when democratic provisions are not implemented. No evaluation of the desirability of referendums is possible until they have been tried. But the referendum is not high on the list of priorities, and one can only wonder when it will be put to the test.

RESTRUCTURING THE JUDICIARY

An early and enduring theme of glasnost and the socialist rule-of-law state has been the performance of the courts. Criticism has been directed against extraneous influences upon judges, including the notorious "telephone law"—the habit of government and party officials to reach for the phone and proffer "advice" to judges on how to handle any given case—a low acquittal rate, the one-sidedness of the investigative and trial stages, the immaturity and inexperience of judges, and the absence of a jury system.

The 1988–89 amendments are in some measure a response to these criticisms. The term of office for judges has been increased from five to ten years; the judges of the lowest courts, called the people's courts, are no longer directly elected by the public at large but rather by the legislative branch of government at each respective superior level; and a Law on the Status of Judges was enacted in 1989 with a view to defining more explicitly the concept of judicial independence. Behind these reforms lies a vigorous and illuminating debate about how these objectives might best be achieved.

Some Soviet jurists have urged that the role of the courts be altered from that of an enforcement organ assigning criminal punishment for crimes committed to one whose task is to guarantee the rights of the individual: "Our court does not occupy the position it should occupy

82

in a rule-of-law state. It is neither a bearer of justice nor a guarantor of the rights of the individual. Regrettably, it is a mere administrative institution dependent upon local and other authorities."[19]

Various methods of securing judicial independence have been discussed, first at the June 1988 Party Conference and subsequently in the press, the technique most favored being the election of each level of judges by the respective *superior* soviet. Since judicial elections are almost invariably uncontested, local nominations of judges are a means of local control and influence that would arguably be forestalled by vesting the election in a higher soviet. The 1988 draft constitutional amendments initially rejected that approach by conferring the right to elect judges on the soviets of the *same* level as the respective courts. Some believed the only solution lay in having all judges appointed for life by the highest legislative authority of the USSR. Whenever a judge is appointed or elected for a term of years, however long, as that term nears its end the concern is that a judge begins to worry about reappointment or reelection and is accordingly sensitive to the wishes of the authorities. Such has been the reported experience in Czechoslovakia and Yugoslavia.[20]

Yet lifetime appointments may well bear the greatest risk. People who are secure in their post for life tend to enlarge their power and connections, and a lifetime appointment may mean a lifetime of illegal behavior and erroneous judgments.[21] Moreover, the best graduates of Soviet law schools are not, as a rule, sent out to be elected as judges; usually this is the fate of average students, and the annual salaries of judges have been described as "miserly."[22]

One counterpoise to the risk of a corrupt or undistinguished judiciary would be a jury system, which existed in Russia from 1864 to 1917. Guilt or innocence would be decided by the independent panel of jurors, who would be subject to the influence of neither the procuracy nor the judges.[23] And as a larger panel of laymen involved in the administration of justice, a jury would be more democratic. In November 1989, union republics were authorized to introduce the use of juries in cases where the penalties could be capital punishment or ten years or more imprisonment. Republics that do not wish to use juries may enlarge the number of people's assessors that sit together with the judge in such cases.

The Law on the Status of Judges is a response especially to the issue of extraneous influence on the judiciary. The "telephone law" is but one form of such influence, and not necessarily the most pervasive. Press comment before and during trials, the climate of public opinion, bribery, and a variety of other means, direct and indirect, of attempting to guide or direct the court may be used.

Nor is influence necessarily confined to or even most common in so-called political cases. Local interest in a civil proceeding may be sufficiently intense to cause a state enterprise or the deputy of a local soviet to attempt to intervene. Soviet jurists are profoundly suspicious of the old-boy network among the district procurator, the local party secretary, the chairman of the local soviet executive committee, and the people's judge, especially in smaller communities. Granting that "influence" can be extremely difficult sometimes to define precisely, and that judges should not be wholly isolated from their communities, the Law on the Status of Judges has nonetheless undertaken to determine the nature of improper influence, and to devise institutional guarantees of independence. The 1988 constitutional amendments properly speak not of "influence," but of "interference," and proscribe "any interference whatever" in the activities of judges. A definition of "interference" will go some way towards strengthening the heretofore eloquent but unobserved stipulation of Article 155 of the USSR Constitution: "Judges . . . shall be independent and subordinate only to law."

JUDICIAL REVIEW VS. CONSTITUTIONAL SUPERVISION

As amended in 1988, the USSR Constitution (Article 125) provides for a USSR Constitutional Supervision Committee of fifteen persons who are specialists in law and politics and elected for a term of ten years. In performing their duties the Committee members are to be "independent and subordinate only to the USSR Constitution." Although many Soviet jurists believe a constitutional court should be created,[24] the preferred concept of "supervision" [nadzor] is quite different. In effect a supervisory body, the USSR Constitutional Supervision Committee offers opinions to the Congress of People's Deputies as to whether draft laws are consistent with the constitution. It may also pass similar judgment on drafts or final laws enacted by the USSR Supreme Soviet or its two chambers (Soviet of Nationalities and Soviet of the Union), as well as on whether those laws are consistent with laws of the USSR Congress of People's Deputies; it may observe whether union republic constitutions, and laws or decrees of the USSR or union republic councils of

WILLIAM E. BUTLER

ministers, conform to the USSR Constitution and laws; and it may also offer opinions as to whether normative acts of other state agencies and social organizations conform to the USSR Constitution and laws.

If inconsistencies are discovered, the USSR Constitutional Supervision Committee is supposed to send its opinion to the agency at fault. By doing so, the defective act or individual provision thereof is suspended, and is sent to the USSR Congress of People's Deputies, the USSR Supreme Soviet, or the USSR Council of Ministers for the purpose of reviewing or repealing acts contrary to the USSR Constitution or laws. These are weak powers, rather akin to a "constitutional ombudsman," and they are at odds with the principle of parliamentary supremacy. Yet the latter is readily preserved even if the committee were transformed into a constitutional court with powers to strike down enactments, or individual provisions thereof, as contrary to the constitution. If the Congress of People's Deputies did not agree with the Court, it might alter the constitution or law accordingly. In its present guise, the impetus for constitutional interpretation lies ultimately with the Congress of People's Deputies, which by its size and composition is ill equipped to cope with the technicalities of the constitution and poorly placed to secure rational and consistent constitutional growth.

Parliamentary bodies are essentially political in character, not legal. They assess constitutional concerns in light of current political concerns rather than the verities of constitutional doctrine. In a parliamentary order it is appropriate that the courts be rectified when they stray, but it is unrealistic to expect a parliament to give reasoned consideration to a series of constitutional advisory opinions submitted year in and year out. The Congress of People's Deputies ultimately may have to form a special committee to consider the submissions of the Constitutional Supervision Committee, thereby compounding or protracting the process even further.

The Constitutional Supervision Committee has another weakness. Although individuals and bodies have the right to raise a constitutional issue, this is not done in the form of a contentious proceeding. The committee is invited or undertakes at its own initiative to evaluate the texts of enactments against the text of the constitution without the benefit of the weight of argument and circumstances thrown up by litigation, by the peculiar circumstances of competing rights against the fabric of real life.

This too seems likely to encourage a mechanistic and literalist attitude to constitutional matters and to diminish the opportunities for the rule of law through constitutional maturity.

FAIR TRIALS

An early cause célèbre of glasnost has been the problem of enhancing (or perhaps more accurately, truly introducing) the presumption of innocence in Soviet criminal proceedings. The term itself, proposed for inclusion in the 1958 USSR Fundamental Principles of Criminal Legislation, was dismissed by one deputy in the USSR Supreme Soviet as a "worm-eaten dogma of bourgeois law," a political characterization sufficient to bind jurists "hand and foot."

Some time in the past (the precise date is not known), a special commission was formed which included the USSR procurator general, the chairman of the USSR Supreme Court, and others. The commission reportedly concluded that irrespective of whether the presumption of innocence existed in Soviet law or not, it was unnecessary to write about it. And all Soviet publishing houses at once began to remove the term from manuscripts in process.[25] In 1968 the preeminent Soviet criminal procedure specialist, the late M. S. Strogovich, included a sentence in his two-volume work: "We suggest that there are sufficient grounds to incorporate the formula of presumption of innocence in prevailing criminal procedure legislation as a separate legal norm." This passage was discovered shortly after the book had been printed: most copies were recalled, the offending passage removed by apparently inserting an entirely new signature in the book, and the volume rebound. Apparently a single individual within the apparatus of the Central Committee of the CPSU had the authority to effect this change.[26]

Some Western scholars have argued that the essential features of what Anglo-American lawyers understand by the presumption of innocence have been accepted as present in Soviet law even though the term itself was not employed and was in fact rejected.[27] Whatever the precise truth of this assertion, the issue ultimately comes down to striking the proper balance between prosecution and defense in a criminal proceeding, rather than the formal existence or nonexistence of the presumption. And here there is general consensus that much needs to be reformed within the Soviet model of criminal justice.[28]

The ideological barrier to discussing this concept has been surmounted: Article 160 of the USSR Constitution set out the essence of the principle, reinforced by a Decree of the Plenum of the USSR Supreme Court adopted June 16, 1978 and by the Resolution of the Nineteenth Party Conference in June 1988. In November 1989 the term "presumption of innocence" was itself introduced into the Fundamental Principles on Court Organization of the USSR and Union Republics.

The presumption of innocence is being invoked on behalf of other criminal-procedure reforms. After years of obstruction, defense counsel will be admitted at the arrest or preliminary-investigation stages of all criminal proceedings. Judges are being cautioned to review the conclusions of preliminary investigations far more rigorously than before, and the acquittal rate reportedly is beginning to increase. But many Soviet jurists would like to restructure the investigative, trial, and appellate procedures more drastically, in line with what they see as values implicit in the rule-of-law state. This might include, for example, abolishing party disciplinary proceedings in advance of criminal proceedings in the courts as prejudicial to the court deliberations on the matter.

CONCLUSION

In June 1988 a respected legal journalist reproached Soviet legal scholars for a certain "passivity" in discussing the concept of a socialist rule-of-law state.[29] Other media characterized Soviet jurists as "conservative." Both accusations are too harsh, yet both contain an element of truth. Legal journalism and legal scholarship in an era of glasnost serve one another, but the relationship is often an uneasy one.

Journalism thrives on anecdote and sensation, yet legal journalists find themselves provoking profound discussions about the role and fate of law itself in a way their Western counterparts are not experiencing. Within the larger context of legal principles and institutions, it may be that individual accounts of abuse are not significant—merely part of the expected range of behavior in an imperfect world. It likewise follows that jurists may not have ready panaceas for society's legal problems. What has been construed as "passivity" in many instances is professional restraint and balance. It is easier to diagnose the shortcomings than to propose foolproof solutions: the jury system may have its attractions and virtues, for example, but any specialist on comparative law in the late 1980s is acutely aware of its shortcomings. However, under Soviet conditions the merits of a jury system are more than likely to outweigh its disadvantages.

Legal scholars nonetheless seem to be taken by surprise at the pace and direction of perestroika. The "origins" of the rule-of-law state are obscure precisely because individuals cannot speak with confidence about the recent past; glasnost is still being used primarily for reacting against abuses and empty slogans rather than identifying positive strains on which to build. The rule-of-law state challenges assumptions about the state and the law that few legal scholars would have been inclined to realistically espouse in the recent past, although many of their writings were edging in that direction.

Much of the criticism of the legal system by legal scholars is journalistic, that is, anecdotal. The hard empirical evidence needed to evaluate the efficacy of legal rules and institutions either is not being released or is simply unavailable. Many of the early reforms being discussed appear to be slightly recast versions of draft enactments haunting legal research institutes and drafting commissions for several years. Where the proposals are genuinely new, the legal community is not ready to relate them easily to the rule-of-law state.

The 1988–89 constitutional amendments, despite the understandable objections raised by the Baltic republics (some of which were in fact adopted at the June and December 1989 sessions of the Congress of People's Deputies), enjoyed basic consensus. The process of generating amendments may be more important than their formal substance, such that when the second round of constitutional changes is approached people will be more experienced and the debate more responsive.

Each debate over draft legislation or constitutional procedures adds to the reservoir, still low, of experience with the new thinking and new democratic processes. Although many of the Baltic proposals were declared unconstitutional by the Presidium of the USSR Supreme Soviet in November 1988 (recognition of private property, union republic sovereignty over natural resources, the right of a union republic to suspend or otherwise limit the effects of USSR legislation, the supremacy of union republic legislation, and others), the issue of all-union versus union republic authority and responsibility has been placed at the top of the agenda for the next round of constitutional reforms. In November 1989 a working group of the USSR Supreme Soviet was charged with drafting a new USSR Constitution; no timetable was fixed.

The long-awaited revision of Soviet criminal legislation—the third thorough reworking of criminal law since the October 1917 Revolution (the previous major reforms were in 1926 and 1958)—has reduced the scope of capital punishment, eliminated or restricted some of the criminal law restraints upon the freedom of speech and the press, and contributed generally to a reduction in the number of criminal offenses and a more humane attitude towards punishment. This is suggested by the draft of the Basic Principles of Criminal Legislation, published in early 1989; from the information available to this author at the time of writing, the criminal codes of the RSFSR and of the other union republics are likely to reflect these changes.[30] New legislation on inventions, no less controversial than constitutional and criminal legislation and also the object of public discussion, is one of the keys to Soviet technology policy and the success of economic reforms. These will be joined by countless other enactments, each enriching the debate on the rule of law in their own way.

★

HISTORY RECLAIMED

✩

JUTTA SCHERRER

AT A MEETING WITH A GROUP OF SOVIET writers in June 1986, Gorbachev referred—to my knowledge for the first time—to "blank [or white] spots" (*belye pyatna*) in official accounts of the history of the USSR. In February 1987, at another meeting with editors and leading media personalities, he again mentioned those "spots," this time not only in history, but also in literature.[1] For Gorbachev, it had become clear that Soviet society could be transformed or "restructured" only if the country's past were thoroughly reexamined and the roots of its current problems fully acknowledged; and he called upon his interlocutors—indeed, upon the Soviet intelligentsia—to play a major part in this process.

Since that time, not a month, not a week has passed without ever more startling disclosures and ever more vigorous debates about the country's history after as well as before the Revolution. At first it was the writers, literary critics, journalists, filmmakers, sociologists, and economists who were at the forefront of this process. Only later did historians enter the fray. By now, so much material on this subject has accumulated that any attempt to keep track is likely to be out of date by the time the results appear in print. Yet a review of this process is mandatory, for it will indicate the direction and nature of one of the most remarkable products of the policies of glasnost and perestroika.

FORETASTE OF THINGS TO COME

That there are gaping "holes" in the knowledge and consciousness of the historical past is not the exclusive discovery of the Gorbachev era. Under Khrushchev, and in the years following his dismissal, important developments in literature and the arts were paralleled by equally important discussions concerning Soviet historiography. Historians called for more rigorous historical scholarship, and for more sophisticated methodology (i.e., the adoption of the tools of empirical social research). Their quest for truth as against myths led to the publication of new research, as well as of archival materials and original sources previously out of reach to scholar and average reader alike.

After the Twentieth Party Congress in February 1956, writers began—however timidly—to tackle topics such as the collectivization of Soviet agriculture, various aspects of Stalin's reign, the role of the Bolsheviks at the time of the revolution, the intraparty opposition, the history of the Mensheviks and Socialist Revolutionaries, and the Second World War. Defending his own exposure of Stalin, Khrushchev argued that knowledge of the historical truth of the Stalin period was essential to social health and economic productivity, thus suggesting that historical accuracy and documentation had above all a functional value.

The Brezhnev years, despite their current characterization as the "period of stagnation," were not devoid of historical research. True, some of the studies produced at the time, such as V. P. Danilov's major book on collectivization, (*Kollektivizatsia selskovo khozayistva v SSSR*, 1964–65), were never allowed to circulate in the late 1960s. Some work, however, was published, such as the studies of war communism by E. G. Gimpelson (1973), and V. S. Lelchuk's book on the Soviet chemical industry (1964). All these volumes were paralleled by the publication of literary works dealing with the Stalin era, such as, in 1966 (though in drastically censored form) Anatoli Kuznetsov's novel *Babi Yar*.

As the Brezhnev reign continued, however, the process of reclaiming the past ground to a halt. The most prominent scandal occurred in February 1966, in connection with Aleksandr Nekrich's devastating portrayal of Stalin's failure to prepare the country for the Nazi attack. His

22 June 1941 had been published a year earlier, but in 1966 it was withdrawn from circulation, and its author expelled from the party.[2] These actions elicited a sharp protest—characteristically, not from historians, but from twenty-five famous scientists, writers, and artists (including Pyotr Kapitsa and Andrei Sakharov and the writers Viktor Nekrasov, Konstantin Paustovsky, and Kornei Chukovsky, all party members)—who warned against any departure from the destalinization begun by Khrushchev.[3]

While the liberals attempted to proceed with the destalinization process, the conservatives pressed for a partial rehabilitation of the dead dictator. A brief period of indecision resulted in silence on this issue at the Twenty-Third Party Congress in March 1966, ten years after the Twentieth Congress. A month earlier, the Brezhnev regime tried and sentenced two Soviet writers, Andrei Sinyavsky and Yuli Daniel, for publishing works in the West (under assumed names) "slanderous" of the Soviet Union.[4]

The trial marked the onset of the rapid expansion of "samizdat" in Soviet literature and scholarship. Works such as Roy Medvedev's *Let History Judge*, Zhores Medvedev's *The Rise and Fall of T. D. Lysenko*, Yevgenia Ginzburg's *Journey into the Whirlwind*, Anna Akhmatova's "Requiem"—to mention just a few—began to circulate in the Soviet Union and to be reprinted abroad.

One of the first to denounce the corruption of historical research in the Brezhnev era was the historian P. V. Volobuyev, a victim of the "anti-thaw" campaign. Author of a book on the two revolutions (1905 and February 1917), Volobuyev was forced to resign from his post as director of the Institute of History of the USSR in 1972. At a round-table discussion organized by the Institute of Marxism-Leninism in the summer of 1987, Volobuyev argued that the historical research which had been pursued in the spirit of the Twentieth and Twenty-Second Party Congresses "was interrupted by incompetent and authoritative interference from people whose scholarly equipment did not go beyond the framework of the *Short Course in the History of the CPSU (B)* and its enforced dogmatic concepts." Another participant in the same discussion followed up: "It is no secret to anyone that many qualified historians have left the discipline of history of Soviet society and the party to turn elsewhere; gifted young people practically never take it up anymore."[5]

THE USES OF HISTORY

As illustrated earlier, historical revisionism was not high on Gorbachev's original agenda. It was only in the course of seeking to legitimize his reform that he realized the importance of Soviet history as an instrument for change.[6] His shift was also conditioned by other factors, such as the traditional role that history, already for Marx the "science of sciences," has played in the Soviet Union in justifying and legitimizing given party policies.

Once launched, however, the pace of historical revisionism quickened, and by the summer of 1988, when the Soviet authorities abolished the history examinations in primary and secondary schools, it radically accelerated. An important role in Gorbachev's own evolution in this area has no doubt been played by Aleksandr Yakovlev, a trained historian and member of the Politburo.

True, Gorbachev's speech of November 2, 1987, and the ouster of Boris Yeltsin—until then one of Gorbachev's most ardent followers— seemed like a serious reversal. Yet in fact it was but a temporary concession to the conservatives on the Politburo, who were incensed by Yeltsin's uncompromising stance and who demanded that Gorbachev make some changes in the text of his speech. The address was disappointing. It emphasized how "the country had moved forward" despite all the "mistakes" and the sufferings engendered by forced collectivization and industrialization. Gorbachev's treatment of collectivization as a necessary response to the threatening international environment (German fascism), his distortion of the role of Trotsky, and his portrayal of Stalin's role in the 1920s as the custodian of Leninism seemed starkly at odds with his own earlier pleas for historical truth. So did his dismissive attitude towards Bukharin (whom everybody expected to be fully rehabilitated by that time), and even more so his justification of the German-Soviet Nonaggression Pact of 1939, to which he referred without mentioning the secret clauses permitting the Soviet Union's incorporation of eastern Poland and the Baltic States.[7]

Nonetheless, the public discussion of major historical topics did not halt. If anything, it proceeded apace, thus demonstrating a new autonomy from official pronouncements. Within a few months, a large number of Stalin's party victims were rehabilitated, among them Nikolai Bukharin and Aleksei Rykov. The innocence of military commanders such as M. N. Tukhachevsky, Pyotr Yakir, and Jan Gamarnik, rehabilitated under Khrushchev, was reaffirmed. Several months later Grigori Zinovev, Lev Kamenev, Karl Radek, and Georgi Pyatakov were fully rehabilitated.

ARTISTS OUT OF UNIFORM

Most of these subjects have not been treated by professional historians, certainly not in major historical works. Indeed, the role of what Yuri Afanasev, the rector of Moscow's Historical-Archival Institute, called "the pioneers in opening history"—that is, historian-journalists, playwrights, filmmakers, and writers—remains paramount to this day. It is a role that can by no means be gainsaid, since their work has appeared in the mass media, thus reaching millions of ordinary Soviet citizens who would be unlikely to read academic journals or scholarly books.

Among the most well known of these "pioneers" are the playwright Mikhail Shatrov, the filmmaker Tengiz Abuladze, writers such as Anatoli Rybakov, Boris Mozhayev, and Daniil Granin, political journalists like Fyodor Burlatsky, the editor of *Ogonyok*, Vitali Korotich, the editor of *Moscow News*, Yegor Yakovlev (an historian by training), and editors of literary journals such as Grigori Baklanov (*Znamya*) and Sergei Zalygin (*Novy mir*).

Shatrov, like many other prominent supporters of perestroika, belongs to the Khrushchev or 1956 generation sometimes referred to as "children of the Twentieth Congress," "children" who are today in their late fifties and early sixties. In his recent play "Further . . . Further . . . Further!"[8] Shatrov raises some of the most taboo questions in Soviet history: Was Lenin to be blamed for Stalin? Did the Stalinist system emerge out of the Leninist Revolution? Were there alternative socialisms? These questions amounted to confronting, if not explicitly challenging, the legitimacy of official Soviet history.

Many of Shatrov's plays were written during the Khrushchev "thaw." Central to them is the emphasis on Lenin's quest for a system based primarily on conscience (*sovest*) and moral worth (*chest*). "The Dictatorship of Conscience" (*Diktatura sovesti*)[9] is the characteristic title of one of his most popular works. Staged for the first time in 1986, though written many years earlier, it represents a fictitious trial of Lenin, in which the brutalities of war communism are placed on the dock. "The Brest Peace" (*Brestski mir*),[10] his first "documentary drama," introduced that genre to the Soviet stage; it was written in 1962 but—with its scenes of Trotsky and Bukharin—waited twenty-five years for its debut. In the same year Soviet television broadcast four films of the cycle "Toward a Portrait of Lenin" (*Strikhi k portretu V.I. Lenina*), made twenty years earlier and saved only by chance.

In all his historical dramas Shatrov shows—if at times in a caricatured fashion[11]—not only Lenin's "comrades-in-arms" who had until recently been "unpersons" (Trotsky, Bukharin, Zinovev, Kamenev), but also Mensheviks (Yuli Martov and Fyodor Dan), Socialist Revolutionaries (Maria Spiridonova), the liberal P. B. Struve, and Rosa Luxemburg. In "Further . . . Further . . . Further!" for instance, Lenin praises Rosa Luxemburg. "Bravo, Rosa," he applauds when she gives her own evaluation of the post-October situation in Russia:

> Without general elections, without unrestricted freedom of the press and assembly, without a free struggle of opinion, life in every public institution dies out, becomes a mere appearance, and bureaucracy alone remains active. . . . Freedom only for active supporters of the government . . . is not freedom. Freedom is always and uniquely for those who think differently.

The play represents a series of dialogues between Bolsheviks who look back on history with the full knowledge of what came later.[12] At a time when Gorbachev still praised Stalin for upholding Leninist principles against the views of Trotsky, Shatrov painted Stalin as an enemy of Lenin, the betrayer of the principles of Bolshevism, as the man responsible for Kirov and Trotsky's murders, and, most important of all, as one whose heritage still lives among Soviet people today.

Shatrov's admiration of Lenin and Lenin's legacy can certainly not be reduced to an exercise in "Lenin worship" or "the saccharine Lenin of the sacred heart," as Joravsky puts it in his otherwise excellent essay.[13] In an interview with a French scholar, Shatrov made the point that his plays "are not about history; they are contemporary." Even if he considers his objective to be the same as those of historians, literature cannot in his eyes replace history, "though it may answer those questions which historians are unable to cope with."[14] To the silence of historians he opposes his outrage over Stalin's role in history, his plea for a moral imperative in politics. As he has said on numerous occasions, "Theater is our conscience."

The Georgian filmmaker Tengiz Abuladze, another member of the Khrushchev generation, created in *Repentance* a fictional incarnation of Stalin and Beria in his paranoid totalitarian dictator Varlam. The film was completed in 1984, and its release in 1986 was doubtless one of the most important cultural political events in Soviet life since the publication of Solzhenitsyn's *One Day in the Life of Ivan Denisovich*. The film's title became emblematic of the liberal intelligentsia's attitude towards the past. Sin must be repented and the memory of the past be preserved.

From the long list of novels dealing with the Stalin period, a few must be singled out. Anatoli Rybakov started writing *Children of the Arbat* in the late 1950s; it was published only in 1987.[15] Through a prism of individual destinies he describes the Soviet Union of 1934 with its repressions, imprisonments, annihilation of the intelligentsia, and the cult of Stalin. *Belye Odezhdy (White Robes)* was written by Vladimir Dudintsev, the author of one of the major "thaw" novels, *Not By Bread Alone* (1956). In *White Robes* Dudintsev describes the state of Soviet biology at the time of Lysenko's destruction of genetics, and the cult of a single line of thought (*kult yedinstvennovo mnenia*), when the fight for truth demanded not only scholarly but also human courage.[16] Daniil Granin's novel *Zubr (Aurochs)* examines a similar subject, the scientific milieu of the Soviet Union and its persecution in the 1930s.[17] In *Muzhiki i baby (Peasant Men and Women)* Boris Mozhayev describes the peasants' resistance to collectivization and criticizes the role of local party secretaries in those years.[18]

Some of the novels most harshly critical of the Stalinist period were originally published in the West, but only now are accessible to the Soviet reader. Among these are Aleksandr Bek's *Novoye naznacheniye (The New Appointment)*, an exposure of the flaws in the administrative-command system written in the early 1960s,[19] and Vasili Grossman's *Life and Fate*, in which the Soviet Union under Stalinism is compared to Nazi Germany.[20] The writings of Aleksandr Solzhenitsyn—except for his novel *One Day in the Life of Ivan Denisovich*—were at first under a ban, but in 1989 a number of his outspoken statements as well as literary works (among them *Cancer Ward* and *Gulag Archipelago*), began to appear in Soviet literary journals.[21]

In throwing a harsh light on a system based on fear and brutality, all these works pose a question central to the current reforms: How can you restructure the Soviet system without coming to grips with the forces that brought it into being? In addition, they help to elucidate the paucity of Khrushchev's explanations. In his secret report to the Twentieth Party Congress on the "cult of personality"—published finally in the Soviet Union in April 1989[22]—Khrushchev ascribed Stalin's crimes exclusively to subjective causes. Yet this explanation begged some very real questions. What was it about the Soviet system that enabled Stalin to grasp and exercise so much power? Who were the people and institutions that stood behind him, and whose interests did they represent?

These are questions which only professional historians can truly grapple with. Newspapers and magazines have published an astonishing array of political documents, testimonies, diaries, correspondence, and reminiscences of camp survivors and relatives of Old Bolsheviks, and other material long hidden from the public eye. But it is up to the historians, as Yuri Afanasev has repeatedly stressed, to do more than simply correct facts or shed light on hitherto taboo topics. History must be treated as an autonomous discipline if it is to cease being a hand-maiden of propaganda and a means of legitimizing any regime in power.[23]

A ROUND OF ROUND TABLES

It hasn't been easy to achieve this goal. Only a few historians have joined the ranks of those examining the crucial junctures in their country's history. Many of the "establishment historians" have steered clear of the previously forbidden territory despite the new possibilities, thus leaving the field by and large to members of the so-called creative intelligentsia. As a result, historical science in the Soviet Union today finds itself in a state of crisis.

Nevertheless, an attempt to bring historians into the battle for reclaiming the past has been made, and is gaining ground. The first efforts took the form of round-table discussions, in which not only historians, but also economists, philosophers, and writers participated. The discussions centered—in rather general terms—on what is wrong with Soviet historiography. For example, one such discussion was organized by the party's Central Committee journal *Kommunist* (a journal that has become a leading forum for the reformers) on the occasion of the seventieth anniversary of the October Revolution.[24]

Many of the participants did not shy away from the most astringent criticism as well as self-criticism (*samokritika*). Soviet history, said the historian M. P. Kim, has been treated too schematically—for instance, by abstractly counterposing capitalism to socialism, or by justifying the headlong collectivization drive on the grounds of the danger of an imminent war. Another historian, Yuri Polyakov, urged that historical scholarship take into account real people, human beings motivated by fundamental concerns, needs, interests, hopes, and prejudices. The same scholar, as well as one of his colleagues, V. A. Kozlov, called for an end to the use of Marxism as a dogma, rather than as a creative method. Everybody agreed that the professional level of historians must be improved, and that they should learn to advance arguments and compelling data instead of relying on the usual "safe" quotations.

While the participants also agreed on a long list of neglected topics that require objective study (e.g., the period of the 1930s, the growth of bureaucracy, and the tensions between social groups such as the intelligentsia and the working class), the discussion of the need for a new periodization of Soviet history proved more problematic. The version advanced in official party histories, said Kim, which first posits the "transition period" and then goes on immediately to the "accomplishment of socialism" and then to the "transition to communism" is "unscientific."

But when it came to concrete proposals, neither Kim nor any of his colleagues, such as I. I. Mints or V. Z. Drobyzhev, proved capable of explaining why their country has not yet reached the point of "achievement" (Kim) or even the "victory" (Mints) of socialism. The question of how perestroika fits into this new periodization was answered rather unconvincingly by Drobyzhev, who proposed terming it as the "stage of the struggle for the renewal of socialism," which, curiously enough, follows the stage of the "achieved" or "victorious" socialism. Thus the debate exposed the congenital dilemma of Soviet historiography, at one and the same time claiming that socialism has already been constructed while also asserting that it is still in the state of construction.

Another stimulating if not indeed provocative discussion took place in May 1988 under the auspices of the journal *Voprosy istorii* (*Problems of History*). Its topic was "The Soviet Union in the 1920s"[25]—a topic of momentous contemporary significance, since its centerpiece, the New Economic Policy, has in large measure been the model and point of departure for Gorbachev's reforms.

The most outspoken participant in this round-table discussion was the aforementioned Viktor Danilov, the leading specialist on the peasant question in the 1920s and 1930s, who had already revised some of the views advanced in his earlier work on collectivization. The New Economic Policy, said Danilov, introduced in 1921 and scuttled by Stalin in 1928, is crucial for an understanding of the entire history of the USSR. In fact, socialism has not been achieved largely because many of the problems engendered by the NEP remain unresolved. Gorbachev's perestroika, he went on, which is to say the social processes initiated by perestroika, provides the foundation for the real transition from capitalism to socialism.

Danilov stressed in particular the autonomy of the kolkhozes during NEP, their cooperative character, as well as the relative freedom that existed in market relations. When Stalin demolished NEP and replaced it with his "bureaucratically controlled system of command mobilization" (*komando-mobilizatsionnaya sistema byurokraticheskovo upravlenia*), he did so without having laid the basis for a collectivized (which is to say, in Danilov's interpretation, a cooperative) agriculture—a task to be performed by perestroika. In addition, Danilov raised the question of alternatives to Stalin's "revolution from above," alternatives that would have maintained and developed the New Economic Policy as the politics of a transitional period.[26]

For Danilov, Bukharin represented a real alternative to Stalin (at least until 1927, when Bukharin capitulated to Stalin and voted for the exclusion of Trotsky, Zinovev, and Kamenev from the party), and the first Five Year Plan (1928–33) was a "variant of the Bukharin alternative." Not so, however, the other participants. V. A. Kozlov, for instance, sharply disagreed with Danilov, calling attention to some of the huge differences between Lenin and Bukharin, which the latter freely admitted. He suggested that Bukharin was in no way the person destined to accomplish Lenin's policy. Kozlov insisted that 1925 was the crucial year when the party was presented with the choice of either developing the NEP or embarking on the policy of rapid industrialization. Other participants, such as V. S. Lelchuk, saw the roots of the "administrative-command system" already in the intraparty struggles which prevented the Central Committee from "objectively" implementing the directives left to them by Lenin.

The problem of alternatives to Stalinism was also the subject of a round-table discussion organized by *Kommunist* in the spring of 1989. The exact title was "The Deformation of Socialism" that resulted from the "great turning point" (*veliki perevot*) in 1929, and the participants included a number of distinguished historians and economists. The central question was posed at the very start by the deputy editor of *Kommunist*, Otto Latsis:[27] What was the role of Marxist-Leninist doctrine in shaping the industrialization and collectivization drives that were launched by Stalin at that time?

According to the historian V. Kozlov, the theory of "building socialism in one country" represented by its very nature a departure from reality. Furthermore, he said, nobody either then or since has provided a satisfactory theoretical answer to the question of what kind of socialism would ensue under those conditions. Other participants, such as V. Lelchuk, insisted that Marx's theories applied to highly industrial countries, and not to overwhelmingly peasant societies. As for Lenin, all the participants agreed that it was in his last writings, where he elaborated a new concept of socialism based on a network of cooperatives (*kooperativny stroi*) in all branches of the economy, that he provides the only methodological guideline for the definition of a socialist society.

WHERE DID WE GO WRONG?

As opposed to the once official line, therefore, that from the day of its inception the Soviet Union had developed along a path that was both correct and unavoidable, the evolving view now holds that there *were* alternative paths—indeed, "alternative socialisms"—and that the tragedy of the past six decades of Soviet history consists precisely in the fact that those alternatives were crushed. It is a view that is gaining more and more adherents.

The historian Mikhail Gefter, whose work went unpublished during the Brezhnev period, has made a signal contribution to the discussion of this issue. In his essay under the remarkable title "Stalin died yesterday" (*Stalin umer vchera*),[28] he states that the year 1917 did not offer the possibility of a free "choice" (*vybor*) in Russia's "historical path." The choice *within* that path came in 1921, with the introduction of the NEP. Further alternatives, he says, arose in 1923, in 1928, and in 1934, each of them linked respectively to the names of Trotsky, Bukharin, and Kirov.

Gefter links the current "thirst for historical truth" with the sense of moral responsibility for the heritage of Stalinism—"It's not just Stalin, but us." Like Shatrov, he too depicts Lenin as a tragic figure. He quotes one of Lenin's last statements, dictated as he lay on his deathbed: "I am deeply culpable before the workers of Russia . . . I put too much hope in my recovery."[29] The words referred specifically to Stalin's treatment of the nationality question, which Lenin fiercely condemned, but they have a more general resonance. If Gorbachev's Lenin is almost exclusively the Lenin of the last years of his life, the man who implements reforms (e.g., the NEP), Gefter's Lenin is one tormented by the recognition of "failures," "delays," and "reversals," painfully trying to transform revolution into reform, a man who does not follow a "simple, straight path," but is characterized by the "disrupted unity of his thinking" (*razorvannaya tselost yevo myshlenia*).

Some writers have gone further. While not questioning the legitimacy of Lenin and Leninism in general, they nevertheless suggest—ever more strongly, as time goes on—that Lenin helped to prepare the ground for Stalinism. Thus in his article "Istoki" (Sources), the economic journalist Vasili Selyunin praises Lenin for introducing the NEP, but goes on to say that Lenin's severe restriction of freedom within the party, approved at the Tenth Party Congress in 1921, helped to consolidate the general secretary's—that is, Stalin's—power.[30]

Similarly, the historian Nikolai Popov, while explaining Lenin's violations of constitutional norms by the exceptional circumstances of the Civil War, nevertheless points to Lenin as the source of the political norms of the Stalinist state.[31] So does the former "dissident" historian Roy Medvedev, who in some of his recent works singles out elements of continuity between Leninism and Stalinism.

In 1987, Fyodor Burlatsky demanded that Leninism be "cleansed" of "Stalinist distortions and deformations."[32] By now, the "cleansing" process has been extended to Marxism itself. In four major essays titled "Sources of Stalinism" (*Istoki stalinizma*), the philosopher and Central Committee member A. S. Tsipko argues that many of Stalin's most disastrous policies may be traced to the errors in the works of Marx and Engels themselves—which is to say that Stalinism has a doctrinal origin. A theory conceived in the nineteenth century, said Tsipko, cannot be regarded as one impervious to the march of time. Instead of venerating Marx and Engels as prophets, the Soviet intelligentsia must cultivate a "healthy skepticism" with regard to some of their "propositions," and continuously verify them against concrete reality.[33]

Tsipko's was not the last word on this subject. On April 22, 1989, the 119th anniversary of Lenin's birth, Mark Zakharov, the director of the Lenin Youth Theatre, appeared on the popular television program *Vzglyad* (View) to plead for an end to the "religious cult of Lenin," for giving Lenin a proper burial in a "pantheon of Russian history" that would replace the mausoleum on Red Square and would also contain the bodies of other revolutionary heroes. Six weeks later, the historian and philosopher Yuri Karyakin, in an address before the first session of the new Congress of People's Deputies, asked that Lenin be buried next to his mother in Leningrad's Volkov cemetery, as he had requested in his will, and that the mausoleum—nothing but a "monument to Stalinism"—be done away with.[34] What with the "cleansing" process steadily accelerating, it is safe to assume that by the time this essay reaches the reader, more and perhaps even bolder reassessments of the founding fathers' legacies will have taken place.[35]

GRIM RECOUNTINGS

Yet another subject that has claimed the attention of historians is the magnitude of the Stalinist terror, and more specifically the number of his victims. In his aforementioned speech of November 2, 1987, Gorbachev spoke of the "thousands" who died during the Great Purge. This "disclosure" was not followed by any mention of the victims of collectivization, nor of the mass deportations of entire ethnic populations during World War II.[36]

In the spring of 1987, a twenty-two-year-old student by the name of Dmitri Yurasov, who had worked in a number of official archives, revealed that he had personally compiled a list of about eighty thousand people "repressed" during 1935–40 and 1953–57 (which is to say, after Stalin's death). This figure, he indicated, should be considered but a modest beginning of the grim recounting that awaits Soviet historians.[37]

Yurasov's initiative proved another stimulus to the creation of the organization Memorial, dedicated to the full elucidation of Stalin's reign of terror, the construction of libraries, a documentation center, and a monument honoring Stalin's victims. The creation of the society, in turn, encouraged further disclosures, such as the mass graves of hundreds of thousands of people executed by the NKVD near Minsk, Belorussia.[38]

In the meantime, other historians have turned their attention to this topic. Thus Danilov criticizes Western writings on the famine of 1932–33 and the "demographic catastrophe" of the 1930s and 1940s, particularly the works of Robert Conquest and Steven Rosefielde.[39] While Danilov regards their estimates of victims as too high and offers alternative estimates, his article is noteworthy for being the first by a Soviet historian to treat seriously the work of Western scholars in this field. (In the meantime, incidentally, Conquest's book *The Great Terror* has been published in the USSR.) Other scholars (the economist Nikolai Shmelyov, for one) have offered statistics on people deported and killed during the collectivization that in fact exceed the highest estimates of Western specialists.[40]

In the autumn of 1988, Roy Medvedev offered his own "rough calculations" on the number of Stalin's victims. According to Medvedev, collectivization alone resulted in the deportation (*vyseleniye*) of ten million peasants, of whom two to three million lost their lives. The 1932–33 famine, Medvedev estimates, claimed six million lives. All told, at least seventeen to eighteen million people were "repressed" before 1937–38, of whom ten million died. As for the height of the Great Terror, five to seven million people were arrested, of whom more than seven hundred thousand were shot. The figure for 1941–46 (excluding those killed in the war) is ten million, and for 1947–53 one million.[41]

STORMING THE VAULTS

Full and unrestricted access to Soviet archives is still another issue central to the pursuit of historical truth. For years, all documents relating to the history of the USSR have been sequestered in archives, some of them administered by ministries (e.g., of defense and foreign affairs), others by the party, and all of them accessible only to holders of special permits.

The battle for opening the archives has been spearheaded by Yuri Afanasev, rector of the Historical-Archival Institute, and one of the sharpest critics of the state of Soviet historical science in general. It was he who was behind the November 1988 letter addressed by the Council of the Institute to the Presidium of the USSR Academy of Sciences. In it the council urged the publication of a White Book on Stalinism, and an end to restrictions on archival material.[42] His uncompromising stance has antagonized not only the official establishment, but even some of the "liberal" historians who feel that their erstwhile efforts to write decently under conditions of unconscionable pressure should be fully recognized.

One of the strongest statements by Afanasev is his "Energia istoricheskovo znania" ("The Energy of Historical Knowledge"), which was published in *Moscow News* in early 1987. In this piece, Afanasev attacked the academic bureaucrats who dominate historical research and publications. The writing of history, said Afanasev, was still a matter of political accommodation—that is, of opportunism. The article elicited a sharp rebuke from four party historians, who reproached Afanasev not only for abandoning the Leninist principle of *partinost* (roughly, adherence to the party line), but also for embracing some of Trotsky's views—at that time still a very serious accusation.

Undaunted, Afanasev counterattacked, and stayed the course.[43] He criticized the new version of Trotsky that no longer presents him as "an enemy of the people" (i.e., a "spy," "saboteur," "agent of foreign intelligence") yet fails to mention that Stalin ordered the assassination of Trotsky in 1940, that Trotsky had in fact been a close associate of Lenin, the virtual creator of the Red Army, the first Soviet foreign commissar, a man with a devoted following in the party.[44] What Afanasev has been demanding in general is that Soviet historians broaden their methods of research by taking into accounts fields such as structural linguistics, ethnology, psychoanalysis, and psycho-history, stop ignoring Western writers, among others Durkheim, Jaspers, Weber, Toynbee, Freud, Spengler, and Marcuse as well as the writings of scholars of Soviet society such as E. H. Carr, Moshe Lewin, Alexander Rabinowitch, and Robert Tucker.[45]

The struggle led by Afanasev and others has resulted in turning his Historical Archival Institute into one of Moscow's outstanding intellectual centers. There have also been positive developments in historical journals, some of whose editorial boards have been overhauled, thus enabling bona fide scholars to publish searching and forthright studies. The works of prerevolutionary historians are to be published over the next decade—among them those of V. O. Klyuchevsky, S. M. Solovyov, N. M. Karamzin, S. F. Platonov, and many others. In addition, among the books to be published are the works of Bolshevik and other revolutionary as well as anti-Communist leaders such as Nikolai Bukharin, Nikolai Sukhanov, A. A. Bogdanov, and Aleksandr Denikin. The list also includes hitherto proscribed works by nineteenth- and early twentieth-century philosophers, political and cultural figures such as

Nikolai Berdyaev, P. A. Florensky, Pyotr Chaadayev, A. S. Khomyakov, Pyotr Kropotkin, and Mikhail Bakunin.[46]

In addition, Western scholarship is no longer out of bounds. Soviet scholars frequently pay tribute to their foreign colleagues, past and present, and some of the latter's works have already or are about to be published in the USSR (e.g., Stephen Cohen's book on Bukharin and Franco Venturi's *The Roots of Revolution*). Western scholars travel frequently to the Soviet Union and participate in scholarly conferences, and Soviet scholars, in turn, are travelling in ever greater numbers to the West.

UNFINISHED AGENDAS

The historical debate now taking place in the Soviet Union has an importance and intensity very difficult to imagine in Western countries. Decades of suppression and manipulation of history have created an overwhelming desire among many Soviet citizens to learn more about their country's past. Startling disclosures about World War II bring even more startling disclosures (e.g., about Stalin's massacre of the officers corps in 1938, and his disastrous role as chief of staff during the war years). It is now permissible to compare Stalin's and Hitler's forms of totalitarianism: one eminent sociologist, for instance, discussed Elias Canetti's *Masses and Power*, using the chapter on "The Question of Guilt" as a model for the need of collective repentance by the Russian people.[47]

The Molotov-Ribbentrop Pact has finally been put on the agenda, as has the incorporation of the Baltic states in 1940.[48] Many Western writings bearing directly or indirectly on Stalinism—e.g., Victor Serge's *The Case of Comrade Tulaev*, George Orwell's *Animal Farm*, Arthur Koestler's *Darkness at Noon*, and Arthur London's *Confession* (the latter an account of the 1952 Slansky trial in Prague)—are now appearing, many of them in mass-circulation journals. Finally, certain areas of Russian history of relevance to current realities are also being reexamined, such as the nineteenth-century debates between Westerners and Slavophiles, and the role of Christianity in the history of Russia.

For Western specialists, as well as for independent-minded Soviet historians, there is little that is truly new or revelatory in the Soviet writings. What is absolutely new, however, is the amount of publicity they receive and the excitement they generate. One reason for it is the fact that there is now almost no generally recognized official history. The old textbooks, full of "blank spots," have been withdrawn from circulation, and for a time history examinations were suspended. (Only in September 1989 did a new book on the history of the USSR appear. But it is not the last word on the subject.) Another reason is the dearth of good, particularly young, historians: many years will be needed to restore professional standards, and to persuade young academics not to turn exclusively to medieval studies or ethnography, but to the recent past. The first step in this direction was already taken in the summer of 1988, when a number of young historians created a national Society of Historians.

The flowering of glasnost and of a new historical consciousness has given the liberal and enlightened members of the Soviet intelligentsia an opportunity to make their voices heard and to shape public opinion. But other voices, too, have emerged into the open, most brashly those of the Russophiles (*russisty*). Already present during the Brezhnev period, the *russisty* demand the revindication of Russia's "glorious past," and a cleansing of Russian culture from the insidious influences of Western values and fashions (such as rock music). Largely grouped around the magazines *Nash sovremmenik* (Our Contemporary) and *Molodaya gvardia* (Young Guard), writers such as Yuri Bondarev, Valentin Rasputin, and Vasili Belov, among others (the latter, incidentally, frequently evoking in his writing the specter of a "Judeo-Masonic conspiracy") regularly attack magazines such as *Ogonyok*, and its editor, Vitali Korotich, whom they hold responsible for encouraging "licentiousness" and destroying "national values."

At the present time, it looks as if the liberals for whom perestroika is "our last chance" (*nash posledni shans*) have gained the upper hand. It remains to be seen whether they have won a battle or the war. What is absolutely certain, however, is that the explosion of interest in the past goes far beyond Gorbachev's initial—and traditional—view of history as the legitimation and ideological justification of his policies.

In 1987, Gorbachev went farther by pleading that the "lessons of history" be so applied as to enable "us to live and act according to our conscience."[49] The avidity with which these lessons have been learned has led not only to a remarkable diversity of opinions. It has also brought about the steady erosion of official Soviet historiography, and indeed of the legitimacy of the regime itself. For the time being, the journalists and writers are in the forefront, and "historical scholarship," in the words of the historian K. F. Shatsillo, is still "lagging behind perestroika." But more and more historians are now joining the process of reclaiming the past, filling in the "blank spots" and training their sights on territories once feared and forbidden.

★

NATIONALITIES
AND NATIONALISM

☆

R O N A L D   G.   S U N Y

AS GORBACHEV'S PERESTROIKA ENTERS ITS
sixth year, the most insistent voices for radical political and social change
are heard not so much from the heart as from the national peripheries
of the Soviet empire. To the surprise of many journalists and Soviet
specialists in the West, who had either tended to treat the USSR as a
single ethnic unit or regarded the national question as a marginal nuis-
ance, the first massive displays of popular politics occurred in Armenia,
Georgia, the Baltic republics, and, more brutally, in Azerbaijan.

The gradualist politics of perestroika were quickly radicalized into
the ethnopolitics of national self-determination and democratization,
while long-latent interethnic hostilities erupted into protests and massacres. Already in late 1986 Gorbachev faced his first major crisis in the
national republics when supporters of ousted Kazakh party chief Dinmukhammed Kunayev rampaged through the streets of Alma Ata to
protest his replacement by an ethnic Russian. For the next year demonstrations were held in the Baltic republics and in Armenia around
diverse complaints, ranging from environmental pollution to immigration policy to the infamous "blank spots" in Soviet history. As ethnic
assertiveness took bolder form and expanded out from intellectuals to

108

include broader strata of the population, it metamorphosed into something both deeper and more inclusive than a simple cultural nationalism. Besides the issues of democracy and openness, the Gorbachev initiative had raised questions of the limits of central authority and local autonomy and had given a new political significance to persistent frictions caused by a central state widely perceived as pursuing a policy of russification.

In February 1988, tens of thousands of Armenians marched through the streets of Yerevan in support of their compatriots in Nagorno-Karabakh in neighboring Azerbaijan, who wished to join their region to the Armenian republic. Even in their defiance the Armenians proclaimed themselves loyal to Soviet power and to the ideals of perestroika. Then, tragically, Azerbaijani youth, incensed at what they thought was a threat to their people, went on a rampage in Sumgait in the last days of February, killing their Armenian neighbors indiscriminately.

In the Baltic countries—Latvia, Lithuania, and Estonia—a national protest over Russian dominance, embracing all social strata, led to demands for greater national autonomy and to the creation of alternative political fronts. In Moldavia, a movement focused on the issue of the Moldavian language. It proclaimed (rightly) that Moldavian is not different from Romanian, and demanded the restoration of the Latin script (replaced by the Cyrillic alphabet when Moldavia was incorporated into the Soviet Union in 1944) and the recognition of Moldavian as the national language of the republic. After several stormy months, the local party leadership—and Moscow—were forced to yield. In Belorussia and Ukraine, issues from the unburied past, fears about the threat to the native languages, and anxiety about demographic and linguistic russification brought intellectuals together with their ethnic compatriots in common protests. Peaceful marches, mass meetings, and hunger strikes became daily challenges to the entrenched national party apparats.

While in the Baltic new party leaders found a common language with the popular fronts, making concessions and even supporting national demands, in Azerbaijan and Armenia martial law and the arrest of the leaders of the protests brought the movements to a temporary halt. And in early April 1989 hundreds of demonstrators in Tbilisi were hurt, and several dozen killed, when Soviet troops acted swiftly and brutally to quell demands for Georgian independence. Just as each mobilized republic raised its own national flag and resurrected its particular national symbols and myths, so each of these movements developed its own agenda—some consonant with the plans of the Kremlin reformers,

others a deadly challenge to the more tentative process of democratization initiated from the top.

NATIONALISM AND RUSSIFICATION

In the conventional interpretation of Soviet nationality policy, the emergence of nationalist protest is explained as the predictable response of
the indigenous peoples to a consistent state practice of forced russification. National consciousness, or at least inherent, perhaps even primordial, national feelings that have been long suppressed exploded in
reaction to long-term oppression. In this view, once opportunities for
public expression appeared after the death of Stalin, non-Russians once
again took up their struggles for national freedom that had been broken
off half a century earlier.

As seemingly compelling as such an interpretation is, it fails to account for the full complexity of the national question in the USSR—the
russophilia of many non-Russians in the USSR, the power of assimilation, the acculturationist pressures of modernization, and the conflicts
between non-Russian peoples themselves. Assuming a relatively consistent and usually oppressive policy from the state neglects the indigenous
social, political, and cultural developments among the non-Russians,
explaining everything instead as the result exclusively of the clash between state policies and frustrated ethnic aspirations.

A more useful way to approach this subject is to focus on the social,
historical, and intellectual developments among the non-Russian peoples. Such an approach reveals the profound changes in Soviet society
that have taken place outside or even despite the policies of the state,
and avoids lumping divergent peoples into a single pattern of development. On one level all the Soviet people, non-Russians and Russians
alike, shared a traumatic and often tragic evolution that turned largely
peasant peoples into urban, educated, industrial citizens and created a
literate, mobile population; on another, equally determinate level, the
collective history of the Soviet peoples has been one of "making nations"—nations which for specific historical and cultural reasons have
to a greater or lesser degree successfully resisted "merging" into a homogeneous "Soviet people."

Attacks on nationalism and efforts at linguistic russification have
undeniably been part of Soviet nationality policy at specific times. How-

ever, state policies have fluctuated from enthusiastic encouragement of native cultures to brutal repression of ethnic uniqueness to "benign neglect" of nationality problems altogether. In addition, Soviet policies and social developments have benefited some ethnic groups more than others. The differential effects of the Soviet experience on the Slavic peoples of the West, the Muslims of Central Asia and the Caucasus, the Armenians, the Georgians, and the Baltic peoples have created a variety of national responses, some more pointedly anti-Russian, others directed against non-Russian neighbors.

Investigation of the different national histories of the nations of the USSR supports the conclusion that nationalism and the accompanying social movements stem from two sources: first, an increased capacity of ethnic populations to act in their own interest (and not only because of a freer political atmosphere but also because of greater coherence and consciousness of the nationalities themselves); and second, perceptions of non-Russians (and Russians!) that their nations are in danger, either demographically, linguistically, or culturally. Whatever the intentions and predictions of self-styled Marxist internationalist officials and theorists, the actual history of most of the major Soviet peoples has been one of greater consolidation of ethnic nations, heightened national consciousness, and increased capacity to act in defense of their perceived national interests.

PERESTROIKA'S DILEMMAS

These developments by the late 1980s presented the reformist leadership in Moscow with a dangerous dilemma rivaled only by chronic economic stagnation and the dangers of international conflict. Unlike ethnic minorities in the United States or in many parts of Western Europe, most of the non-Russian peoples of the Soviet Union are demographically compact, culturally coherent, and socially and politically conscious nations within a large multinational federation dominated by the largest ethnic nation—the Russians. Moreover, they understand their present situation and their historic evolution in specifically cultural terms, viewing the world through their own perceptual framework (or what anthropologists call "root paradigm") and interpreting and reinterpreting their experience through codes that may be impenetrable or appear irrational to outsiders.

111

Thus, what to a Russian official in Moscow might seem a reasonable policy of bilingualism and promotion of a *lingua franca* for the whole union appears to an Estonian or Georgian as another rude attempt to russify the culture of an historic nation. Whereas the killings in Sumgait in February 1988 seemed to ordinary people on the streets of central cities a shocking case of interethnic hatred, or of unbridled hooliganism, to Armenians in Yerevan and Stepanakert they immediately revived ever-present memories of the 1915 genocide.[1] A variety of discourses operates among the non-Russian peoples and competes with those of the Russian people and the official viewpoint of state and party officials. In the new era of glasnost and perestroika, the power of the deep and varied national cultures of the Soviet peoples in the peripheries of the empire means that central Soviet authorities must contend with the influence of historically rooted alternative understandings, some of which are fundamentally alien to the "root paradigm" of the Kremlin.

The small peoples of Transcaucasia and the Baltic region, apprehensive about the threat to their national survival, rallied around issues central to their history and experience. For Armenians the issue of Karabakh was foreshadowed by and linked to earlier campaigns against environmental pollution. A "gray genocide" has long been threatening the smallest (in size) Soviet republic, and ecology became a rallying point around which general discontent with material shortages, an unresponsive and venal local leadership, and neglect of the national culture coalesced.

The struggle over Karabakh, a region inhabited by close to two hundred thousand Armenians, took on a heightened meaning to a people whose central experience in modern times was near annihilation at the hands of the Ottoman Turkish government in 1915 and the subsequent loss of four-fifths of the territory that made up historic Armenia to the newly formed republic of Turkey.[2] Long subjected to Azerbaijani neglect (and even active persecution) of Armenian culture and education, the Armenians of Karabakh had steadily lost the possibility of contact with the Armenian republic only a few miles away. Armenian education was curbed, roads leading to Yerevan were left to rot, and even television reception from Yerevan was restricted. The demographic dominance of Armenians in this historically Armenian region was still high (seventy-six percent in 1979), but in certain areas, like the former cultural center of Shushi, Azerbaijanis overwhelmed Armenians.

The Karabakh Armenians began their open street protests in February 1988, after quieter complaints, petitions, and letters had repeatedly failed to bring any response, either from Baku or Moscow. Startlingly, the first few demonstrators in the Karabakh capital of Stepanakert were soon joined by thousands, and within days sympathizers in Yerevan were marching around the clock. Most unexpected was the rapid collapse of official authority. Popular committees—*Krunk* (Crane) in Karabakh and the Karabakh Committee in Yerevan—became the *de facto* leaders of the popular resistance. The formerly obedient local soviet of Karabakh voted—against all precedence and with no sanction from above—to raise the question of secession from Azerbaijan and incorporation into the Armenian republic. The local Communist party organization soon followed the soviet's example.[3]

Like the Armenians, the Baltic peoples felt that their national existence was imperiled. Having enjoyed independence during the interwar period, and annexed to the USSR only at the end of the Second World War, Estonia, Latvia, and Lithuania all had preserved a clear memory of Stalin's pact with Hitler that had permitted Soviet troops to move into their countries in 1940. All remembered the savage purges of the local populations that had effectively decapitated their nations, destroying those intellectuals and political leaders who had not managed to escape to the West.

Even in the relatively peaceful post-Stalin period, when the Baltic region was widely recognized as the economically most advanced and culturally most Western part of the Soviet Union, hostility toward Russian inroads remained high. With industrialization, planned and directed from Moscow, came Russian workers and specialists. In one generation Latvians became a minority in their own republic, while Estonians barely held a majority in theirs. Resistance took the form of retreat into the native culture, refusal to learn or speak Russian, and determined efforts to increase ties with the West.

When the policies of glasnost and *demokratizatsia* permitted more open expression and political activity, the Baltic peoples rallied quickly around the most potent symbols of their independent past—the flags and anthems of the interwar republics—and spontaneously organized national fronts to express their cultural and political demands. History, so long denied, was rapidly recovered, most importantly the truth about the annexation of the Baltic republics by Stalin. Though few had ever accepted the official version of three simultaneous "popular revolutions" petitioning for entry into the Soviet Union, the full facts of the Nazi-

Soviet Pact of 1939 and its so-called secret protocol that placed the Baltic republics in a Soviet sphere of influence had never been publicly aired. In Riga, Tallinn, and Vilnius crowds numbered in the tens and even hundreds of thousands marched to mark the anniversary of the pact, and the "secret protocol" to the Molotov-Ribbentrop agreement was published for the first time in the Soviet Union by the Estonians.

Russians reacted quickly to the Baltic protests. In Tallinn local Russians formed an "international front" as a counterweight to the national popular front, and massive demonstrations were held to protest the planned laws insisting on Estonian language competence for non-Estonians. In *Pravda* a crude attempt was made by the then head of *Novosti*, V. M. Falin, to deny that the "secret protocol" had ever existed; and top party leaders, even those sympathetic to greater autonomy, warned that talk of full independence was utopian.

In an extraordinary display of political flexibility, the Baltic Communist parties negotiated with the popular fronts and managed to prevent violent confrontations between nationalities and between the fronts and the government. The historical debate, never simply a discussion of the past, continued, however, and seemingly academic arguments implicitly undermined the legitimacy of the annexation and provided support for calls for full independence of the formerly sovereign republics.

While Armenians and the Baltic peoples organized mass demonstrations, strikes, and national front organizations, Ukraine, Belorussia, Moldavia, and Central Asia were slower to act openly. Exposures in the press of the horrors of Stalinism, however, took on a national coloration. The Ukrainian famine of 1932–1933, already called a genocide by emigrants and their supporters in the West, was shown to have been artificially created, either as the callous consequence of an ill-conceived and ruthless policy of collectivizing agriculture or as a deliberate effort to punish specific ethnic groups.[4] Belorussian newspapers told the horrific story of mass executions of their republic's citizens by Stalin's police, who economized on ammunition by lining up two heads so that one bullet would suffice.

In Ukraine and Belorussia intellectuals passionately condemned the erosion of native language schooling and the state's promotion of Russian. In Moldavia the linguistic and cultural affinity of Soviet Moldavians with Rumanians across the border no longer was an unmentionable theme. In Tataria a quiet discussion was held in the press and at meetings in the Kazan stadium on whether a people's front should be formed.

114

Some speakers favored making the front an oppositional party; others called for support of the local Communist party and perestroika. At first the discussion was centered primarily around local issues like pollution in Kazan rather than on ethnic questions, but by the time of the Constituent Assembly of the Tatar Social Center (*Tatarski obshchestvenny tsentr*) in mid-February 1989, specific issues concerning Tatar national history and language were central to the debates.[5]

The differential response to the possibilities of glasnost—mass mobilization in Armenia and Karabakh, Azerbaijan, and the Baltic republics; patience and caution in much of the Soviet Muslim world; and intellectual ferment in the major Slavic republics—was rooted in the complex and contradictory experience of Soviet development and may be illuminated by examining the historic process of the "making" of Soviet nations.

WHAT'S IN A NATION?

Before the revolutions of 1917 most of the constituent peoples of what now makes up the Soviet Union were not yet fully formed, self-conscious nations. Though ethno-linguistic communities with distinct religious and ethnic cultures had existed on what is now Soviet territory since prehistoric times, few of the peoples of the Russian empire had coalesced around the more modern notions of a secular, territorial nation. Most had never had a state in the past, and nationalist ideas expressed by urban intellectuals had not yet spread to the less educated, either in towns or the countryside.

Even during the years of revolution and civil war (1917–1921), when independent and semi-independent national states appeared on the borders of ethnic Russia, nationalism was still largely a phenomenon centered on the educated townspeople, students, and the lower middle classes, with only an unstable following in the countryside. Among Belorussians, Lithuanians, and almost all the Muslim peoples of the empire, the paramount identification was with people nearby with whom one shared social and religious communality. Muslims saw themselves as part of a world religious community or as natives of a region such as Turkestan rather than as members of an ethnic nation. For these peoples neither nationalism nor socialism was able to mobilize large numbers of the peasant population into the political struggles that were being waged across the land.

For several other nationalities, among them the Latvians and Georgians, class-based socialist movements were far more meaningful than political nationalism. Socialism as espoused by the dominant intellectual elite offered a solution to both social and ethnic inferiority as well as to the dual oppression determined by class and nationality. For still other nationalities, like the Ukrainians and Estonians, nationalism competed with class loyalty. Neither nationalism nor socialism could find majority support or even a reliable social base that could withstand the armed intervention of the West or the Bolsheviks. Ukrainian peasants, for example, most often identified themselves with their village or locality rather than with any abstract notion of a Ukrainian nation.

The Jews, at once a dispersed people and heavily concentrated in the western parts of the Russian empire, were divided between a variety of contenders for their political loyalties—Russian Marxism, the Jewish socialist Bund, and Zionism. Finally, among Armenians, a people divided between the Russian and Turkish empires, without a secure area of concentration, and faced by the imminent danger of extermination at the hands of the Ottoman Turks, a nationalism unifying almost all social strata overwhelmed all competitors.[6]

With the end of the Civil War several major nationalities found themselves independent of the Soviet Union. As a result of Soviet weakness, effective resistance to native Bolsheviks, and Western intervention, the Poles, Finns, Lithuanians, Estonians, and Latvians created their own independent states. Those left under Soviet rule—Russians, Ukrainians, Belorussians, Moldavians, Armenians, Georgians, Azerbaijanis, and other Muslim peoples—were organized in a new federal state, the first ever to base its political units on ethnicity. Marxist theory at the time maintained that nationalism and national exclusivity could eventually be eliminated through the development of socialism, but even this simplistic reduction of ethnic culture and national formation to the economic base recognized the contemporary power of the appeal of nationality.

FROM LENIN TO KHRUSHCHEV

Ever flexible, Lenin, who espoused "national self-determination," proposed a compromise: to maximize national political and cultural autonomy within a federation dominated by the Communist party and to condemn the overcentralizing tendencies of more Russian chauvinist members of the party (among whom he included Stalin).[7]

Although the republics quickly lost real state sovereignty, each nationality maintained its own republic or autonomous district in which the national language and culture were to be encouraged and where native cadres were to dominate in administration. This policy of "nativization" (*korenizatsia*), encouraged by Lenin and supported by Stalin until the early 1930s, produced impressive results. The ethnic republics became demographically and culturally more ethnic. In the Ukraine, as in other republics, a cultural renaissance blossomed. Russians seeking higher education there had to learn in Ukrainian.[8] Many smaller peoples who had never had a written language were provided alphabets, and campaigns for literacy promoted both socialism and national culture simultaneously. Even the Jews, who did not have a republic of their own, benefitted from this policy, enjoying a revival of Yiddish learning and culture, the formation of a Jewish section of the Communist party, and new security from a state that legislated against manifestations of anti-Semitism.[9] Ironically (and this is a point often overlooked by many Western observers), the emergence of a broad national consciousness among most Soviet peoples, rather than a primordial or even prerevolutionary phenomenon, was primarily the result of Soviet nationality policies and indigenous cultural development.

At the same time, however, the Bolshevik program of modernization had a more contrary effect on the nationalities. It undermined native cultural institutions, often brutally attacking the church and subverting traditional patterns of authority. At the same time, the shift from village to town, farm to factory, gave millions of ethnic peasants greater social mobility, as well as potential access to higher education and a wider variety of cultural experiences.

By the early 1930s, once Stalin had consolidated the hegemony of his faction within the party, the imperatives of rapid industrialization and the massive effort of forcing peasants into collective farms carried the party leadership toward a more expedient nationality policy. Nativization as a deliberate state policy almost immediately suffered from the Stalin revolution of the 1930s and the revival under his personal autocracy of Russian chauvinism. Stalin had never reconciled himself to Lenin's notion of federalism. He maintained and strengthened the power of the centralized state, with no real political autonomy left to the peripheries. Through the instrument of police terror, Stalin destroyed the last vestiges of national communism—the policy favoring greater ethnic political autonomy—and imprisoned or executed tens of thousands of ethnic Communist leaders in the Great Purges. All hints of small-nation nationalism were severely punished, and Russian culture was promoted as the most advanced in the USSR.

At the end of the 1930s study of the Russian language was made compulsory in all schools, although the non-Russian languages continued to be taught in most of the ethnic areas. Even when some accommodation was made to national and religious feeling, as during the struggle against the Nazis in the Second World War, the new emphasis on Russian patriotic themes and national heroes subordinated the non-Russian peoples to the state's primary emphasis on defense and economic development. Several small peoples—the Crimean Tatars, Meskhetians, Volga Germans, Karachai, Kalmyks, Balkars, Ingush, and Chechens— were condemned as traitors to the Soviet state and forcibly removed from their homelands and sent into Central Asian exile.[10]

Nevertheless, despite the political repression of the Stalin years and the abandonment of much of the cultural program of *korenizatsia*, the non-Russians managed to maintain their demographic and cultural hold on their republics. By the time of Stalin's death the so-called titular nationalities dominated in numbers in most of the republics, even though they had been unable to establish any real political autonomy or carry on any nationalist expression for nearly a quarter of a century.

When the worst excesses of Stalinism were eliminated by Khrushchev in the early 1950s, tentative national expression reappeared—first in the form of reprinted writers, rehabilitated victims of the *stalinshchina*, and new themes in art, film, and literature. A part of the national heritage of non-Russians was officially sanctioned, promoted, and, in a sense, appropriated as part of the collective Soviet past. At the same time significant historical figures, even whole movements central to historical understanding, were beyond the newly established limits of discussion. Armenian Dashnaks, Georgian Mensheviks, nationalist poets, and those who had fled abroad were ritualistically condemned by officialdom. Yet in the atmosphere of increased freedom the border between the forbidden and the acceptable was constantly crossed by emboldened writers and principled dissidents.

TABLE 1: Republics and Nationalities

In 1959, the first post-Stalin census showed that only two nationalities with their own soviet republic, the Kazakhs and the Kirgiz, made up less than a majority of the population of their own republic, and only the Kazakhs were outnumbered by Russians:

Republic	% of Titular Nationality	% of Russians
RSFSR	83.3	83.3
Ukraine	76.8	16.9
Belorussia	81.1	8.2
Uzbekistan	62.2	13.5
Kazakhstan	30.0	42.7
Georgia	64.3	10.1
Azerbaijan	67.5	13.6
Lithuania	79.3	8.5
Moldavia	65.4	10.2
Latvia	62.0	26.6
Kirgizia	40.5	30.2
Tajikistan	53.1	13.3
Armenia	88.0	3.2
Turkmenistan	60.9	17.3
Estonia	74.6	20.1

[Tsentralnoe statisticheskoe upravlenie pri sovete ministrov SSSR, *Itogi vsesoiuznoi perepisi naseleniia 1959 goda SSSR (Svodnyi tom)*, (Moscow: Gosstatizdat, 1962), 202–8.]

THE WEEDS THAT BLOOM IN THE SPRING

Khrushchev also established a more decentralized political and economic system, though this limited political autonomy was far from democratic. With less control from the center, but in the absence of any real democracy, limited political autonomy resulted in the strengthening of local elites, most of them carryovers from Stalin's time. In Transcaucasia and Central Asia particularly, local ethnic "mafias" gained control of the economy and political patronage systems. Corruption, bribery, and the advancement of friends and relatives into positions of power became the norm for local administrators.

As long as the Communist leaders in the republics could placate Moscow by maintaining stability, keeping some restraints on nationalism, and showing economic growth, they remained relatively free from reprisals from the center. The perverse result of the end of terror and centralization was the strengthening of already powerful ethno-political machines that plundered the state economic sector, patronized the "second economy," and satisfied certain parts of the local population who either benefitted from the spoils system or enjoyed the usually freer way of life in their homelands. To the dismay of many Russians, life appeared gayer and richer in Georgia or Armenia than in their own republic. "Diamond" Anton Kochinyan, first secretary of the Communist party in Armenia, and the rapacious Vasili Mzhavanadze, his counterpart in Georgia, were matched in their venality and brazen disregard of the law by petty party potentates in Central Asia, most notoriously Uzbekistan's Sharaf Rashidov.[11]

For nearly a decade after the fall of Khrushchev in 1964, little changed for the national elites. The conservative cadre policy of "chairman of the board" Leonid Brezhnev encouraged corruption until it enveloped all parts of the Soviet Union and reached into the family of Brezhnev himself. No attempt was made at structural reform, however. The problem of the non-Russian regions was dealt with administratively and only very rarely by changes of the top leadership.

In Central Asia and the Baltic republics party chiefs stayed in power for decades.[12] In Transcaucasia, where the "second economy" had grown to gargantuan proportions by the early 1970s and economic indicators dipped ever lower, attempts were made to bring in personnel from outside the patronage system. In 1969 Heidar Aliyev, a career KGB officer, was named first secretary of the Azerbaijani Communist party. Three years later Eduard Shevardnadze, also from the security apparatus, became head of the Georgian party, and in 1974 Karen Demirchyan, an engineer educated outside of Armenia, was brought in to head the Armenian party. Their mandates were similar: to end the corruption and system of favoritism in personnel decisions, to contain the growing nationalism, and to stimulate the local economies.

Success was mixed. Purges of thousands of officials only temporarily affected "business as usual." Corruption and bribery were too deeply imbedded in kinship networks and local cultural prohibitions against betrayal of friends, patrons, and clients to be eradicated or even seriously injured by changes at the top.[13] As Brezhnev, ever more feeble, clung to power, the local "mafias" held sway in the border republics and former reformers, like Aliyev and Demirchyan, became the beneficiaries of their

own power networks. Cynicism, disillusionment, and a growing pessi-
mism marked the dominant mood in the population. As economic and
political stagnation spread, some people gave up on the Soviet Union
altogether and sought refuge abroad. Many retreated into the details of
daily life. And still others turned toward nationalism as an internal refuge
from the mundane burdens of a spiritless modernization.

INTO THE FRAY

The uneven and contradictory development of nations in the Soviet
Union—at the same time consolidating ethnically in some republics while
threatened by assimilation, in-migration, and linguistic Russification
elsewhere—gave rise to a variety of nationalist responses in the 1960s
and 1970s. Some of the deported peoples who had lost their homelands
under Stalin, most courageously the Crimean Tatars, organized daring
demonstrations in the heart of Moscow. Newly inspired by Israeli military victories and encouraged by supporters abroad, Soviet Jews agitated
after 1967 to emigrate to Israel or the West. At first defiantly and later
with permission, Armenians marched year after year, beginning in 1965,
to commemorate the genocide of 1915. When in April 1978 the Georgian
party tried to remove a clause in the republic's constitution that established Georgian as the official state language, thousands marched to the
party headquarters and forced Shevardnadze to reverse the decision.

That same year Abkhazians protested against poor treatment by
their Georgian overlords and petitioned to join the Russian federated
republic. Karabakh Armenians repeatedly raised objections to Azerbaijani restrictions on Armenian culture and learning, though with no results. Ukrainian writers, teachers, and journalists protested against
Russian inroads in their republic and were subjected to arrest and exile.
Lithuanians rallied around the Catholic Church, protesting restrictions
on religious observance; in Kaunas a student immolated himself by fire.
In Muslim Central Asia there was generally little open protest, but many
Western observers believed that Islam presented a potential source of
cultural resistance to Soviet authority. And perhaps most ominously of
all, the same economic, social, and cultural discontents that gave rise to
non-Russian nationalism also affected the Great Russians as well.

Like the national consciousness of smaller nations, that of the Russians was centered on a perception of national danger, of the erosion

121

and irreplaceable loss of culture, of a sense of the past. Like Armenian, Estonian, and other national movements, the Russian movement was at first concerned with environmental destruction, with threats to Russia's natural habitat, and with the brutal treatment of cultural and religious monuments.

In time, however, this relatively benign affection for the village and the church was molded by some groups into a vicious, xenophobic, anti-Semitic chauvinism that pictured the Russians as a disadvantaged nation victimized by foreigners and the non-Russians of the USSR. Religious nationalists, neo-Slavophiles emphasizing the innate virtues of Slavic peoples, "National Bolsheviks" combining a thirst for Stalinist "law and order" with Russian chauvinism, and outright fascists emerged on the right wing of underground Russian nationalism in the Brezhnev years, and less virulent versions of their russocentric ideas could be read in official journals like *Molodaya gvardia* and *Nash sovremennik*. When a prominent party official (now a close advisor to Gorbachev), Aleksandr Yakovlev, strongly criticized the ideology of the nationalists, he was "exiled" to Canada as ambassador.

Clearly russophilia, so alien to Lenin,[14] had deeply penetrated his party in the six decades since his death, and much of the Russian intelligentsia openly admired the sensationalist depictions of tsars and priests of the painter Ilya Glazunov or the religious nationalism, with its explicit authoritarianism, of Aleksandr Solzhenitsyn. With the coming of glasnost, a Russian nationalist organization called *Pamyat* (Memory), stealthily protected by highly placed officials, combined russophilic themes, a xenophobic sense of national danger, and the now fashionable anti-Stalinism to blame Jews, Latvians, and other non-Russians for the repressions of the Stalinist past and the evident degeneration of Russian life.[15]

GORBACHEV AND THE NON-RUSSIANS

Were the integrated political and social movements of the non-Russians reducible to the policies of russification and state restriction on nationalist expression, the dilemma facing the Kremlin would be more manageable than it is in reality. The Soviet experience has produced something far more potent than frustrated nationalists—new nations, stronger in numbers and in self-awareness, newly mobilized around culturally defined concerns.

As the Stalinist police state was dismantled piece by piece, the Soviet government was left with completely inadequate means with which to deal with its ethnic constituents. The Soviet constitution, which had operated only symbolically during the decades of Stalin's autocracy and the subsequent party oligarchy, offered no guidance whatsoever on how best to resolve interethnic conflicts. The rights of the union republics and autonomous regions and republics were nowhere clearly defined. No Commissariat of Nationalities or other permanent authoritative body existed (as it had in the 1920s) to which ethnic issues could be referred, though temporary commissions began to provide the nucleus of future institutions. In the absence of dictatorship, instruments and institutions for negotiation between an aroused society and a more flexible state had to be created. But even as Gorbachev spoke of democracy and the rule of law, the potential range of republic autonomy was being worked out in the streets of Yerevan, Tallinn, and Tbilisi.

Gorbachev's aim to promote economic reform, greater productivity, and efficiency throughout the country, while at the same time stimulating local initiative, required that the immovable structure of the Stalinist administrative-command system be shaken by greater decentralization, more regional autonomy, more open and frank discussion of shortcomings and problems, and, eventually, increased democracy. For the non-Russian republics two roads lay open: either undemocratic national autonomy (the further strengthening of the local mafias) or democratic national autonomy (fundamental restructuring with broader participation). The consequences of the former road were well known—corruption and stagnation; the consequences of the latter began to reveal themselves in the course of 1988 and 1989.

The axes of conflict within the USSR are not only between Russians and non-Russians but between various non-Russian peoples who have had long religious, cultural, or territorial disputes. The Abkhaz-Georgian hostility of 1977–1978, which revived in 1989, was a foretaste of the more tragic Azerbaijani-Armenian clashes a decade later. In his interventions in the Supreme Soviet debate on Karabakh, the general secretary made it clear that both stability and progress, the goals of perestroika, were undermined by nationalism and ethnic conflict. Only political compromise offered a solution. Repeatedly affirming that there could be no winners and losers at the expense of another ethnic group, Gorbachev pushed hard for satisfying some grievances of each of the parties. Rather than granting the Armenian demand of incorporation of Karabakh into Armenia—a political impossibility after the killings in Sumgait—a program of reforms was set out that implicitly recognized the long record of Azerbaijani discrimination against the Karabakh Armenians. Even more importantly, Azerbaijani sovereignty over Karabakh was replaced *de facto* by the appointment of a commission from Moscow to oversee the implementation of reforms in the autonomous region.

Following the devastating earthquake of December 7, 1988, the Soviet authorities arrested the Karabakh Committee—the leadership of the national democratic movement in Armenia—in an attempt to restore authority to the discredited Armenian Communist party and to gain time for the implementation of a solution from above. In Azerbaijan leaders of the nationalist protests were also arrested, and in January 1989 Karabakh was placed under the direct rule of Moscow. Though this compromise satisfied neither the Armenians nor the Azerbaijanis, it permitted some "breathing space" for the passions and hostilities of the past year, but by the fall of 1989 the Azerbaijani Popular Front organized an effective railroad blockade of the Armenian republic. In frustration, Moscow gave in to the Azerbaijanis, and in November formally returned Karabakh to Azerbaijani suzerainty.

In neighboring Georgia the growing nationalism of the intelligentsia gave rise to fears on the part of local minorities, particularly Abkhazians and Osetins, who felt discriminated against by the majority. When the Abkhazians renewed their demand for secession from Georgia and merger with Russia, Georgians began massive counterdemonstrations calling for Georgian independence. On 9 April 1989, one such demonstration was attacked by army troops in Tbilisi. At least twenty people were killed either by beatings or a powerful gas.

The dramatic mobilization of Armenians and Baltic peoples in 1988 ended the long period of benign neglect of the nationality question. While Moscow might have preferred that this "problem" await its considered solution in the repeatedly delayed Central Committee plenum on the nationality question, the contours of the issues were being shaped by people in the streets, by ad hoc committees and their intellectual leaders, and by sensitive Communist leaders, like Vaino Valas in Estonia, who worked with rather than against the local popular fronts. The Baltic strategy of cooperative competition between party and popular front contrasted with the harsher policy of martial law, arrests, and shootings in Transcaucasia. Yet in neither the Caucasus nor the Baltic were state policies able to end the national movements.

In the age of perestroika, the thrust of the more mobilized peoples has been simultaneously toward a recovery of the past, the removal of local mafias, the end of demographic and linguistic russification, a struggle against environmental pollution, greater local autonomy, republic-level *khozraschyot* (self-financing), and real democracy. The interests of the non-Russians could no longer be sacrificed on the altar of economic development. For Estonians this meant an end to placing plants in their republic and importing Russian workers without the agreement of the local people. For Uzbeks it could mean the end of exclusive planting of cotton, so necessary for Soviet independence from foreign cotton, but ruinous to the land, resources, and diversity of the economy of Uzbekistan.

Though ethnic conflict and nationalism cannot be crudely reduced to economic causes, part of the toxic mix that produced ethnic discontent was prepared by the chronic material shortages and slow economic development of the whole country. At times Kremlin leaders appear to hope wistfully that their policies of economic stimulation, if blessed by the fruits of prosperity, will dampen the ardor of the nationalists. While that certainly might help, the prolonged failure to solve fundamental economic problems promises a greater danger of material and psychological discontents being expressed in ethnic struggles.

Gorbachev has spoken of a return to Lenin. In the area of nationality relations this would mean resurrection of *korenizatsia* with its consequent fostering of national communism—greater self-rule in the ethnic republics and tolerance of national differences and cultures—but also with opposition to separatism and national exclusivity. With the steady growth of democracy—autonomous political and social organizations, contested elections, and full freedom of expression—the ruling party has been forced to accept a degree of instability, unpredictability, and disunity that it had resisted in the past. By the end of 1989, the failure to improve the economic situation and the reluctance to grant meaningful political concessions to non-Russians had intensified their strivings for autonomy if not outright independence.

125

POINT COUNTERPOINT

As destabilizing, decentralizing, and centrifugal as the divergent national aspirations of non-Russians are at the moment, they have coexisted with strong integrating processes. Economically the whole Soviet Union is intricately tied together, with cheap resources from less developed regions fueling the industrial growth of the more advanced. No ethnic republic is homogeneous in its population but includes minorities, including Russians. Armenia may present an admired picture of ethnic hegemony (eighty-nine percent Armenian) to Estonians and Latvians. Each year Georgia may grow more Georgian, as Jews and Russians leave the republic. But even as nationalities consolidate their demographic hold on some republics, they are losing in others. And rather than single nation-states, in much of the Soviet Union the republics remain binational or multinational states.

Estonia, Latvia, and Kazakhstan with their large, even overwhelmingly Russian presence, are the clearest examples of binational states, but elsewhere, in Central Asia and Ukraine, largely Russian or Russified cities exist in non-Russian societies. The twenty-five million Russians who live in the non-Russian republics are a powerful lobby for Soviet unity. Moreover, Russian intellectual culture, if not ethnic culture, continues to dominate many non-Russian cultural elites, as it has since the eighteenth century. Russia remains the road to the West with its cosmopolitan, denationalized technology, science, art, and literature. The Russian language continues to be the vehicle for communication with the world outside one's ethnic community, and whatever the hidden intents of the Soviet central authorities might be, the widespread use of Russian coexists with the use of non-Russian languages in an uneasy bilingual symbiosis.

In addition, some peoples, like the Armenians, depend on Russian protection for survival in a region where they are nearly surrounded by hostile Muslims. Central Asian peoples, who might be attracted by the Muslim fundamentalism across the border in revolutionary Iran and Afghanistan, may more likely value the security, tranquility, and material improvement provided by the Soviet system. Certainly the real benefits of a system that educated, urbanized, and industrialized the steppes and deserts and for which much has been paid in labor and even blood are not easily discarded. The costs of attempting to separate from the Soviet Union vie with the less than self-evident benefits of remaining part of a superpower, especially with the current promise of greater freedom and popular participation.

BIRTH PANGS OF A NEW ERA?

By now it has become a cliche to speak of the death of Marxism—or any form of socialism—in the Soviet Union and to speak of a form of Russian nationalism that will take the place of a discredited ideology. Yet in the world of real politics useful myths and ritual language are not easily discarded. The pattern of Russian dominance in the party and state apparatus is conveniently, even if transparently, masked by the language of national equality and self-determination.

While it is evident that Soviet patriotism and ethnic nationalism have been far more popular and potent than the symbols of "Marxist internationalism," for those in the political elites an extranational ideology retains its utility as an essential cement for a multinational state. Now freed of much of its Stalinist baggage, the language of democracy and self-determination has taken on a new power as both a tool in the hands of the disenfranchised and a means of linking the efforts of Kremlin reformers and their supporters. The debasement of Marxism into an empty rhetoric, the Gorbachevites must hope, can potentially be reversed by the reinfusion of meaning into the current leadership's effort to construct a new model of socialism. On the other hand, failure to democratize and modernize further reinforce popular perceptions of the bankruptcy of any socialist model.

In many ways Gorbachev's task in changing Soviet society while preserving state stability (and party power?) is even more difficult than was Lenin's, for his chosen ends preclude the use of terror and sustained coercion. Gorbachev seems to accept the idea that the employment of Stalinist methods has already corrupted and will continue to taint the original goals of socialism, as well as the path to it, namely democratization and glasnost. He seeks to reconcile two political ends that have seldom coexisted in history: democracy and empire.

Faced with a fundamental challenge—how to hold together the largest multinational state on the globe while stimulating social change and economic development in a freer, more democratic environment, Gorbachev must realize that he can neither take for granted the support of non-Russian peoples nor neglect the separate agendas of the nationalities

127

that could create dozens of points of opposition. In a very real sense the banner of the demonstrators in Yerevan proclaimed a harsh truth: "Karabakh is the test of perestroika." How Moscow deals with the non-Russians will to a large extent determine the fate of the most significant political and social transformation that the Soviet Union has undergone since the 1930s.

★

LYRICS:
THE PAIN
OF DISCOVERY

★

VERA S. DUNHAM

IN 1830, THE RUSSIAN POET FYODOR
Tyutchev wrote a poem called "Silentium," whose most urgent and
disturbing lines rang like a reproach—or appeal—to himself and to his
fellow poets:

> *Mysl izrechyonnaya yest lozh;*
> *Vzryvaya, vozmutish klyuchi—*
> *Pitaisya imi—i molchi.*

> A thought expressed is but a lie;
> Stir up the springs, and you will cloud them—
> Drink of them, and be silent.[1]

Tyutchev's alarm about the disfiguring gap between thought and
language stands in contrast not only to his own work but also to the
tenacious longevity of the Russian traditional view of poetry as Holy
Communion with Truth. Yet it may serve as a fitting introduction to
this essay, which will examine the "springs" stirred up by Soviet poets—

not, as Tyutchev warned, in order to "becloud" them—but to find a meaning in their battered lives.

Let me start with the Leningrad poet Ilya Fonyakov, perhaps less awed by the poet's prophetic potential than Tyutchev was, but clearly not afraid of its consequences:

> There are books of red-hot tension,
> Of uneven and passionate script
> As if their authors were pushed
> By life itself or death itself.
>
> You open such a book and suddenly turn pale
> As you read your life in a stranger's fate.
> You turn pale as if from a page somebody
> Hits you in the heart with a bullet.
> That with which you had shielded yourself
> Has been punctured and shattered
> And you die. And you are reborn at once
> Just as you had been and not at all as you had been before.[2]

Fonyakov, born in 1935, belongs to the pivotal yet uncomfortable age group squeezed between the Stalinist war generation, which was either stained or victimized by Stalinism, or both, and their younger colleagues, who command a combative and skeptical clarity far greater than that of any previous generation of Soviet poets. In the complex reality of Soviet tensions, it is not at all clear to whom Fonyakov's "you" refers. Is it the reader of his own verse? Is it the author-as-reader? His reverence for the moral power of art is patent: less so, perhaps, the anchorage for that reverence. Who else accepts it, and to whom is his awed eloquence both familiar and cathartic?

Dmitri Prigov, Fonyakov's coeval, is considerably more self-mocking. He writes of the displacement of the poet in an amoral world with wry detachment, turning a Soviet cliche inward in semiskeptical, semiserious query:

> I am, let us say, an ordinary poet,
> But Russian fate by some caprice decreed

That one should be the conscience of the nation.
But how be conscience where there's none?
Verses they may be, conscience—no.
What's to be done?[3]

Indeed, what's to be done? Grandiloquence has been compromised
for its previous services to ideological cant. Its opposite—purification—
is far too demanding a goal. In the climate of glasnost, even plain and
simple eloquence is not above suspicion. Perhaps this is one of the reasons
why poetry is presently yielding to prose, while prose itself seems to veer
toward *melkotemiye*—the proliferation of small, not to say petty, concrete, and private themes.

Still, glasnost seems not to have changed two fundamental aspects
of the cultural conundrum of Soviet life. First, Soviet literature continues
to be at once culture-ridden and culture-forming: it continues to report
and to create. Secondly, no matter how seemingly apolitical its topic
and authorial posture, the literary work itself remains politicized.

Of course, the first of these two traits is true of every literature.
What seems to be characteristic of the Soviet literary process—what
Soviet scholars like to call the relationship of author, critic, and reader—
is the tension between the two literary functions—preservation and innovation. It is augmented by the burden of cultural leadership placed
on the writer's shoulders as well as by the sometimes excessive public
admiration with which he is rewarded.

Thus, for example, a perusal of Prigov's skeptical—not to say cyn-
ical—verse brings into focus the belief that cliquishness must not be
confused with solidarity, and that the concept of *grupovshchina*, adherence to like-minded circles, is inauthentic and even destructive in a
society so flagrantly rent by divisiveness. Perhaps one day in the future
the apolitical and the political will no longer be bound to each other.
But not yet.

Within the parameters of these unaltered realities Soviet literature
has reacted to glasnost with a vengeance, unrolling a rich thematic
tapestry with an unsparing, if often weary, clarity. One of the most
prominent images is of the embattled family in the urban professional
setting. It is not a new theme, though Soviet writers are still expected
to apotheosize the "Soviet family." Yet while the authorial respect for
the family nexus remains intact, more and more works suggest that the

stability of that nexus, at least in the urban setting, is rapidly eroding. Obviously, closely related subthemes orbit around the core: unhappy love, abandoned women, loneliness, and the most important and melancholy of them all—*bezotsovshchina* ("fatherlessness," quite different from "orphanhood"), the harrowing break in the male generational linkage. This in turn overlaps another major theme: the lingering memory of war.

In the last several years, memories of war have flooded journals and filled books. It is not a new subject, of course, nor could it be easily repressed, as so many other themes were. But under glasnost it has assumed a new meaning—above all, as the background for debates between different Soviet generations.

Within this flood one problem stands out above all others—that of children and youth. Anatoli Pristavkin's novella *I nochevala tuchka zolotaya* (And A Golden Cloud Spent the Night), for example, depicts his own evacuation from Moscow to a children's home in Siberia during the war. Written in 1981, it was published only six years later.[4]

In Pristavkin's words, it took him six months to write the novella, "plus my whole life. The writing was fast, because I couldn't take long over it. The story literally burned within me."[5] The hunger and death suffered by children in wartime, as well as the forced deportation of the local Chechen population, is delineated with painful attention to detail. "By showing the events through the eyes of teenage boys," Pristavkin explained, "I wanted to show their encounter with pain, injustice, and fear, the latter being all the greater for its being incomprehensible and mysterious."

Difficult childhood is also the subject of "From the Length of Days," written by the eighty-one-year-old poet and literary scholar Vladimir Admoni:

Childhood is not a preface.
It is an independent text.
We remember loving even
The bitter faraway years.

Sometimes there comes to the surface
The memory of such childhood days

That we ourselves can't fathom
How we managed to live with it.[6]

Many Soviet children did not. Many were saved. Many perished at
the front. Yuri Petrovich Voronov, born in 1929, was awarded the medal
"For the defense of Leningrad" in 1943. He was not quite 15 years old.

> During the days of siege
> We truly failed to find
> The dividing line
> Between our youth
> And our childhood!
> We were given medals
> In nineteen forty three
> And passports
> Only two years later.[7]

Yulia Drunina volunteered at the age of eighteen to go to the front,
where she served in the medical corps till the end of the war.

> By birth I am not from childhood,
> I am from war,
> And, therefore, probably,
> I value more than you can value
> The bliss of stillness
> As well as each new day
> I live.
>
> By birth I am not from childhood,
> I am from war. Once, on my way
> Through a guerilla path,
> I firmly grasped that
> We must love
> All tender blades of grass.
>
> By birth I am not from childhood.
> I am from war.

133

And, therefore, possibly,
Not well protected.
Front soldiers' hearts are scorched
And you, your hands are rough.

By birth I am not from childhood.
I am from war.
Forgive me,
It is no fault of mine.[8]

And finally another poem, perhaps the most haunting of all. It is called "Age," and it was written by Aleksandr Mezhirov, born in 1923. Mezhirov, too, went to the front at the age of eighteen, managing to survive the hell of the Leningrad siege. His lines are clearly addressed to poets like Yevgeni Yevtushenko and Andrei Voznesensky, of like minds but born too late to have endured the single most formative experience of Mezhirov's generation.

The difference in age between us is small,
Some five years, no more.
Yet you see an old man in me for good reason.
And I am ready to agree with you.

The cruelty of your naïve judgment
I shall not hold against you
Because, indeed, I am by the years
Of the Fatherland war older than you.[9]

Every era deserves its own apocalypse. The unspeakable tragedy of Stalinism is one thing, corporate responsibility for it another. And as time goes on, the country's efforts to reconstruct its own history run deeper and more contentious. Mezhirov's talk with a brother-in-arms— in a poem published in 1988—speaks for millions of soldiers who fell, as well as for those who survived and must now carry the shame of Stalinism on their shoulders.

What is it you are crying about, old wreck—
Where is it—your sacred faith

In the revolution and in Stalin
And the class essence of life?

We were inspired by Stalin's plans,
We soared into Stalin's heights.
You and I, we are brothers in arms.
We pledged allegiance to Stalin's banner.

We marched accompanied by explosions.
We marched through our own fault and that of others.
Oh, how happy would we have been
Had we been killed in that war.[10]

Mezhirov's stark and heretical poem sounds flat in translation. Even so, it is hard not to be struck by its gnawing pain. Glasnost has spawned a heady mixture of exhilaration, acrimony, chaos, and hope. The wish of death alone lifts "Age" high above the tumult of today's battlefield.

Yet Mezhirov's cold despair is alien, if not actually anathema, to many for whom memories of idealism, practiced or proclaimed, are tenacious. So are memories of courage. Today's memories of war—doleful, disparate, and combative—present a tangle of problems, even in the climate of glasnost. During the war, Stalinism blended with patriotism in a form of communism that neither Soviet nor Western scholars have properly studied. In the first, "critical" (read: disastrous) phase of the war, the fusion took place under the healing aegis of populism. Those who witnessed and participated in the wartime *sobornost* (that old Russian term that stands for brotherhood *in extremis*) and their children as well have had a hard time beating their chests in shame and admission of guilt.

Again, what is to be done? Does shame substitute for guilt and responsibility? Is glorification of shame helpful? Hardly, one suspects. But advocacy of shame is now a frequent—and enlightening—phenomenon. It suggests that the search for explanations for Stalin's crimes, a process well under way in scholarship and the popular press, is bound to accelerate. More: it suggests that the explanation will focus on endemic social and institutional factors—that is, on the Soviet system itself.

As an example, take Yevgeni Yevtushenko's poem published in 1985—

A dish with wax
turned dim in darkness.
A melted candle
cannot be restored. . . .

He who broke up a family
will not accommodate the next.
Friendship crushed underfoot
Cannot be restored. . . .

Mugs with honey on their lips
show stains of blood.
A face turned into a mug
Cannot be restored. . . .

Revolt of shame alone
against the lack of shame
will help avoid Last Judgment's
total emptiness.

Only the revolt of a face
against facelessness can
restore life in all its
majesty and grandeur.

Shamelessness can devour
children. It stops at nothing.
But shame is not terrible.
It is not death.
Everything will be restored.[11]

—to whose curiously didactic and reassuring tone one might be tempted to respond with "That's what *you* say!" But what outsider has the right to utter such words?

The seemingly inescapable politicization of Soviet literature calls into question, if it does not entirely destroy, the distinction between public poets, like Vladimir Mayakovsky and Sergei Yesenin on the one hand, and private poets, like Boris Pasternak, Leonid Martynov, and Arseni Tarkovsky. Yet the lives of some poets have become quiet legends.

Olga Berggolts, a faithful and forceful chronicler (and survivor) of the Leningrad siege, was one of Stalin's martyrs. Her quietly legendary life was destroyed when her husband, the poet Boris Kornilov, perished in the camps. A severe alcoholic, she died in 1975. It is only recently that Vitali Korotich, the editor of *Ogonyok*, published one of her heretofore unknown poems. In a vein reminiscent of Anna Akhmatova (yet another victim of Stalin's murderous lunacy) she speaks of her love of *rodina* (motherland)—*no matter what*:

> You have chased me and
> slandered me.
> You have taken my children
> away.
> And my fame.
> But I have not stopped
> loving you
> Because I know that you are
> savage but
> not evil.
> I watch you and faithfully
> believe in you.
> I have become stronger
> and more grim.
> But I know how majestic is
> my lofty love for you.
> It has never wavered.[12]

A "savage but not evil" homeland still commands Berggolts's devotion. But the gradual and most likely irrevocable process of privatization of just about everything spells out, among other shifts and changes, the demise of the ideological and idealistic verbiage of formerly worshipped collective values. So what *does* man live by? Surely not bread alone?

Vitali Korotich, now chiefly known as the editor of the weekly *Ogonyok* and as a powerful foreman on the cultural reconstruction site, is also a poet; and a good one at that. And it is important to ascertain what *he* lives by. He tells us just that, with unmistakable clarity.

What is there in the end?
Mother, friends, work
Love . . .
What else contains one's soul?
Life's glitter and simplicity are both
Unthinkable without this stronghold.
This is the essence.
The rest is fuss and nonsense.[13]

And if the stalk of life, unharmed,
Starts growing in your wound,
Well, press your lips
Or eat your tears.
Their salt is clean as bread.
To lose your mother, your beloved,
Your friends, your work is terrible.
They hold the stubborn light
Of meaning.
            The rest is fuss and nonsense.[14]

In a few lines, Korotich disposes of a bagful of orthodox verities, such as the sanctity of "socialist labor," the worship of the "collective," the apotheosis of statism, and the rejection of personal (that is to say, "petty bourgeois") pursuits. Korotich's plea for the defense of truly personal priorities expresses an urgency that transcends political differences. Take, for instance, the following lines from a story by the increasingly xenophobic Valentin Rasputin:

> Man has four props in his life: his house with his family; his work; people with whom he spends holidays and workdays; and the earth on which his house stands. And of the four each is more important than the others. If one of the props caves in—your whole world is on the skids.[15]

The demise of ideology has not been succeeded by a new all-embracing faith, certainly not among those impervious to the blandishments of either nationalism or to the poisonous brew peddled by "societies" such as *Pamyat* and the like. The end of ideology has left them with a powerful sense of *pustota*, that is, spiritual emptiness. Even the warmth of compassion and of *chelovechnost* (very loosely, humanness), a concept which has become almost synonymous with glasnost itself, is not a substitute for the props once provided by canonized values. Thus in one of the first published poems by a young poet from Gorky, the traditional "props"—party, ideology, civic devotion—are entirely absent.

Three things matter most in the world.
They embrace everything.
Children are most important in the world.
Thereafter—truth and a friend.
And possibly the world was made
Because from age to age the child
Reaches out to fruit, people to the stars
And man reaches out to man.[16]

The child as highest value links with the saddest of all glasnost themes, mentioned earlier: the damaged child in the battered urban professional family—another child, if you will, in another kind of war. And no one has cast a sharper light—without the slightest bit of sermon or drama—on *bezotsovshchina* (fatherlessness) than Yuri Nesterov, a young Kuibishev poet. This is how the adolescent narrator of his poem "For the First Time" thinks and feels:

Passing through our town,
My father stops for an hour or so.
I have heard about him more than once.
But I see him for the first time.
He resembles me. He is straightforward.
But he acts like a stranger.
We raise a silent toast to this encounter
As we clink our glasses by the wall.

The wall can't be broken.
Why should one even try?
He prefers to live the way
His heart commands him.

139

I won't reproach him.
My mother is silent. She is pale.
For the first time I drink in her presence
And the wine is bitter for the first time.

For the first time the wine has
No effect at all.
Evening has come long ago
But he keeps waiting for something.

The silence is difficult, heavy.
It would seem that father should go.
But it's painful for me
To tell him so.[17]

The next poem turns the situation around: the father, separated
from his child and weighed down by sorrow and guilt, speaks in his
verse what he cannot say aloud. The author, like Nesterov, is young,
and "To My Daughter," too, comes from his first published work:

She asks me questions
And I can't find the answers . . .
How can I explain to you
That you are the Eighth Wonder of the world?

Our meetings are infrequent and not easy.
The bond is a cantata on the phone.
How can I explain to you
That you are my penitence forever?

We walk once more along the streets,
Those where we did not walk before,
How can I explain to you
That you are both my joy and hope?

The dark firmament of your eyes,
The smiling dimples.
How can I explain to you
That you are the beautiful price of an error?[18]

And what of the women—the "silent, pale" mother of Nesterov's poem, the custodial parent of Dorin's? They speak for themselves, voicing their pain and loneliness, the difficulties and absurdities embedded in life *à deux*, the shock of discovering a third person in what turns out, unbeknownst to them, to be life *à trois*. They are women's cares, articulated in women's voices, occasionally with a sad smile, as in these lines by the young Leningrad poet Irina Moiseyeva:

> No sooner are we both alone,
> How painful it becomes
> As well as awkward.
> Such a splendid myth
> And such a stupid stage production.[19]

More often there is no smile, especially when the production folds. The anguished yet simple words that follow are a woman's, but in no way suggest the demeaning connotations of "women's poetry," *damskaya poezia*, with its whiff of gentility, crooked pinkies and china tea cups. They were penned by Maya Borisova, one of Russia's best poets:

> A break-up is hard to carry
> Especially when
> You do not know
> What made us part.
> Coolness, duty, sudden trouble?
> If only some sign had been given . . .
> So many days now
> I drag the break-up like
> A suitcase without straps or handle.[20]

Increasingly, a note of self-reproach, of self-laceration, is heard in these poems. Even in one imbued with the whimsical mood of a *chastushka*, a folk ditty:

> Again I squander myself
> On a man who gives nothing.

141

Let him live a long life.
I have forgiven even him.

I am alone to blame. Alone.
I always, always wait
For someone I shouldn't wait for,
And I remember what I shouldn't.[21]

Another woman poet, resigned to her fate, harbors no bitterness
against the one who left her. He is, as the title observes with melancholy,
"Like All the Others":

You come to me like all the others
To swallow tea just like the others do.
It is as if nostalgia for a long lost country
Were to gnaw at the heart. . . .

No, I will not call you nor reproach you,
We are neither friends nor foes by now.
How sad and pitiful and lonely
Do your steps sound down below.[22]

And then the *malaise à trois*:

Let's part—I shall not see the eyes
of the woman who in time will enter
as mistress your cozy house.
A nail on a faded stain on the wall
May not fill her with joy.
My photo used to hang there.
She will keep quiet. She'll hang her portrait
on that nail.
But in the silence of your rooms
Your glance will come sometime upon that nail.
Her portrait will remind you of my portrait
without fail.[23]

142

Commonplace, pedestrian occurrence, of course. Universal, of course. But of late so often repeated, so obsessively examined, that its eloquence suggests a wholly fractured world of love, broken along the fault line between the sexes. What is the price of loneliness? "Talks, meetings, phone calls," writes Natalya Babitskaya—all of which she would "exchange / for friendship / friendship / from heart to heart."[24]

Still, loneliness is an honest emotion, and as such is to be preferred to specious hustle and bustle, with its overtones of the now rejected *kollektivnost*.

I have learned to live alone,
To cry silently at dawn,
To sit aimlessly by the window,
To wander past the summer homes.

And to buy your flowers,
To let my heart drink their pain and freshness,
And quietly—just like you used to do—
To chide the tom-cat and caress him,

To talk with him the way I talked with you—
To share my thoughts with him,
To value his purring
When it's impossible to sleep all night.

To rise when it is dark,
And flowers in the garden keep their silence,
To let the cat out the window
And fall into a light sweet sleep.

By morning, making rapid order,
To settle at the table all alone
And, having kissed the sheet of paper,
To write without a deadline or a break.

So that, resigned, as if in a dream
And powerless over a cup of tea turned cold,
To burst out laughing in the silence,
Noticing neither the walls nor my tears.

Yet the sky is blue, the sky is blazing,
Yet there is life and somewhere there are people.
Forgive me and rejoice with me
that I am sheltered by your dream.

Your warmth lives in me. So does
The rapid voice of your heart.
And it is difficult no end
To be so happy without you.[25]

Because the author of this poem, Nina Ostrovskaya, belongs to
Mezhirov's and Voronov's age group; because she, too, went to war at
the age of seventeen, it is difficult to resist the impression that while
grieving over a personal loss, she has more than that in mind, and that
her grief and search are thus imbued with a transcendental quality.

Let me close with an excerpt from a poem—a question—that en-
capsulates the themes touched upon in this essay. The author is the
young Assia Veksler, and like so many poets quoted in these pages, she
comes from Leningrad.

What do we live by?
After discounting a heap
of excuses and insults,
there looms that last question:

Over there, when life,
unrepeatable, is over,
What will we leave behind
the inseparable boundary?[26]

★

LEARNING TO LIVE
AND LET LIVE

⭐

DAVID HOLLOWAY

IN ADDITION TO PERESTROIKA AND GLASNOST, the Gorbachev era has bestowed to the world another term, "new political thinking"; and like the first two, this term also has given rise to no end of interest and controversy in the West. Some American and West European commentators have dismissed it as mere propaganda, designed to hide a real Soviet threat from Western public opinion. Others have seen it as nothing more than an attempt on the part of the Soviet government to obtain a breathing space so that it can restore its ailing economy before redoubling its efforts to achieve military superiority and expand its power. Still others have seen it as evidence that the new Soviet leadership has changed its basic priorities and now places global interests above those of the USSR. And there are those who argue that a change in domestic politics entails a change in foreign policy, that the new political thinking is to be understood merely as the external expression of perestroika.

The explanation we give for the emergence of the new thinking necessarily affects the significance we ascribe to it in East-West relations. Those who interpret it merely as a tactical device obviously regard it as introducing nothing new into international relations. Those who see it as forced on the Soviet Union by economic constraints assume that it would disappear once the economic difficulties are overcome. It is therefore important to ask where the new thinking has come from, why it has been adopted by the Soviet Union, and what its implications are for international relations.

THE OLD AND THE NEW

The new thinking embraces a number of propositions about the nature of international relations in the modern world: human interests take precedence over the interests of any particular class; the world is becoming increasingly interdependent; there can be no victors in a nuclear war; security has to be based increasingly on political rather than military instruments; security, especially in the context of Soviet-American relations, must be mutual, since if one side is insecure it will make the other insecure too.

As other aspects of the current reforms in the USSR, the new thinking did not spring into existence fully armed like Athena from the head of Zeus. None of its propositions is new; many may be found in such Western studies as the Palme Commission's report on common security;[1] others can be found in Soviet writings of the 1970s and early 1980s. But taken together they provide a framework that orients Soviet foreign policy in a new direction.

The new thinking has found expression not only in the speeches of party and government leaders, but also in newspaper and journal articles by specialists in international relations and military affairs. Glasnost has opened foreign and defense policy to broader and freer discussion and to a wide spectrum of views. But the discussion of foreign policy is more limited than that of domestic political affairs; and this is true also of the history of Soviet foreign policy. Stalin's policies on the eve of the Great Patriotic War and his conduct of the war have been severely criticized. However, Stalin's postwar foreign and military policy has not been subjected to careful scrutiny. Nor have Khrushchev's and Brezhnev's policies been the subject of detailed critical analysis. Some specific decisions, such as the ones to deploy the SS-20 missile, to send Soviet forces into Afghanistan, and to use military power in the Third World in the 1970s, have been criticized in the press. And Soviet academics and former officials have participated in meetings with American counterparts to explore the history of the Cuban missile crisis. Altogether, discussion of foreign policy is much more open than it was eight years ago; but compared with what it might be, it is rather restrained, though that may well change as glasnost continues.

This does not mean that Soviet foreign policy in the postwar period is now regarded as correct or successful. On the contrary, Soviet specialists (as well as, increasingly, journalists) reject and criticize many basic assumptions of earlier foreign policy, especially as it was conducted under Brezhnev.

To make this argument is not to slight the domestic sources of the new thinking or its importance for perestroika. The foreign policy crisis that Gorbachev inherited when he became general secretary in March 1985 was only part of a broader economic and social crisis affecting the country. The build-up of Soviet military power had been accompanied by an erosion of the economic and technological basis of that power, and by a general demoralization of society, as evidenced in such social ills as alcoholism and corruption.

It is this general crisis that has been Gorbachev's first priority. His intention is not to patch up the Stalinist system, but to replace it with a more efficient and more open model of socialism. It is conceivable that in 1985 another leader might have tried to muddle through, or adopted a more repressive policy at home and a more rigid policy abroad. But Gorbachev has shown his determination to deal with the crisis of the Stalinist system by far-reaching economic and political reform, and this has shaped his foreign policy, too.

One of Gorbachev's top priorities has been an attempt to create a more stable and predictable international environment, necessary no less for the conduct of foreign policy than for domestic reforms. One reason for wanting such an international environment is to create conditions in which defense spending can be restrained, or even cut. In the words of Foreign Minister Eduard Shevardnadze, the main objective is to ensure

> that our country no longer bears additional expenditures in connection with the necessity of supporting our defense capability and the defense of our legitimate foreign policy interests. That means that we must seek paths to the limitation and reduction of military rivalry, to the removal of confrontational moments in relations with other states, to the damping down of conflicts and crises.[2]

The needs of domestic policy have thus impelled the Soviet Union to look for new approaches to foreign and military policy. The domestic factor alone, however, is not enough to account for the new thinking, the most important of whose propositions should be understood as responses to the foreign-policy problems that the Soviet Union faced in the early 1980s.

THE PRICE OF DOGMA

It was a central premise of Brezhnev's foreign policy that the world's "correlation of forces" was shifting in favor of socialism. For the Soviet leaders this idea provided the basis for detente: as a result of the growing Soviet power, the West (so the reasoning went) would find it impossible to deal with the Soviet Union from a position of strength, and would therefore be more willing to reach agreement on arms control, on trade and technology, and on political issues. Although the concept of the correlation of forces embraces political and economic forces as well as military power, Brezhnev and his colleagues clearly regarded the growth of Soviet military power, and in particular the attainment of strategic parity with the United States, as a crucial factor in the move to detente.

While both the Soviet Union and the United States subscribed to "détente," each of them had a different conception of what it meant and of what it should entail. Both believed that the Soviet Union was growing more powerful, yet each of them drew its own conclusions from it. The Soviet leaders thought that the stronger their country, the more accommodating the West would be. The United States, especially during Nixon's presidency, wanted to temper Soviet power, curb its growth, and restrain the way in which it was exercised.

By the mid-1970s, however, American critics of détente were claiming that the hope of restraining the growth and exercise of Soviet power was an illusion. They argued that, in spite of SALT I and the Basic Principles Agreement,[3] the USSR was building up its forces in a determined drive to achieve strategic superiority, and using its military power to make political gains in the Third World. They quoted Soviet military writings to show that Brezhnev and his colleagues were convinced that they could fight and win a nuclear war, and that they were therefore not deterred by the threat of assured destruction.

Though many of these criticisms were exaggerated, they contributed to the sense of alarm at the growth of Soviet military power that impelled the Carter Administration to embark in the late 1970s on its own military buildup. When Deng Xiaoping came to Washington in January 1979, he called for an anti-Soviet united front, thus conjuring up for the Soviet leaders the specter of encirclement by a Sino–American–Japanese–West European coalition. Even before the Soviet invasion of Afghanistan in December 1979, it was clear that Soviet expectations about the deepening of détente were not being realized.

In the 1970s Soviet analyses of world politics assumed that the growth of Soviet military power and the extension of Soviet influence would curb American power and elicit American cooperation. But this conception proved to be a poor guide to international relations. The growth of Soviet power did not elicit accommodation from the Soviet Union's rivals, but evoked an effort to counteract that power. As the Soviet historian Vyacheslav Dashichev has written, in the 1970s the Soviet Union "erred in assessing the global situation in the world and the correlation of forces."[4]

Whether this failure resulted more from incompetence and bureaucratic sluggishness than from conceptual blinders remains unclear, but preconceptions about the nature of international relations may have played a role. One Soviet author has suggested that the effect of Soviet Third-World policy on the United States was well understood at one level by Soviet diplomats, but discounted because it was assumed that peaceful coexistence at the interstate level would not be affected by the "world revolutionary process."[5] Similarly, it may be wondered whether the correlation of forces model, by suggesting that the West would remain committed to détente because of the growth of Soviet power helped to blind Soviet policy-makers to the effects of their own actions on other governments. It may have encouraged them to believe that foreign leaders, no matter what harsh rhetoric they used, would in time accommodate themselves to the new realities of power.

Brezhnev was slow to recognize the failure of his policies. At the Twenty-sixth Party Congress in 1981 he remarked that the previous five years had been a "complex and stormy" period in international relations, but offered nothing to guide foreign policy into calmer waters. It was only in October 1982, a month before his death, that he gave a more urgent assessment, declaring that the United States had "launched a political, ideological, and economic offensive" against the Soviet Union and had begun an "unprecedented arms race."[6]

In 1983 Soviet foreign policy was at an impasse. The Reagan Administration's military build-up was well under way, and the president's

"Star Wars" speech threatened the Soviet Union not only with a less predictable strategic relationship, but also with an intense technological arms race. In Western Europe, which had seemed to be the weakest link in the presumed "encirclement" of the Soviet Union, the deployment of GLCMs and Pershing 2s began. The invasion of Afghanistan had resulted in a debilitating war rather than political control of that country. Soviet policy in the Third World had brought few significant political gains, and had compelled the Soviet Union to support weak governments that faced economic problems and strong domestic opposition. East-West relations were at such a low ebb that many people began to speak of a new Cold War. A slight thaw had begun in Sino-Soviet relations, following China's adoption of an independent foreign policy, but the three obstacles remained; and relations with Japan were chilly, too.

During Andropov's brief term in office, little was done to improve the situation. Andropov withdrew from the INF and START talks when the NATO INF deployment began in November 1983. This decision, Shevardnadze said in 1988, had made it easier for the United States to create "a second strategic front" against the Soviet Union in Europe.[7] In September 1983, after the KAL 007 incident, Andropov issued a statement declaring that "if anyone had any illusions about the possibility that the policy of the present American administration would change for the better, then the events of the recent period have finally dispelled them."[8] Soviet policy towards the United States was defiant and rigid under Andropov; only under Chernenko was there some slight movement out of the impasse, when the Soviet Union and the United States agreed, in January 1985, to start the nuclear and space arms-control talks in Geneva. The problems that the Soviet Union faced in its foreign and defense policy in the mid-1980s were, in some measure, the consequence of Brezhnev's policies. One of Gorbachev's main tasks has been to devise a strategy to extricate the Soviet Union from this unfavorable and threatening international position.

AGONIZING REAPPRAISALS

The failure of Brezhnev's foreign policy presented Gorbachev not only with practical policy problems, but also with conceptual challenges. The collapse of détente had discredited the premises on which Brezhnev's policy had been based. The presumed shift in the correlation of forces towards socialism had not brought about a reduction in tension; on the

150

contrary, the world in 1983 and 1984 seemed a more dangerous place than it had been ten years earlier. If the growth of Soviet military power and its use to further Soviet foreign policy (in line with the notion of the correlation of forces shifting towards socialism) made the world more tense by evoking dangerous countermoves from other states, what should the Soviet Union do? Should it conclude that its primary goal is to increase its own power, or should it strive above all to secure a more peaceful and cooperative relationship with the West? As the issue was to be framed in the post-Brezhnev discussion, if a potential conflict exists between peace and socialism, which should receive priority?[9]

Gorbachev's response to this question has been to point to the overriding importance of peace. In October 1986 he referred to Lenin's "immensely profound idea concerning the priority of the interests of social development, of all-human values, over the interests of one or another class." Gorbachev went on to speak of the importance in the nuclear age of the "thesis of the priority of the all-human value of peace over all others to which different people are attached."[10] Taken by itself this proposition may seem banal, but it is significant in the Soviet context because it implies that the goals of peace and socialism may come into conflict, and because it provides a justification for giving priority to the pursuit of cooperation with the West over the search for unilateral advantage.

The argument that peace has priority has aroused controversy in the party leadership. In July 1988 Shevardnadze said that "peaceful coexistence" was acquiring a new meaning in the light of this concept, and condemned as "mistaken" and "anti-Leninist" the view, which was expounded in the Brezhnev years, that peaceful coexistence is a specific form of the class struggle.[11] In the following month Politburo member Yegor Ligachev responded by implying that there is—and can be—no contradiction between peace and socialism:

We proceed from the class nature of international relations. Any other formulation of the issue only introduces confusion into the thinking of Soviet people and our friends abroad. Active involvement in the solution of general human problems by no means signifies any artificial 'braking' of the social and national liberation struggle.[12]

Two months later Vadim Medvedev, the new party secretary responsible for ideology, reasserted the importance of universal values. "Today," he said, "when universal values are embodied with utmost specificity, primarily in ensuring mankind's survival, they come to the foreground of international relations and constitute the nucleus of the new political thinking."[13] In his speech to the United Nations in December 1988 Gorbachev stressed again the importance of human values, and argued that differences in ideology should not be allowed to affect relations between states.

The thesis that all-human values take priority is closely linked to the argument, also advanced by Gorbachev, that the world is increasingly interdependent. Capitalism and socialism cannot develop in isolation from each other, because they are part of one and the same human civilization. Neither the Soviet Union nor the United States can feel secure if the other feels insecure. In an interdependent world it is not the conflict between capitalism and socialism, but rather cooperation in defense of universal values that is at the heart of international relations. This argument provides the basis for Soviet proposals to make greater use of the United Nations and other international organizations in maintaining peace and dealing with global problems.

In criticizing Brezhnev, Gorbachev is certainly not returning to the premises of Stalin's foreign policy. For instance, the arguments that have been aired in the Soviet press about the Nazi-Soviet Pact of 1939 have had more to do with assessing Stalin's leadership than with elaborating new concepts. But just as Gorbachev is trying to replace the Stalinist system at home, so he is rejecting the unilateral, territorial approach to security characteristic of Stalin, who thought that Soviet security depended on the insecurity of others.

EXPANSIONISM AND POWER POLITICS

Some commentators have argued that the new thinking marks the end of Soviet expansionism. The term "expansionism" implies that there is something inherent in the Soviet system that drives the Soviet Union, more than other states, to seek to expand its power and influence. Stalin did of course exploit the dismemberment of Poland in 1939 and the defeat of Germany and Japan in 1945 to expand Soviet territory and Soviet control over other states. This expansion reflected his belief that the more territory the Soviet Union controlled, the safer it would be. And in his dealings with other states Stalin displayed a characteristically great-power attitude, regarding the interests of these states as important only if they were backed by power. The bases of expansion under Khrushchev and Brezhnev were different. In the nuclear age a territorial conception of security loses some of its meaning. The breakup of the Western colonial empires did, however, give the Soviet Union the opportunity to expand its influence throughout the world, and both Khrushchev and Brezhnev took advantage of this opportunity, in the belief that the expansion of Soviet influence would move the correlation of forces in favor of the USSR.

Soviet leaders today clearly reject the premises that underpinned both the Stalinist and post-Stalinist expansion of Soviet power and influence. This is not to suggest that the Soviet Union wishes to abandon its role as a world power. Rather, the current view provides a different picture of the world and redefines the Soviet role in it. It assigns a less important place to conflict in international relations, and calls for the Soviet Union to base its world role not on military power and the search for unilateral advantage, but on a more cooperative—more normal—involvement in the international system.

MILITARY POWER AND FOREIGN POLICY

The growth of Soviet military power in the Brezhnev years was not accompanied by commensurate gains in foreign policy. Far from making the Soviet Union more secure, it merely provoked the United States and its allies into building up their own forces. This in turn created new threats to Soviet security and imposed new military requirements on the Soviet Union. According to Shevardnadze, "one of the most unfavorable phenomena of the period of stagnation, which had a negative influence on our international positions, was the discrepancy between military and political directions."[14]

What should be the relationship, then, between "military and political directions"—that is, between military power and foreign policy? The debate on this question was serious and resulted in a startlingly new consensus: security should be based not on the accumulation of military power, but on such political measures as arms control, the settlement of regional conflicts, and the removal of irritants in relations with other states.

The acceptance of this general proposition led, in turn, to the elaboration of a new conception of Soviet military doctrine in which its military-technical aspect dovetails with its political premises. This was not prompted by a passion for intellectual tidiness, but by pragmatic considerations. Since it was precisely the conceptual inconsistencies in the erstwhile military doctrine that contributed to the Soviet Union's political problems in the 1960s and 1970s, it was now mandatory to revise the doctrine so that it would not hinder the new foreign policy line.

To illustrate the impact of doctrine on the actual conduct of Soviet foreign policy, let us take a look at the inconsistencies of the Brezhnev era. When the Soviet military first acquired nuclear weapons in the 1950s, it regarded them largely as a means of increasing the firepower available to the armed forces. In the 1970s and 1980s, however, the rapid growth in the number of nuclear weapons and delivery systems led, in the words of Marshal N.V. Ogarkov, former chief of the general staff, "to a radical review of the role of these weapons, to a break with previous views of their place and significance in war, of the methods of conducting battles or operations, and even of the possibility of waging war at all with the use of nuclear weapons."[15] This shift in thinking was reflected in a series of speeches in which Brezhnev elaborated a deterrent rationale for Soviet strategic forces, emphasizing that it would be suicidal to start a nuclear war, and declaring that sufficiency, not superiority, was the Soviet goal.

The Soviet High Command concluded in the 1970s that, because nuclear war would be so destructive, a major war might remain conventional even in Europe. Many Western analysts believed that, if there were a war in Europe, the Soviet military would mount rapid conventional offensive operations into Western Europe in the hope of achieving a quick victory. Improvements in Soviet conventional capabilities seemed to support the argument that the Soviet Union was indeed giving particular importance to conventional offensive operations.

Soviet policy appeared to the West to be at best ambiguous, at worst dangerous and menacing. Although Brezhnev and other Soviet leaders made it clear that they wished to avoid nuclear war, the Soviet military stressed the importance of preparing to fight and win such a war. And while the Soviet leaders asserted that Soviet military doctrine was profoundly defensive, the military emphasized that the offensive was the primary form of military operation. These inconsistencies, especially when viewed in the context of growing Soviet military power, aroused suspicion and mistrust in the West and helped to fuel political support for strategic programs like the MX ICBM and the Strategic Defense Initiative, and for efforts to improve NATO's conventional forces. Soviet military doctrine contributed to the image of a Soviet threat abroad, and by provoking a military reaction from other states imposed new military requirements and new economic burdens on the Soviet Union.

Gorbachev has introduced the principles of defensive (or reasonable) sufficiency and defensive (or nonoffensive) defense in order to bring both the economic costs and the political effects of Soviet defense policy under control. In the last three years Soviet leaders, both party and military, have made it clearer than ever before that a nuclear war cannot be won, and that a large-scale conventional war in Europe would be almost as devastating in its consequences. The military has now been instructed to take the prevention of war, not victory in war, as its overriding goal. This implies that the Soviet Union should not try to build forces to win a major war, but should aim for "defensive sufficiency."

At the strategic level, sufficiency has been defined as the ability to retaliate under any and all circumstances. What that means in operational terms is not clear, since the targets to be struck in the retaliatory strike are not specified. At the conventional level, defensive sufficiency implies a rejection of the view that the Soviet Union should be prepared to win a major war in Europe by rapid offensive operations. In May 1987 the Warsaw Pact adopted a Statement on Military Doctrine which stressed the defensive nature of the Pact's doctrine, and called for the reduction of armed forces on the continent to a level "at which neither side, in guaranteeing its own defense, would have the means for a surprise attack on the other, for mounting offensive operations in general."[16] The implementation of this concept would remove the inconsistency in Soviet doctrine between defensive intention and offensive capability.

This shift in doctrine was not only the work of the party leadership. Some members of the High Command, too, seem to have had doubts all along about the feasibility of winning a conventional war in Europe by means of rapid offensive operations. Such a strategy had obvious problems: the political decision to strike would have to be made at just the right moment and would require precise and reliable intelligence; the danger of escalation to nuclear weapons could not be excluded; and NATO was trying to develop a deep-strike strategy to counter Soviet offensive operations. Besides, the forces needed for the conventional option would be very expensive. Thus a military reassessment has combined with political and economic considerations to move military

155

doctrine towards the principles of defensive sufficiency and defensive defense.

Defensive sufficiency and defensive defense have been widely debated in the Soviet press. No one rejects these principles outright, but there has been much discussion as to what they really mean.[17] Western governments have been skeptical of Soviet statements about defensive sufficiency and defensive defense because, until Gorbachev's United Nations speech in December 1988, they had seen no sign of a major redeployment or restructuring of conventional forces, or of a major reduction in defense expenditure or weapons procurement. Gorbachev's decision to cut the Soviet armed forces by 500,000 men over the next two years indicates, however, that there is more to this than words alone. He has promised to withdraw and disband six tank divisions from Eastern Europe, and to remove river-crossing and assault units. These are key elements of Soviet offensive capability in Europe, and their withdrawal will be a significant practical step towards the adoption of a more defensive posture. Gorbachev has also said that the remaining Soviet divisions in Eastern Europe will be reorganized, and their tank complement reduced, in order to make them more clearly suited for defensive operations alone.

SUCCESSES AND PENDING AGENDAS

The new thinking was at first dismissed by some commentators as little more than propaganda, intended to lull the West into complacency. Certainly there is propaganda here, for the new concepts and policies are designed to improve the image of the Soviet Union abroad and to reduce the perception of the Soviet Union as a threat. One of the great failures of Brezhnev's foreign policy was his mismanagement of relations with the United States. By the same token, one of Gorbachev's most important goals has been to convince the United States, which has often appeared unpredictable and erratic in Soviet eyes, that it should seek a stable and cooperative relationship with the USSR. His effort has met with considerable success, partly because he has taken practical steps— in signing the INF Treaty, in withdrawing Soviet forces from Afghanistan, in working for the settlement of regional conflicts, and in announcing unilateral troop cuts—to show that he is interested in far more than scoring propaganda victories.

In pursuing a more cooperative relationship with the United States,

Gorbachev has not neglected the other great powers. He has managed to reduce West European suspicion of the Soviet Union. He has succeeded in improving relations with China to the point where the danger of an anti-Soviet united front no longer exists. He has pursued better relations with the countries of Asia and Western Europe not as an alternative to good relations with the United States, but rather as a way of influencing the United States by depriving it of the capacity to organize an anti-Soviet coalition.

All in all, Gorbachev has succeeded in extricating the Soviet Union from the foreign-policy crisis of the early 1980s. Progress has been made in settling some of the regional conflicts that embittered US-Soviet relations in the 1970s. Soviet arms-control policy has become more flexible and more dynamic, while the Stockholm Agreement of 1986 and the Intermediate-Range Nuclear Forces Treaty of 1987 have given a new impetus to the whole enterprise of arms control. The improvement in political relations between the United States and the Soviet Union offers some hope that the military competition too will be restrained. And Gorbachev's oft-repeated assurance that the course his country has embarked on is of a lasting and fundamental nature, that it not only meets Soviet interests, but also responds to changes in the nature of international relations, is likely to pave the way for broader agreements in the future.

The most compelling reason for regarding the new thinking as more than a tactical device is the dramatic change Gorbachev has allowed—even encouraged—in Eastern Europe. Ever since the mid-1950s the countries of that region have grappled with the system that Stalin imposed on them in the late 1940s. Efforts to reform the Stalinist system were hampered by opposition from entrenched bureaucracies at home and by the threat—as well as the reality—of Soviet military intervention. Perestroika widened the opportunities for change in Eastern Europe, however. In his speech to the United Nations in December 1988, Gorbachev spoke of freedom of choice for all countries without exception. In 1989 the Soviet Union condemned the 1968 invasion of Czechoslovakia and the 1979 invasion of Afghanistan, and renounced the Brezhnev doctrine, which had asserted that the Soviet Union had the right to intervene with military force in other socialist states if it deemed that the socialist order was in danger.

Gorbachev has abandoned the assumption, which Soviet leaders have made since the 1940s, that Soviet security depends on political domination over Eastern Europe, and that such domination in turn depends on a particular kind of political system in those countries. In the course of 1989 the ruling parties in Poland, Hungary, East Germany, Czechoslovakia, and Bulgaria were forced by democratic movements to abandon their monopoly of power and to begin to move towards free multi-party elections and economic reform; Rumania's reverse was more sudden and violent, but apparently no less complete. Although the Soviet Union still maintains hundreds of thousands of troops in Eastern Europe, the possibility of military intervention to reverse the move toward democracy must now be considered remote. This is not only because Gorbachev approves of the changes in Eastern Europe, but because the costs of reimposing Soviet control would be enormous. Military intervention would have a devastating effect on Soviet citizens, especially those that pin their hopes on the further development of *demokratizatsia*, glosnost, and perestroika, and thus constitute Gorbachev's most loyal constituency. It would more than likely meet fierce resistance, not only by the populations of Eastern Europe but also by sections of the East European military. And finally, it would destroy the gains of Gorbachev's policies by subverting the effort to remove the image of a Soviet threat.

Gorbachev's policies have undermined the Cold War system of international relations; this has been most clearly symbolized by the opening of the Berlin Wall. The political changes in Eastern Europe have greatly reduced—if not completely eliminated—the conventional military threat to Western Europe. This threat provided the main rationale for the establishment of NATO in 1949, and has been the main focus of NATO's policy ever since. Gorbachev has altered the political conditions on which the division of Europe into two blocs is based. This means that a new security system will have to be devised for Europe. The opportunity now exists to create a less dangerous and less costly security regime. The opportunity poses new questions for the Soviet Union as well as for the other European powers. For all its disadvantages (which are many and serious), the existing confrontation between two military blocs is something that governments have become accustomed to and understand. Will a new regime be less stable than the existing arrangement? Might it lead to the reunification of Germany? Would that be tolerable for the Soviet Union? If so, under what conditions? There is no sign that either Gorbachev or anyone else has clear answers to these questions.

THE ROAD AHEAD

The new thinking has helped to guide Soviet policy in new directions, thereby extricating the Soviet Union from the crisis that it faced in foreign policy in the early 1980s. At the same time, it has raised new issues and new dilemmas for Soviet policy. In his UN speech in December 1988 Gorbachev remarked that there were those in the Soviet Union who regarded his view of international relations as romantic. In announcing unilateral force cuts, Gorbachev apparently overrode objections from senior officers who had argued that movement towards a purely defensive military policy would have to be based on reciprocal cuts; and military spokesmen have since pointed out that there is a limit to unilateral reductions.[18] Nevertheless, the changing strategic environment, coupled with the desire to reduce defense spending, suggests that more unilateral cuts may be forthcoming. These might be combined with far-reaching military reforms designed to improve the quality of the Soviet armed forces.

Recent political changes in the Soviet Union may help to create a new balance between the political, economic, and military bases of Soviet security. Gorbachev told the Congress of People's Deputies in May 1989 that Soviet defense expenditure in 1989 amounted to 77.3 billion rubles, or about nine percent of GNP, and he stated that this figure would be reduced by 10 billion rubles in 1990–91.[19] Although there is some doubt (because of the vagaries of the Soviet pricing system) as to whether this figure reflects the true cost of defense, the new figure will make possible some level of public discussion of the priority and cost of defense, and of waste in the defense sector. The Supreme Soviet now has a committee for defense and security, and this may become an important vehicle for public oversight of this important area of policy. As glasnost develops, we may expect to see the emergence of open politics in the realm of military affairs, something without precedent since the 1920s.

Gorbachev's foreign policy has been designed to provide favorable conditions for economic and political change at home. At the same time, its success has depended and will continue to depend on domestic reform. The improvement in human-rights policy and the relaxation of censorship have raised Soviet prestige abroad and helped to convince Western governments that Gorbachev is serious in his efforts to reform the Soviet Union. So have all the fruits of glasnost, from the wide-ranging debates in the press all the way to the erosion of the Soviet obsession with secrecy, once regarded as one of the essential features of the Soviet ethos writ large. The future of Soviet foreign policy is bound up with the future of domestic reform.

New thinking has led to new realities. In meeting the foreign-policy crisis of the early 1980s, Gorbachev has ushered in a new stage of international relations, thereby creating new opportunities and new problems for the Soviet Union and other powers alike.

PART TWO

FROM
THE OTHER SHORE:
Commentaries

★

★

T O W A R D
A   N E W   M O D E L
O F   S O C I A L I S M

★

B O R I S   P.   K U R A S H V I L I

IN HIS ESSAY, PROFESSOR BROWN
rightly observes that until quite recently the very topic of "different
models of socialism" could not be brought up, much less discussed, in
our country. The reigning orthodoxy prescribed only one single model,
slightly diluted in the 1950s by the proviso allowing for the existence
of "different paths to socialism." Under perestroika and glasnost, this
is no longer the case. And so I should like to use this opportunity to
discuss my own views about the models of socialism that existed in the
Soviet Union heretofore, and the kind of model we should strive for.

Any revolution, and a socialist one in particular, may tend to get
carried away by the demons of "purity," extremism, and implacability.
The realization of socialism in our country has not come to pass without
utopian attempts to abolish market production. For a long time a number
of surrogates were devised to limit the meaning of socialism and (to this
day) the meaning of democracy: one such surrogate is the concept of
"supportive democracy" (the leadership correctly expresses the interests
of the people; the people approve and fulfill the leadership's plans). In
part, this was the consequence of incomplete theoretical preparation for
the building of a new society, and of a low level of mass political culture,

but mainly it was the result of extreme conditions of development, of inexorable historical circumstances, and of a violent struggle between two social systems in which socialism was forced to defend its right to exist.

Under these conditions, we have gone through several models of socialism. First, there was "war communism," an authoritarian-utopian socialism. Then, under the New Economic Policy (NEP), an authoritarian, multifaceted socialism began to emerge. It was replaced by a long period of authoritarian-mobilizational socialism with totalitarian perversions. When, as a result of epochal victories, gained at the expense of millions of victims, socialism was finally provided with an opportunity to shed its "extraordinary" nature and embark on a course of normal development, it found no better option (after a rather brief "thaw" and "semireform") than becoming bogged down in stagnation and decay. There arose (under the name of developed socialism) an authoritarian-bureaucratic socialism. This in turn provided the impetus for perestroika. Such is the service record of Soviet socialism.

Some say that this is not socialism at all, that a society characterized by lack of democracy and by the virtual alienation of the producer from the means of production cannot possibly be called socialist. This proposition is only partially valid. A socialism "agreeable in every respect" cannot appear as if by magic. Actual, real socialism, as with modern developed capitalism, arises through a long evolution, passing through stages that are far from perfect.

The main element in our historical legacy consists of the fact that public and cooperative property has been preserved as the basic means of production; there is no need to wrest them from anyone, no need for a revolution in the strict sense of the word—that is, a transfer of political and economic power from one class to another. If a revolutionary change is required, it is one that would bring about profound reform, political breakthroughs, and victories over indecisiveness and weakness of will.

Perhaps a "new class" has emerged—a bureaucratized ruling apparatus that has appropriated public property? Not quite. The apparat, however powerful, does not truly own this property, but rather disposes of it in the role of the empowered representative of the presumed owner—the people. The dignitaries and bureaucrats have no class-based rights, but managerial—one might say squatters—rights to the property. In principle at least, these rights end with the termination of their duties. The point of "expropriating the expropriators," of the "revolution" as

TOWARD A NEW MODEL OF SOCIALISM
★
BORIS P. KURASHVILI

a whole, can be summed up with one simple phrase addressed to the apparat: "Know your place."

The bureaucracy is necessary and irreplaceable for managing public property. Without it, the property cannot be put to proper use, nor can there be any production. In a democratically organized society, however, this function does not lead to the alienation of the producer from the means of production. Although at this time the bureaucratized ruling apparatus constitutes a conservative force, the solution is not to liquidate it (that would be administrative Luddism), but to subject it to a thoroughgoing structural and functional reorganization, to subordinate it to representative government organs, to place it under effective control. Without the support of a sizeable progressive element in the apparat and a reorganized apparat as a whole, perestroika may grind to a halt amid colossal disorganization and confusion that could pave the way to a new dictatorship championing order and discipline.

It is becoming generally accepted that the current historical task of Soviet society is to create democratic socialism. This term is not ideal. It encompasses various ideas with a variety of meanings. But the main thing is surely that the epithet *democratic* characterizes this new socialism, this neosocialism, to which perestroika almost certainly will eventually lead.

What is this democratic socialism? Briefly stated, it is a social structure distributing goods according to work, and based on public, primarily commonly held property, commodity production, and extensive political democracy—that is, participatory democracy. Communism, not currently a reality, remains the hypothetically final stage in socialist development, the final goal of socialism, and signifies a social structure distributing goods according to need and based on public property, unmediated public control of the means of production, and public self-government.

More concretely, democratic socialism is a social structure with several key characteristics. It provides for the full personal development of each member of society, distributing material and nonmaterial benefits among workers, labor collectives, and territory-based communities according to actual, publicly recognized results of their labor. Production is based on state enterprises, cooperatives, and individuals having complete economic control of the property that they own or that has been turned over to them by the state. Competitive commodity production, its effectiveness and remuneration to be determined by the market, is limited only by state regulations (mainly legislative and economic) directed toward the general good of the nation. Public life, within the framework of a "state of law," is organized on the basis of broad political democracy, including majority rule, respect for the rights of the minority, government accountability to its citizens and vice versa, separation of powers, and a multiparty system.

Perestroika, which grew out of stormy criticism of the past and was not initially conceived in concrete terms, has tended naturally to extremes, seeks easy solutions, and tries one thing after another. One assumption envisions the future society to be similar to what existed during the NEP period. The basis of NEP—near-total financial autonomy of state enterprises—is indeed destined for rebirth. (Such financial autonomy essentially acknowledges, however abashedly, the law of prices.) But what about the status of smaller-scale private property? Will "privatization" of property and capitalist enterprise become an element of the economic structure of democratic socialism?

The future democratic socialism should be able to get along without "privatization," though mixed enterprises are profitable and often essential. It is perfectly possible for the worker in the state sector to identify himself—technologically as well as organizationally—with the means of production and to maintain a keen interest in increasing its efficiency, but only on one condition: that he has complete economic control. In the case of what is loosely called "leasing," commonly held property remains under the economic control of the group involved (family, partnership, enterprise) for an open-ended or substantial period of time. The enterprise thus gains virtually complete freedom in its economic strategy and in disposing of its property. All the ingredients for rational economic management of private property are available without private property itself. So why do we need "privatization?" Do we really long for the power of the purse?

It is absolutely true that Soviet society has no alternative to perestroika, but several variants of perestroika are possible. Democratic socialism is already a genuine breakthrough for Soviet society as it moves toward what really can be a bright future. Two other types of development are possible as well.

The less probable and in any case less desirable regressive variant involves returning to a multifaceted socialism such as existed during the NEP, a kind of hybrid socialist-capitalist system. Some authors have in

TOWARD A NEW MODEL OF SOCIALISM
★
BORIS P. KURASHVILI

mind this variant when they propose "privatization," and when they look further back "from October to February," without saying so directly. They often fail to consider one danger. Their hopes for full democracy notwithstanding, such a two-tiered system would bring back political instability, and with it the need for a harsh authoritarian, possibly even Bonapartist, political regime. Genies will appear that were not summoned.

A "semiprogressive," moderately authoritarian form of socialism is more probable. This suggests a society within which individuals are guaranteed a substantial amount of room for personal development. Their work, and the work done by labor collectives and land-based communities, would be evaluated by the state, and moderately differentiated rewards distributed according to the quality and quantity of that work. Production would be centered on public property, allocated by the government to state enterprises for systematically controlled use, though with some cooperative and individual property as well. An overall state plan would distribute assignments to enterprises, mandating relative competition in commodity output. Although market factors would play a role, they would in part remain under state control: the state would set prices for a majority of goods and services, for instance. Public life, democratically organized, would include such features as majority rule, respect for the rights of the minority, reciprocal responsibility of citizens—with rights and freedoms guaranteed—and state, and a system of state power in which representative bodies would dominate. Within a limited multiparty structure, the Communist party would remain as the ruling party; other parties or quasi-parties would participate in managing society.

Their eclecticism and inconsistency notwithstanding, the measures already implemented in the process of perestroika seem to tend toward the "semiprogressive," moderately authoritarian model of socialism. One can discern some elements of democratic socialism, but as a model it is still only dimly perceptible.

In the early stages of socialist development, the single-party system and the effective concentration of power in the hands of the ruling party seemed to be inevitable in a proletarian dictatorship. With the transition toward a genuine people's state, this situation is changing. The negative consequences of a monopoly of power are becoming intolerable. Hence the question of a multiparty system emerges.

The existence of two paths of development for socialist society—

167

toward democratic or semiauthoritarian socialism (the latter under a more attractive name)—creates the basis upon which a socialist multi-party (most likely two-party) system can develop.

At crucial stages in any process of growth, major ideological and political divisions become manifest: those in favor of innovation oppose the orthodox and the fundamentalists. "No schism" most often means "no progress." This is happening now. Soviet socialism is sufficiently mature, its circumstances sufficiently "normal," and its situation so critical (all plausible half-measures having been attempted) that a multiparty system may be the deciding factor in its radical transformation.

When innovators within the party are forced to look over their shoulders every time they make a decision in order to preserve the artificial unity of the party, then the character and pace of change are being dictated by the fundamentalists, who now appear in the role of conservatives. If the innovators do not create their own party, then a multiparty system will form naturally, in response to mounting pressure and outside the framework of the ruling party, which will be driven back into the conservative position. The spread of informal organizations and national fronts is a manifestation of precisely this process. The best way to create a socialist multiparty system is by a timely "de-unification" of the ruling party, to be achieved not as a fight to the death but as a principled rivalry and loyal collaboration between two parties with equally socialist aims.

To be sure, the emergence of a bourgeois-liberal party, which under the banner of "pure democracy" would advocate that much sought-after "privatization," cannot be ruled out. Such a party would not pose a danger to democratic socialism as long as the latter continues to transform itself. Indeed, it might provide a safeguard against the bureaucratization, corruption, complacency, servility, and mania for self-glorification that have taken root in our country because of the absence of a real political arena.

A socialist multiparty system, putting an end to the abnormality of the monopoly of power, will sooner or later become an essential element of widespread socialist democracy. As of this writing (September 1989), the idea of a multiparty system has still not been accepted in this country (as it has been elsewhere in Eastern Europe). At the same time, we must not forget the groundbreaking role of scholarship. What can be discussed only in a theoretical context today may turn into practical reality tomorrow.

★

THE DEEP ROOTS
OF OUR PROBLEMS

✯

OTTO LATSIS

NOW THAT RELIABLE INFORMATION about the Soviet economy is easily accessible and Soviet scholars and journalists are able, thanks to glasnost, to freely analyze the working of the Soviet economic system now and in the past, the writings of Western observers, too, have also become more precise. Thus in this instance I can agree with nearly all the concepts and interpretations contained in Alec Nove's essay. At the same time, it seems to me that such an essay raises many questions in the mind of the reader, Soviet and foreign alike.

The fundamental reasons for the current reform and the magnitude of the obstacles that stand in the way of its realization can be grasped only through an understanding of the entire development of the Soviet economy that had preceded perestroika. The most urgent question—which is also posed by Professor Nove—is "Why now?" One can only regret that so few other Western analysts raise this question. For years there have been signs that structural changes were urgently overdue. After the end of the Civil War, Lenin realized the necessity of reexamining the entire wartime economic system, which he did by introducing the New Economic Policy (NEP). By contrast, in 1947 Stalin confined himself to monetary reforms without changing the way in which the economy was managed; four years later, the rate of industrial growth began to fall.

Khrushchev instinctively perceived the flaws of the economic system, and only a few months after Stalin's death, in the autumn of 1953, proposed economic measures which for the first time represented serious attempts to encourage agricultural growth. Unfortunately, their implementation left much to be desired. In 1957 a number of industrial ministries were abolished. Though a bold political step, this did not, however, improve the overall condition of the enterprises. Within a year of Khrushchev's removal the government made a number of decisions that on the face of it promised to give enterprises a large measure of autonomy. The decisions were not put into effect, but they show that twenty years before today's perestroika there was an awareness not only of the need for economic reform, but also of the direction it should take.

The persistent delay in the implementation of the reforms, then, accounts for many of the difficulties we face today. There is very little time for maneuvering, for reflection, for correcting errors. The stability of the national economy has been undermined, and too much energy has been sapped in a struggle with an ineffectual system of management. Moreover, the population is restless, impatient, and demands swift and palpable results that would demonstrate that this time, finally, the right path has been chosen.

Foreign authors have developed the notion of a "Soviet-style economy." Oddly enough, this notion hardly differs from the conception of a socialist economy that has developed among Soviet citizens over the past sixty years. Almost the only difference between the Western and Soviet perceptions lies in their assessment of this type of economy: until recently the majority of Soviet citizens viewed it by and large in a positive light, while most Western assessments were negative. Despite this difference, everyone agreed that the Soviet economy was centralized, that it was based on government ownership of the means of production, and that it was capable of concentrating and effectively utilizing investments in critical sectors of the economy. An economy of this type is not distinguished by its efficiency, but it can nonetheless guarantee a relative degree of social protection over an extensive range of social services, the absence of unemployment, and minimal social differentiation ("no one is rich, no one is poor").

For a long time no one, or almost no one, was willing to acknowledge that the economic system of the USSR from the beginning of the 1930s until the early 1980s was by no means the only possible version of a socialist economy. It was of course no secret that for nearly the entire decade of the 1920s our country had a different economic model—that is, the New Economic Policy, introduced by Lenin in 1921. But both Soviet scholars and journalists on the one hand and Western propagandists on the other almost without exception denied the applicability of the term "socialist" to that model. Western scholars considered it a "mixed economy," whose positive components were by definition of a "capitalist" nature—i.e., where "free enterprise" and "individual initiative" were given free reign. For their part, Soviet specialists regarded the NEP as a "transitional" phase from capitalism to communism, whose negative characteristics were merely capitalist survivals, to be erased as quickly as possible so as to make way for the reign (*tsarstvo*) of full socialism, itself the first step toward communism. Consequently the basic economic principles and methods of NEP were unacceptable, given the onset of developing socialism.

This attitude proved one of the main points of contention in the debate between promarket and antimarket forces, which took place in the Soviet Union in the 1960s and 1970s, and whose echoes resonate to this day. The "anti-market" spokesmen pointed out that Marx and Engels predicted the withering away of commodity-monetary exchange (i.e., market relations) under socialism, and that economic policies had to be predicated on the inevitable "withering away" of these relations. The "pro-market" spokesmen, on the other hand, argued that Marxists held to this view before the revolution, before acquiring experience in the actual construction of socialism. It was Lenin himself, they reminded their adversaries, who in 1921 reached other conclusions, having proposed to utilize commodity-monetary exchange. To which the "anti-market" proponents replied that Lenin was speaking exclusively about NEP, and that NEP was not socialism.

Accordingly, all recent attempts to apply commodity-monetary exchange more broadly and to institute economic accountability in enterprises were—from the point of view of Stalinist ideology—"unsocialist." By so labelling these efforts, the critics neatly evaded the necessity of tackling the various economic and political questions associated with such attempts.

This situation has significantly changed only in the last few years. Since 1985, the majority of Soviet scholars have admitted that the "infantile socialism" of the 1920s was closer to the ideals of scientific socialism and to the fundamental conception of a just society than the "mature socialism" which came into being under Stalin and which now merits, at best, the appellation "deformed socialism." Thus it has been a mere three years since our society began to reexamine concepts that had gone unquestioned for nearly sixty years, concepts with which the last two generations have lived and labored, and which were used to justify the not insignificant victories scored by their predecessors.

The victories were real and impressive, though in today's difficult situation many are reluctant to recall them. The industrialization of an enormous and backward country was accomplished in a historically brief period of time. During the Second World War, Soviet industry achieved extraordinary results: with a far lesser potential than that of the enemy, it produced more weapons of a generally higher quality than those produced by the German industry. It is true that Stalin attempted to minimize the dreadful sacrifices such achievements demanded of the population, time and again invoking the argument that they were both necessary and unavoidable. The actual cost of what was achieved now appears far greater than what it appeared in the past. Nevertheless, what was accomplished cannot be gainsaid. And it is equally indisputable that both industrialization and wartime industrial productivity were part of that very economic system from which we are now attempting to extricate ourselves.

In the 1930s and 1940s, then, the administrative-command system accomplished what was most important from the viewpoint of the entire society: the defense of the nation against the invasion of a more powerful enemy.

Let me also add that until the early 1970s this system demonstrated its ability to maintain a rather slow but steady rate of growth in the average standard of living, if not of the entire population then at least of its politically influential—that is, its urban—sector. Apart from the war years, the only exception to this continuing growth was the fairly compressed period at the very start of the administrative-command system, from 1929 to 1934. The Stalinist methods of industrialization and collectivization at the time created a horrible famine both in the cities and in rural areas.

Stalin justified the burden of those years with three arguments: the need for rapid industrialization to arm against an external enemy, the liquidation of unemployment, and, against the background of the world-wide depression, the need to accelerate the growth of the Soviet economy. We now know that these arguments, especially the first of them, were only partially valid. In fact, the Stalinist methods of industrialization had delayed rather than accelerated industrial development. But at the time there was no way of substantiating, let alone publishing, the results of such an assessment. And insofar as accelerated industrialization was indeed dictated by external circumstances, that argument seemed especially persuasive.

The postwar years under Stalin's leadership—from 1945 to 1953—brought about a further deterioration in the standard of living of the majority of Soviet citizens—that is, of rural inhabitants whose voices were never heard. At the same time, the government designed a distribution system that guaranteed a relative growth of prosperity among workers and service industry employees, especially in major cities. Older people who spent the postwar years in cities can still remember the deflationary policy which sharply limited wage-raises (effectively a tacit wage-freeze), and the huge annual bond drives which were supposedly voluntary but actually obligatory for the entire populace.

All these policies imposed draconian taxes on the peasantry that brought it to the brink of starvation, but they allowed highly publicized annual price decreases in government markets, thus alleviating some of the pressure on the free pricing of the collective markets. Those urban dwellers have forgotten—if they ever knew—the egregious side of these measures, but vividly remember the occasional prices decreases. Careful analysis has demonstrated that in real terms even city dwellers gained little from these policies. However, their emotional impact was indisputable. To this day a fairly small but highly aggressive segment of the population refuses to hear a bad word about Stalin and his policies only because "he lowered prices." Many of them are profoundly suspicious of all the post-Stalin reforms, in the belief that it would be "simple enough" to return to the economic policies of the Stalinist era.

After 1953 there were salutary changes in the entire planning strategy: sharp reductions in military spending; a shift away from the gigantic, prestigious, but economically senseless construction projects; the channeling of significant resources into agriculture, housing construction, and light industry. These changes resulted in a conspicuous rise in the living standard of both urban and village inhabitants, without rejecting the instruments of economic administration and stimulation created by Stalin.

This, in turn, made it possible to exploit further some significant sources of extensive growth—e.g., the large labor pools in the countryside and raw materials. These sources continued to shrink, yet they permitted the continuation—to be sure, at a decreasing tempo—of economic growth until the end of the 1960s. By the early 1970s, it became impossible to sustain this growth in industry and living standards, though even then the problem was obscured for another decade or so by the drastic rise of the world price of our main export, oil, and by the decline in quality of our manufactured goods.

What, economically speaking, was the "average Soviet man" to make of the bizarre combination of foreign and domestic factors in our history from 1921 to 1985? On the one hand was the period of NEP—brief and subsequently hidden beneath a thick blanket of official lies—a period which saw a system of administrative planning based on the socialist market, on the complete fiscal autonomy of government and cooperative enterprises, and on the unhindered exploitation of commodity-monetary relations. All this was happening, for the first time in history, in a semiliterate country lacking the requisite number of specialists, with no prior experience to go by, no previously formulated theory, and—for the first four years at any rate—in conditions of postwar chaos.

On the other hand, the "average Soviet citizen" sees an administrative system that for nearly sixty years has claimed to be the model of socialist development, a system which had indeed assured the country's historic victory during the war, a certain degree of growth in the standard of living, and the social welfare of most of its citizens. It is during those sixty years that the majority of Soviet citizens were born, grew up, and have spent their lives.

Naturally, it was impossible during Stalin's lifetime to speak of NEP as the embryo of an essentially socialist economic system. For thirty years after his death only carefully worded research which invoked the authority of Lenin as the creator of NEP made it possible to keep alive the idea that the root of socialist construction in the USSR lies precisely in the economic policies of the 1920s. Before 1985, it was virtually impossible to discuss this idea either in the mass media or even in official scholarly publications.

I trust that these somewhat lengthy prefatory remarks will help the foreign reader understand the tenacity of popular stereotypes, and the reason why they constitute such an obstacle in implementing our current reforms. They permeate not only our scholarly literature, but even more so the attitude of a sizeable part of our public toward the kind of society we are trying to bring about.

Unfortunately, prejudices and stereotypical thinking are not our only difficulty. To these must be added the attitudes of certain social groups that are indifferent, hostile to, or insufficiently interested in perestroika, as well as the purely practical problems relating to the economic situation.

Professor Nove touches on these questions, but let me add a few comments. In treating the problem of opposition to perestroika, some Soviet authors make what I consider a simplistic differentiation between the bureaucratic "class" and the working class. What seems to me more accurate is a line that cuts across all social groups: there are both supporters and opponents of the reforms in every group, among "bureaucrats," among intellectuals, among workers, among peasants. At every level there are people ready to take chances and to work more intensively in order to show their worth and to earn more money.

Equally, there are people who prefer less demanding work as long as their pay, however small, is guaranteed, and the requirements about qualifications and work quality are not overly rigorous. There is, of course, corruption at every social level, especially in trade, in the service sector, and in administrative bodies; those involved have learned how to extract as much income as possible not through honest work but through exploiting the flaws of our system, above all by speculating in goods and services that are in short supply. Taken together, such groups pose a major threat to perestroika, but the threat can be overcome. Most such people (e.g., workers who shirk excessively demanding jobs) are politically inert and incapable of organizing themselves. The organized groups (such as the various "mafias") cannot hope to assume mass proportions nor can they act openly, given the antisocial and illicit nature of their activities.

It is therefore the practical difficulties of the current economic situation which are the most formidable, and which are, moreover, exacerbated by the fact that we are trying to put into practice a new economic system, one which neither this nor the preceding generation has actually lived with. Toward the end of 1988 it became clear that the most pressing of these practical problems was the general economic imbalance of virtually every sector of the national economy, particularly conspicuous in the monetary credit system—which is to say in the enormous budget deficit. Because of the ineffectiveness of the command system, a growing number of substantial expenditures was required to satisfy the most urgent industrial and social demands. Government expenditures grew faster than income. In recent years the accelerated growth of expenditures in relation to income became especially acute, when foreign trade earnings diminished as a result of the fall in the world prices of oil. Moreover, government income from the sale of vodka dropped because the demand for alcohol had reached excessively high levels and such sales had been reduced to safeguard the health of the population. At the Supreme Soviet discussion of the annual budget, held in October 1988, the minister of finances of the USSR suggested for the first time approving a deficit budget for the forthcoming year; he calculated the deficit at 36 billion rubles. (The Supreme Soviet adjusted the figure downward to 35 billion rubles.) Many Soviet economists (and most Western estimates) put the actual deficit at more than 100 billion rubles. When that figure appeared in a number of publications after the Supreme Soviet session, no one disputed it. It has been proven universally that such a deficit brings in its wake a triple-digit annual inflation. Because prices of officially sold goods in the Soviet Union are set by administrative decision and not by the free play of market forces, inflation is manifested not so much in higher prices as in longer queues in stores and the disappearance of goods from the shelves. This has a destructive effect in both the economic and social spheres. By 1989 this destructive impact was plain to see for all consumers, inasmuch as it had become increasingly difficult to obtain the most ordinary items of everyday use despite the fact that the same or even a higher volume of such goods was being produced.

An analysis of the events of the past few years reveals that this situation has been brought about not only by the negative vestiges of the past (which in fact have played a decisive role), but also because of certain mistakes involved in implementing perestroika itself. Broadly, those mistakes lay in underestimating the significance of our own correct decisions affecting the economy and implementing those decisions too slowly and too inconsistently. The decision to reform the monetary credit was adopted as early as 1987, as part of a whole cluster of decisions on economic reforms. Another was the decision to curtail an excessively broad investment plan, even to the point of freezing projects already under way if they were not of top priority. A number of such projects were in fact terminated in 1988. At the same time, however, instead of concentrating all resources on completing a selection of ongoing projects, new ones were begun, at twice the cost of those that had been abandoned. As a result the investment burden of the national economy, already excessive, has become even heavier.

It should have been possible to foresee such a turn of events. The reforms gave a good deal of freedom to enterprises, and the chance to use a portion of their profits more independently, whether for purposes of development or for pay raises for personnel. This is absolutely necessary in order to stimulate economic growth, and is generally useful insofar as enterprises now cover their expenses not with money they receive (gratis) from the state budget, but with income they have earned. Naturally, they spend their own money more carefully, hence more effectively, than "nobody's" money. But once money is allocated to enterprises, at least that amount must be taken away from branches of the industrial ministries whose outlays come exclusively from the state budget and that are generally much less effective than those of individual enterprises. That was not done. Ministry opposition was not overcome. Expenses on new construction grew sharply, and projected pay-back periods were either extremely long or simply ineffective.

The leadership recognized the danger. The rigorous measures adopted by the Politburo and published on February 18, 1989, patently met the expectations of the public. They reduced capital investment of state funds in heavy industry and reduced arms expenditures and expenditures in state management. A decision was made—already being implemented—to convert part of the armaments industry, particularly into consumer-oriented light industry.

There is another question: Will the measures now recognized as appropriate be applied quickly and decisively enough? This will become clear in the next few years. In the meantime, however, we are all interested in a more general question: Will perestroika triumph? The following observations may help answer that question:

The old economic system long ago exhausted whatever potential it had for positive and rational activity. Any attempt to return to it would decisively eliminate all chances of achieving any social and economic goals. It is therefore safe to predict that the public will reject such attempts, and seek solutions within the framework of perestroika.

Furthermore, the basic principles of economic reform have been carefully and realistically formulated. The country contains all the necessary material and intellectual resources for implementing this new economic system and for carrying out a restructuring of industry in conformity with the current needs of scientific and technical progress.

The question, then, is not whether the economy will be restructured, but when and how quickly this restructuring will occur and at what price. There can be no doubt that the progress of economic reform will decisively depend on progress in political reform, just as attempts at economic reform in the 1960s failed because of the absence of political reforms. The answer to "when" is *now*.

★

PERESTROIKA
AND THE PRIMACY
OF POLITICS

☆

GAVRIIL POPOV

I

A NUMBER OF WESTERN ECONOMISTS
have rightly called attention to the crucial and long-term connection
between economic and political institutions in the USSR. The contrived
and—as the historical record demonstrates—feckless nature of that relationship arose because, rather than making the economy the bedrock
of a new political system, we did precisely the opposite. And an economy
subordinated to the exigencies of politics is incapable of meeting the
needs of a society.

The first efforts at economic reform, introduced in 1985–86, has led
me—and others—to three conclusions: First, what our country needs is
not reform, but fundamental economic restructuring, that is to say, a
new economic system. Second, the new economic system requires a
political system that is congruous with it. And third, as a corollary to
the above, further economic reorganization is impossible without radical
changes in our political institutions.

These simple propositions concerning the interrelationship between
economics and politics frequently elicit reactions from Soviet citizens

179

ranging from stupefaction to anger. It might be useful, therefore, especially for the benefit of the foreign reader, to examine the reasons for this response.

We have grown up in a country whose political structures arose independently of and indeed without regard to the economic base, and which have in fact served as the principal instrument determining and shaping our economic institutions. In time, the political structures coalesced into what I have called elsewhere the "administrative system",[1] with its powerful and bloated bureaucracy, arbitrary rule, a string of "personality cults," and inherent constraints on scientific, technical, and above all economic progress.

The defects and outrages of the administrative system have gradually seeped into the public consciousness. It is not surprising, therefore, that any suggestion to concentrate on political institutions is met with bewilderment. Again political considerations first and above all? Are we to focus once more on shell rather than substance, albeit this time in the name of democracy and perestroika? Are we again to put the cart before the horse?

These are not mere theoretical questions. They derive from bitter practical experience. True, in the past our political leaders occasionally tried to introduce new economic policies or changes in our economic mechanisms. But the emphasis was almost invariably on technology— e.g., on developing chemical industry, land improvement through drainage or irrigation, or shifts in our military production. All of these efforts, each valid in its own way, came to nothing—that is, resources were invested and used in a fundamentally ill-conceived and ineffective system. The kolkhoz, for example, constituted a kind of one-way pump, draining resources from the countryside, and incapable of providing sustenance in return. Attempts to organize the flow of resources back through the pump to the countryside led only to squandering them in every direction.[2]

Economists like myself had pointed a finger at the politicians as the primary source of our economic woes. We considered our economic structure the only possible model of a socialist economy. And we were never at a loss to support this assumption with apposite quotations from Marx, Engels, and Lenin.

But with the abortive results engendered by the succession of political administrations—Stalin, Malenkov, Khrushchev-Bulganin, Khrushchev alone, Brezhnev-Kosygin, Brezhnev alone—and the failure of the various "scientific and technological" solutions, we concluded that the source of our problems lay not in these programs, nor even in the personalities of the leaders, nor in the apparat. In a word, the source of our problems lay not in the realm of politics at all, but somewhere deeper—precisely in the kind of economic structure that we had fashioned with the help of the administrative system.

Thus a new wisdom came into being: The real problem, it said, lies not in the leadership, nor in the merits or shortcomings of this or that research institute, nor in the structure of governmental bodies, nor in the method of rule; it lies rather in an economy driven not by economic laws and considerations, but by a strictly political-administrative engine. Hence, the economy must take precedence over everything else. If the latter is not altered, political changes will be mere tinsel. If the base isn't changed, all our energy will again be diverted into doomed "chemical-ization" campaigns or land-improvement schemes. The very fate of perestroika, it seemed, hung on the ability to overhaul our economic system.

The agenda seemed disarmingly simple: First get rid of institutions such as the social consumption funds (for education, health, and the like), which are available at virtually no cost to those working in the apparat, and the various institutions that under the pretense of devising and running a coordinated planning system have been little more than a feeding trough for millions of bureaucrats. In other words, eliminate the economic foundations of a parasitic class that impedes progress. Develop new economic structures. Feed and clothe the nation. Instruct it in the art of economic self-sufficiency. And only after this work is done can we introduce democratic changes in the political superstructure. Such changes would then be both logical and durable; implemented gradually, they would inspire neither social unrest nor ridicule. A man who is fed and clothed is receptive to democratic rights; who knows—presented with a long list of candidates running for office, he might even cast his vote for socialism.

That is in fact how capitalism developed. In the course of successful bourgeois revolutions, while the bourgeoisie proclaimed the supremacy of all freedoms, it actually imposed restrictions in the area of politics and ideology. Only after the capitalist economic base had been firmly established did political democracy begin to flourish.

Faced with such compelling arguments, it seems audacious to advocate an opposite course—that is, political changes first, economic restructuring later. For how, some people would ask, can we embark on political reforms in an economy of scarcity? What use can a nation make of greater political rights if it is forced to spend hours standing on lines? What can democracy offer under such conditions? Moreover, any attempt to introduce sweeping political changes might well result in an elemental uprising "from below" directed at the apparat and in the process nullifying the whole perestroika program. Or these changes may result in the apparat, having long ago mastered the art of manipulation, emasculating the new democratic institutions and remaining firmly in the saddle.

We have, after all, some experience with a bureaucracy bent on eradicating every trace of democracy. When collective farms were first established in the 1920s, they were supposed to be run strictly on a *khozraschyot* (self-accounting, or financing) basis. In addition, they disposed of considerable democratic freedoms. Kolkhoz members fought hard at every election for "their" chairman and governing board as against those nominated from above. Yet after a while the interest in elections subsided. When and why? When wages were guaranteed from above—when, in other words, financial accountability was, for all intents and purposes, done away with. If the kolkhoz employee has the basic part of his salary guaranteed "from the top," regardless of the results of the work of the entire working force, it is the top that will in effect be running the farm, elections or no elections. Which is to say that democratic institutions built on authoritarian economic foundations are just a façade.

Let us take a leap into the present. According to the new rules, workers in an enterprise are now supposed to elect their directors. And elections have indeed been taking place. On closer scrutiny, however, it turns out that only in those enterprises—factories, shops, cooperatives— where *khozraschyot* is the norm, that is, where workers have a real stake in productivity, is there a keen interest and participation in the election process. Where self-financing is a mere formality, the elections either serve as a means of settling personal accounts, or they elicit widespread apathy—surely yet another example of the extent to which democratic forms depend on economic realities.

II

A good case, then, can be made for placing the emphasis on economic reforms. Nevertheless, I firmly believe that political reforms must be our first priority right now.

This is so, first of all, because of the peculiarities of our current phase of economic reorganization. Every attempt to implement a more radical model of *khozraschyot* immediately meets fierce resistance on the part of the economic and party apparat. Efforts to temper or overcome this resistance have thus far met with little success, which strongly suggests that unless the very nature of that apparatus is changed—that is, unless it is replaced with a body of officials directly responsible to the electorate and genuinely interested in implementing a radical economic overhaul—the reforms will remain a dead letter. Workers have in many cases taken matters into their own hands, but without the democratization of party and political bodies, their efforts are doomed.

Let me offer a few examples. In a northern Siberian city, workers at a public transportation depot chose a Moscow specialist as their director. The new man asked the City Executive Committee to repair some broken machinery for which it was contractually responsible: the depot—as a self-financing enterprise—found the cost of repairs prohibitive. The city fathers regarded this legitimate demand as outlandish and brushed it off. Our director retaliated by cancelling several bus and tram routes. One might think that he won. Unfortunately not. The City Executive Committee took the name of this insubordinate troublemaker off the list of apartment allocations, thus forcing him to choose between his family and his job.

There are thousands of ways to sabotage an economic planner who relies on his "legal" rights. At the end of August 1988, for instance, a district party committee (*raikom*) asked the director of a bus factory for buses to pick up children at a Young Pioneers camp. The director refused: "I can't," he said, "I'm on *khozraschyot* and without a contract signed beforehand I can't do anything. But it's the end of the month, we're finishing up our orders—if you wait until tomorrow there will be buses available." Not good enough: within two hours inspectors from the Motor Vehicle Bureau were standing on every corner outside the factory, checking the license of every single driver and taking down the plate number of every vehicle. The director got the picture and—orders notwithstanding—sent his buses off to the *raikom*. "The hell with your Motor Vehicle people," he concluded, "and the hell with your *khozraschyot* too."

Examples abound. And they all point to one conclusion: Because the process of dismantling the fetters to progress has thus been directed almost exclusively at the economic system, the latter, too, is incapable of functioning properly.

It is instructive to recall that Lenin himself regarded political reform as essential for successful economic reform. Millions of Soviet citizens repeat this axiom at school examinations, millions nearly choke on quotations from Lenin. But we are loath to apply this fundamental principle to our current problems. And yet time and again it is precisely the hurdles thrown in our way by the party-state machinery that prevent us from undertaking decisive measures in the economy.

How can a crew meet its contractual obligations when it has pared away all its superfluous workers yet is expected to provide a couple of men to clear snow? How can a factory become truly self-financing if hiring and firing decisions are made not by its manager but by the party? The chairman of an *ispolkom*[3] will no longer dare to scoff at a supervisor chosen by the work collective only when *ispolkom* elections themselves are democratic, and a candidate who ignores the law on enterprises can be decisively rejected.[4] At this point *raikoms* still expect factories to produce volunteers to distribute vegetables, clean streets, and the like. That won't stop unless they begin to elect as leaders people who worry less about rotting vegetables *per se* and more about a rotten adminis-trative apparatus that has never learned how vegetables should be dis-tributed—without regional depots and without bureaucratic middlemen, on the basis of economic interests and contracts.

Thus complete and genuine *khozraschyot* and viable economic re-forms are possible only in the context of full-fledged democracy, in both the party and the government. In real life a director can't be split in two any more than a worker can. Half of a director can't sit submissively for two hours at a *raikom* meeting and listen obediently to officious rhetoric while the other half of him returns to his office at the plant and begins to perform miracles of productivity and self-sufficiency. Half of a worker can't applaud at a meeting, echoing ready-made slogans and dropping his ballot into the box without even reading it, while the other half works as hard as he can on contract with his crew.

A person is a single entity. If we want him to take an active, creative role in the factory, in research institutes, in hospitals, in distributing vegetables, or in a sports stadium, we must allow him to be equally active and creative in elections to the local soviet, in deciding what should happen to the atomic electric power station in the Crimea, in solving the fate of the Crimean Tatars or Nagorno-Karabakh. And this can only happen after a radical reform of the party and government mechanism.

Apart from purely economic arguments, there are more general reasons. Fundamental restructuring must of necessity be a mass phenomenon. Both political democracy and internal party democracy are instruments aimed at bringing ever greater numbers of people into the process of perestroika. The forms of such a democracy will change, but the main criterion must be to turn workers into the principal agents of reform.

Democracy is not merely economically beneficial. It is a social good in itself, as well as an incentive to progress in general. At present, we find it impossible to bring about swift improvements in income and living standards. But in the meantime there is something we can and must offer immediately—namely, democracy, the sense of being the master of one's own life, of being able to make decisions for oneself. Only then will we be able to overcome the onerous legacy of the past.

There is a marvelous line in Eduardo de Filippo's play about Aesop: Don't trust anyone who passes judgment on whether someone is or is not ready for freedom. Such judgments sound like the unsuccessful fox, who comforts himself for not being able to reach the grapes by saying they are sour anyway. It is an excellent piece of advice. For the craving for freedom is a universal phenomenon, common even to people who do not fully realize it, or may think that they don't want it. Experience has taught us that all societies are ripe for democracy, for it is something that turns us into full human beings.

The agricultural reform of 1861 offers an interesting historical parallel.[5] It is often forgotten that this reform—incomplete, partial, preceded by two decades of foot-dragging, implemented by the forces of the autocracy's bureaucratic apparat, conceived to defend the interests not so much of the landowners as of the autocracy and its apparat—that this reform within a year mandated not only economic but also political changes. Changes like the creation of the zemstvos (local rural self-governments), trial by jury, the rise of an independent judiciary, and so on. Why? Because the first problem to arise was where the newly freed serf could go to lodge a complaint against a landowner who contravened the 1861 reform, and solving that problem required eliminating the old patrimonial court system and creating a fundamentally different legal system.

A second historical parallel is connected with experiments in economic reform in socialist countries—in Hungary, for instance. Some of the opponents of perestroika point to them as a salutary lesson of how our reforms, too, may end up. To be sure, Hungary faces innumerable

185

problems. But one must remember that for nearly twenty years—a whole generation's lifespan—Hungary achieved something evidently beyond the grasp of an average Soviet citizen: a normal existence, without queues, with enough produce and goods to meet the basic demands of the population. Its present difficulties are the result not of its reformist path but because somewhere along the way the leadership wavered, dawdled, procrastinated, and failed to implement urgently needed measures. It is clear to me, for one, that Hungary's problems are rooted in the failure to restructure its heavy industry. And this failure stemmed precisely from the failure to restructure the party-government apparat, which objected to the industrial reforms because they would have undermined its power and privileges.

Yugoslavia is another case in point. Its problems are many and serious, yet anyone who has been both there and in the Soviet Union over the past ten or twenty years cannot be but struck by how much better and easier life is in Yugoslavia, especially considering the low economic level it started from. Yugoslavia's difficulties—again in my view—are rooted in its political system. I am convinced that its much- and long-touted system of "self-government" (including workers' councils) was much more façade than substance.

We can also see that socialist countries that have implemented economic reforms without radically altering their political institutions can come to a bad end. The recent events in China are a striking illustration of that.

III

This much said, it is necessary to stress that, however important democracy is in general terms, its actual form and shape are intimately bound up with the form and shape of the economic system it engenders. Which is to say that just as no viable economic institutions can be created without correspondingly viable political institutions, so the viability of the latter depend on that of the former.

Let me again turn to the experience of capitalism, which clearly tends to democracy. The reason is that capitalism rests fundamentally on the laborer's ability freely to trade his labor. He is free not only as a laborer, but also as a consumer. Without this condition—which requires at a minimum all formal freedoms—there can be no genuine competition.

PERESTROIKA AND THE PRIMACY OF POLITICS
★
GAVRIIL POPOV

This seems like a self-evident proposition; nonetheless, Soviet text-books on political economy contain not a word about freedoms as the main precondition for the flourishing of capitalist production. This becomes even more bizarre when you consider that it was precisely because the tsarist regime virtually ignored this proposition that capitalism in Russia developed so slowly and that the country was pushed toward revolution.

One of Stalin's blind spots—among so many others—was his failure to understand the way in which capitalism is tied to democracy. He refused to believe that the democratic bourgeois republics would oppose fascism. Rather, it was his article of faith that they would make common cause with fascist regimes. Thence his vacillations in negotiating with England and France, and thence the course of action which led to the pact with Hitler. As it turned out, England fought Hitler to the death—which is to say that it fought precisely against a system which annulled the bourgeois freedom of competition, and which deprived workers of the right freely to hire out their labor, or to choose and quit jobs as they saw fit.

The Soviet Union paid an awesome price for Stalin's failure to understand the fundamental interrelationship of capitalism and democracy, of capitalism and fascism. Fascism was not the only possible and logical result of the development of capitalism, as Stalin thought, but just such a "defect" of capitalism's development as the cult of personality was a deformation of socialism: likely in a given confluence of circumstances, but not an inevitable outgrowth of the system.

While proceeding with political reforms, as we must, we should also keep in mind Poland's experience. Several years ago in Poland political freedoms outpaced economic reorganization; or put differently, economic changes did not keep pace with political changes. As a result, democratic institutions were used to channel mass dissatisfaction arising from the leadership's failure to implement structural economic reforms. Democracy without economic reorganization can lead to this outcome too. If economic reform somehow goes off the track, so will political reform.

To sum up, then, if it is true that economic reform cannot develop without political reform, the opposite is equally true. It is mandatory for us to proceed immediately with a drastic overhaul of our political system, while at the same time keeping in mind the kind of an economic system we want to create.

★

LEGAL REFORMS
AND BASIC
PRINCIPLES

✴

ARKADI VAKSBERG

WILLIAM BUTLER SKILLFULLY CAPTURES
the essence of the legal problems that have generated such sharp debate
in the Soviet Union. The most important of them, in my opinion, is
how best and most precisely to define certain terms that have gained
widespread currency in official documents as well as in scholarly literature, in the mass media, and in statements made by legal experts and
laymen alike.

Until recently the very use of the term "law-governed," or "rule-of-
law state" was seen as an attempt to transplant bourgeois concepts and
legal structures onto Soviet soil. (See, for instance, the writings of Valeri
Savitsky.)[1] Nowadays, on the other hand, hardly any subject elicits
greater interest and arouses more hope within the public at large than
the nature of the *pravovoye gosudarstvo*—in Professor Butler's rendering, "rule-of-law state"—that we hope to achieve.

Let me offer one salient illustration of how poor is the general understanding of the task at hand and how little agreement there is with
regard to definitions of legal terms used in our debate. The preliminary
documents for the Nineteenth Party Conference in July 1988 referred
to "completing the formation" of a law-governed state as one of the

188

major problems facing society. The use of the verb "to complete" is not just a solecism. It reflects a lack of understanding of the true meaning of a rule-of-law state. After much discussion with jurists practicing at the highest level (i.e., judges, prosecutors), I have come to the conclusion that most of them perceive a rule-of-law state simply as one with "good laws," or at least laws that are better than those that existed previously, insofar as they reflect more faithfully the interests and aims of the current phase of social development. These jurists reject as blasphemy the notion that even in countries where the judicial system is subservient to or patently manipulated by the state, there are laws, which in this case reflect the interests and serve the needs of those in power. Indeed, in such countries laws may play an even greater role than in those where the law is above the state.

Thus the definition of the term is by no means a theoretical question. It is a matter of practical urgency. The overhaul of our political and legal structures requires first a basic strategy: Precisely what do we want to establish? Can we *complete* something that has not yet begun? Yes, we must revise our legal system, but in what direction? What should be the legal character of the society that our revised legislation is to serve?

These are some of the fundamental questions that must be resolved if we are to achieve not verbal but practical results. Professor Butler notes the confusion in the minds of many Soviet politicians and jurists between *pravo* (*jus*), and *zakon* (*lex*). This confusion arose because fundamental legal concepts, which existed in their own right from the outset and which needed legislative implementation with juridical guarantees to ensure that implementation, were never discussed. Instead, official thinking had come to be dominated by a scholastic concept of the class nature of rights conferred upon the citizen by the grace of the state, and dependent on his origins, social conduct, reliability, usefulness, and loyalty to those in power.

Butler's essay poses essential questions: precisely what do we mean by a "rule-of-law state?" Is it a state based on law? Is it a state that rules by means of the law? Is it a state in which all officials are subordinate to the law, and cannot act outside or above it? In other words, is it a state that prohibits arbitrary rule and that prevents the concentration of unlimited power in the hands of a few individuals?

The answer to all these questions is "yes." The kind of state we envision entails all these attributes. But the crux lies elsewhere, and has been most closely formulated by Marat Baglai.[2] It seems to me that people are gradually becoming aware of the supremacy of an individual's rights, interests, and freedoms. Which is to say that the ideal of a state ruled by law is one that ensures the freedom of each individual, fully and without exception, by means of reliable juridical guarantees. I here define freedom in the broadest sense, including freedom of self-expression, of professional fulfillment, of how and where and by what means one lives; and I reject the odious and meaningless Stalinist slogans such as "the freedom of society guarantees the freedom of each citizen." Only the guarantee of the whole range of individual rights and freedoms guarantees in turn the freedom of the entire society. And only a legal system that realizes, in practical terms, those guarantees for every individual will lead to the creation of a genuine state ruled by law.

I am expressing, of course, my own point of view. It is by no means certain that this conception of a state ruled by law is widely accepted, nor that those experts who are entrusted with the responsibility of creating the new Soviet legal system share these goals. Which in turn suggests another question: Is there an alternative definition, and if so what is it? All the legislative revisions introduced until now—in amendments and additions to both old and new laws—seem to share the same narrow perspective. They are attempts to react as quickly as possible to immediate problems, to what are perceived, correctly or not, to be the exigencies of the moment. They lack a clear long-range perspective, and they are predicated—naively, in my opinion—on the assumption that corrections and emendations of the laws will be made in the course of time, as their flaws or defects become manifest.

The most glaring example of this is the April 8, 1989 decree of the Presidium of the Supreme Soviet introducing long-awaited revisions of articles 70 and 190 of the Criminal Code of the RSFSR and corresponding articles of the criminal codes of other republics. This decree annulled two dangerously vague formulations, "anti-Soviet propaganda and agitation," which was susceptible to and indeed allowed wholly arbitrary interpretations, as did "slandering Soviet society and the Soviet regime." Unfortunately, what replaced them was no more precise: "appeals for the overthrow of the existing system," and "discrediting of social organizations and their representatives." But what concerns me in this context is less the substance of this decree than the fact that as soon as it was passed it required a whole series of clarifications, commentaries, and explications. Without such corrections, everyone agreed, its implementation could severely hamper the processes of perestroika and glasnost.

LEGAL REFORMS AND BASIC PRINCIPLES
★
ARKADI VAKSBERG

True, after some corrective action by the Supreme Court of the USSR, the first session of the Congress of People's Deputies annulled one of the articles, and severely circumscribed the potential effect of the other by limiting it only to open calls for "the overthrow of the Soviet social and state system," and by explicitly reaffirming the legality of criticism of state officials and institutions.[3] Nonetheless, it must be asked what kind of law is this, if on the very day of its adoption it reveals such fundamental flaws? Why was it so hastily adopted (though preparatory work lasted a long time), when its defects became apparent at first glance? Clearly the answer to these questions has to do not merely with this particular decree, but with more general faults of the current phase of legal reforms. They are part of the tendency of some conservative officials to react quickly to what they anxiously perceive as "abuses of glasnost" (as if glasnost in its truest sense could even *be* "abused"!). They reflect the absence of a commonly accepted and shared concept of legally guaranteed inalienable individual rights, above all freedom of expression and freedom of the press.

All the recent work on legal reform continues to reveal the powerful influence of a traditional negative impulse, a kind of itch to prohibit that seems so deeply rooted in the national consciousness as to be nearly ineradicable. For many of those who actually write the laws, the first and most important function of law is to prohibit, to set limits. This tendency was exacerbated when the old-time slogan, "Everything is forbidden that is not explicitly permitted by law," gave way to "Everything is permitted that is not explicitly forbidden." After all, that means that if something is not forbidden, people will think it's permitted! This led to new legal norms of prohibition, or so severely restricted "permissive" laws with provisos and exceptions that local judicial bodies and authorities have a wide latitude in applying them.

A recent analysis conducted by legal scholars revealed, incidentally, that of the hundreds of thousands of legal provisions operating in the country as a whole, more than forty percent serve to prohibit some action, and prescribe punishment for this or that "transgression." This trend is clearly reflected in the ongoing legal reforms. Overcoming it requires not only a fundamental change in political thinking, but a radical change of legal thinking, in the population at large, but first and foremost in the minds of legal professionals.

In my view a sweeping and comprehensive legal reform should begin with changes in constitutional legislation. The preeminence of the Basic Law should be no mere theoretical postulate, but a reflection of reality.

All other laws must conform to immutable constitutional principles. Instead, these principles have been subjected to sundry "mutations," such as the "Brezhnev" constitution of 1977, which needs to be thoroughly reexamined. Yet although such a reexamination was promised, it's been postponed to the distant future. Thus the cart is placed before the horse. Instead of concentrating on the first priority, which is the constitution itself, and which should be the fundamental source of all legislation, we are busily turning out all sorts of legislative acts that may be altogether at odds with constitutional principles. What criteria, what judicial (not ideological) principles will the new judicial organ, the Constitutional Court of the USSR, adhere to? How will it evaluate whether or not the new legislation is well grounded? Against which constitutional statutes will it measure the laws on which it renders decisions? With statutes that may be revised tomorrow? These are some of the questions that demand immediate attention, and on whose resolution depends the very fate of a law-governed state.

We have passed a new and potentially significant piece of legislation, which requires that all laws considered to be "most important" be first submitted to public debate. But nowhere is it specified exactly what constitutes a "most important" law, and which issues fit that category. Thus the door is opened to the broadest and most arbitrary interpretations. The outcry that greeted the July 1988 decree on public gatherings, which severely restricted this fundamental constitutional right, demonstrated that popular opinion considered this issue of utmost importance. Nonetheless, the draft of this decree had not been submitted to debate, and the public was presented with a *fait accompli*. As a result, no sooner was the decree put into effect than it became the object of widespread anger and criticism.

Professor Butler poses a series of provocative questions, some of which touch on the judiciary. The list could be expanded, though it should be noted that the number of acquittals, to which Butler refers, has risen significantly in the last few years, a fact which has been discussed more than once at plenary sessions of the Supreme Court of the USSR. But a list of problems does not get to the heart of the matter. That, it seems to me, lies in recognizing the need for a complex, all-embracing and integrated reorganization of the Soviet legal system *in toto*. Such recognition would testify to the fruitful and positive changes which are occurring in the Soviet Union in the context of a comprehensive restructuring process.

LEGAL REFORMS AND BASIC PRINCIPLES
★
ARKADI VAKSBERG

An overhaul of our legal system is a matter of urgent priority. But we cannot go about it on the strength of a concept full of hazy generalizations and noble intentions. We need a broad strategy carefully thought out and implemented by parliament, a parliament that itself comes into being out of carefully thought out changes in the electoral law. Only under those conditions will the enormous task we have set ourselves be truly "completed."

★

THE DIFFICULT
AND PAINFUL PATH
TO THE TRUTH

✭

ROY MEDVEDEV

IN APRIL 1985 IT WAS IMPOSSIBLE TO foresee all the difficulties, problems, and contradictions that would come up during the first year of perestroika, and even more difficult to know how to resolve them. It turned out that most of our diplomats don't know how to conduct negotiations, most of our doctors don't know how to cure their patients, the majority of our writers can't write interesting books, the majority of Soviet "businessmen" are devoid of initiative, salesmen don't know how to trade, and politicians can give orders but cannot engage in real political activity.

In addition, it became apparent that most engineers are not familiar with modern technology, most teachers don't know how to teach children, and most students barely know the latest developments in their own subjects. The most capable workers in any field are to be found not at the top of the huge and enormously complicated bureaucratic pyramid, but at the bottom of it. Moreover, our bureaucratic apparatus consists not merely of party and government ministries and offices, but also of organizations like the Writers' Union, the Artists' Union, the Academy of Sciences, the Committee on Soviet Women, the Veterans'

Association, labor associations, and even societies of dogtrainers, stamp collectors, sports clubs, and the Chess Players' Federation.

The biggest surprise turned out to be the scholarly discipline of history. One might have thought that in view of the fact that the history of the Communist party and of the Soviet Union was, from the beginning of the 1930s, a basic part of the ideological training and education of the entire population, from eight-year-olds to eighty-year-olds, and in view, too, of the more than ten thousand professional historians of the USSR and more than one million professional propagandists and teachers of history, at least some of them would have had a grasp of the actual history of their native land. The opposite proved to be true.

More than two years ago our press began to speak about the need to eliminate "blank spots" in the history of the USSR. But in the process of filling in those "blank spots"—which is being accomplished *not* primarily by professional historians, but by journalists, memoirists, writers, members of a specially trained commission of the Politburo of the Central Committee of the Communist party, the Public Prosecutor's Office, and the Criminal Investigation Department—it became clear that the "blank spots" are intimately connected with the darkest and most shameful pages of Soviet history.

Much of the scholarly activity that was until recently praised now proves to be a deliberate and often primitive falsification of history. An avalanche of muckraking articles and exposés continues to pour down on the Soviet reader from the pages of dozens of newspapers and magazines. Assessments, formerly accepted, of the most important events and historical personalities are collapsing, together with officially accepted evaluations not only of NEP, collectivization, industrialization, and Soviet foreign policy, but also of the Second World War, of the Civil War, and to some extent even of the October Revolution and its consequences. We are unable to formulate a scientific or scholarly definition of our own contemporary social structure, our political system, and the nature of property. Not only has the periodization of Soviet history and its familiar values come crashing down, so has the whole network of widely accepted authorities in the area of history.

Many academicians and directors of historical institutes have been silent, while once-unknown journalists are acquiring national fame. Required exams in Soviet and party history were canceled in high schools and colleges, and standard textbooks removed—to be replaced with new ones only recently. But the reassessment of the pivotal events of

Soviet history continues, and there's good reason to think that the fundamental process of overturning familiar myths and dogmatic stereotypes is just beginning.

The failure of an entire realm of scholarship, which today appears not merely unscholarly but meretricious, presents the political leadership of the country with ever-increasing problems. Thus the controversy over the history of Nagorno-Karabakh is one of the main reasons for the acute national conflict between Armenia and Azerbaijan. The demand for historical truth sparked powerful national movements in Latvia, Lithuania, and Estonia. The peoples of Central Asia, Kazakhstan, and even the small nationalities of Siberia and northern Russia will have their own accounts to settle with the rewriters of history, though not yet as urgently as the others.

There are a great many reasons for the crisis in Soviet historical scholarship. It developed within a Marxist and socialist framework, but in the 1920s it still retained the attributes and qualities of a genuine scholarly discipline. In the early 1930s this tendency slowed down, and by the second half of the decade it practically ceased to exist. (I speak here of the history of the USSR, not of ancient Russia.)

Stalin turned the history of the USSR into the history of the Communist party of the Soviet Union, and with the publication of the *Short Course in the History of the Party* (1938) a mendacious account of the Communist party became the basis of a new party ideology that still retained the label "Marxist-Leninist," though neither Marx nor Lenin made a special study of history: they considered their main work to be in the fields of political economy, philosophy, and socialism.

All these paramount elements of Marxism became secondary adjuncts of the short and falsified history of the party. Not only did objective scholarship become a subjective tool of ideology, but ideology itself was subordinated to the interests of current politics.

Even then, politics was understood not in the broad sense that Marx and Lenin construed the word—the party and class struggle, oppressors and oppressed—but in the most primitive sense of a struggle for personal power. (This is characteristic of every totalitarian regime.) Stalin transformed the history of the party and of the Soviet Union into his own personal property, and gave historians only the opportunity to comment on his genius. In its milder form this absurd structure, seemingly stable but in point of fact exceedingly fragile, rested on the personal ambitions of the "Leader" and spurious historical myths about his great actions, with various ideological constructs tacked on. Remnants of what can legitimately be called scholarship about human society were preserved, tucked away here and there, and survived into the Brezhnev era. That structure, which trembled and tilted under the blows of Khrushchev's Twentieth and Twenty-Second Congresses, is now falling apart in front of our eyes.

No nation, no stable human community is capable of existing not only without a commonality of language, territory, and culture, but also without an accepted commonality of fate—or, put another way, without history. No society with pretenses to calling itself socialist is capable of existing without an ideology based on the contemporary accomplishments of the social sciences. A genuinely democratic state ruled by law can be built only on freedom of opinion, of discussion, and of scholarly research. An economic system capable of supporting life can be created only from a free flow of ideas and information.

The more farsighted leaders of the Communist party are now beginning to understand this. Perestroika, which we are witnessing and taking part in, is the most important turning point in our national history since 1917. A new ideology, fundamentally different from what has been labelled Marxism-Leninism, is emerging in the USSR. For the moment both the press and Mikhail Gorbachev prefer to call this ideology "new thinking." Though we cite Marx and Lenin no less than before, we are continually reexamining the central postulates of Marxism-Leninism. Our new ideology does not reject socialism: on the contrary, it is a new level in the development of what used to be called "scientific socialism."

We respectfully recognize, however, the validity of other ideologies and religious and political convictions, and the priority of universal values and interests over class interests. We speak less and less about the struggle against imperialism, and more and more about the defense and protection of universal civilization. We call on all countries in the world to unite and resolve global problems that threaten life on the planet, and we do not repeat the old dogmas about universal coexistence as a new form of the ideological battle.

The new ideology now emerging in our country accepts, though not yet unreservedly, pluralism of opinions and the possibility of free discussion. Together with its emergence and the disappearance of most of the former myths about Soviet history, a genuinely objective and honest discipline of historiography is developing. Not too many historians now in their fifties and sixties are capable of doing the work that is now required of them. It is still the journalists and essayists who are in the forefront, debunking old myths and criticizing former leaders and their transgressions. Many of them are discovering and disclosing extremely important details and events which we knew little if anything about.

But a properly systematized and conceptually sophisticated scholarly discipline requires professionalism of the highest order and more than a little time. This work is going on with the support of influential political leaders, but in the teeth of desperate resistance from conservative forces that are losing their former authority, their monopoly, and their privileges. The fight goes on, and as it continues the opponents of "new thinking" and new historical concepts resort to baser and more despicable tactics. Support for perestroika grows among the intelligentsia and young people, but a large and important part of the nation is barely active. Hence the abundance of ever more interesting articles and books on Soviet history is accompanied by an increase in inflation and the disappearance of the most essential goods. Unfortunately, economic growth is not keeping pace with intellectual development. We have retained intellectual values accumulated over centuries; however, we have no such "surplus" in the economic sphere to supplement a basic scarcity of goods.

But economics is not my subject here. In history and culture, we still have substantial reserves despite the crises and dismay in official institutions and despite the efforts of previous leaderships to conceal those reserves from the nation. For me personally, perestroika and "new thinking" have materially changed my position as a historian. Since the end of April 1988 I have published more than thirty articles and interviews on various historical subjects in a variety of newspapers and magazines. Three or four times a week I lecture on the history of the USSR to all kinds of audiences—students, high school history teachers, professors at colleges and universities. I have spoken to huge crowds at the Higher School of Komsomol Workers and at the Diplomatic Academy, at the Zhukovsky Military Engineering Academy and the Research Institute of the Russian Language, at the Ministry of Foreign Economic Relations and the Ministry of Foreign Affairs, in the Palace of Youth, the Cinema Workers' Club, the publishing house Prosveshcheniye (Enlightenment), and in clubs of history buffs and bibliophiles.

Each time I receive hundreds of notes asking me to shed light on one or another historical event or express my opinion about this or that political figure. In 1988–89, twelve of my books, almost all of them already published in the West, will have come out in the Soviet Union, as well as two new volumes: a handbook for teachers, *Teaching the History of the USSR in a Time of Perestroika*, and *L.I. Brezhnev: A Political Portrait*.

My official status has only recently altered: in May 1989 I was readmitted to the Communist party and in the summer I was elected to the USSR Supreme Soviet. But I am mindful of the past: of the fact that the KGB twice searched my apartment—in 1971 and 1975—and confiscated my scholarly archive and historical volumes important to me, including books by Trotsky and Solzhenitsyn, and that only since late 1989 have I been given permission to travel abroad. The path to the truth still stretches long before us. But I hope for the best, and I am prepared to work even harder today, when I am in my sixties, than I had to thirty years ago. I shall do so in the belief and in the hope that my work will thus contribute to the further development of freedom and historical truth.

★

THE RISE OF ETHNIC
ASSERTIVENESS

★

JULIAN BROMLEI

RONALD SUNY IS GENERALLY OBJECTIVE
in discussing the history of nationality relations in the USSR. He does
not engage in exaggerations and he relies on facts. Some observations
and stereotypes, such as the term "Soviet empire," can be attributed to
the Sovietological tradition in the West. However, some of the author's
observations on past and present aspects of the nationality problem in
various regions, as well as his conception of the current correlation of
factors of integration and disintegration, are curious and arguable.

Suny narrows the social base of socialism in the USSR to a few elite
political and intellectual groups in the population, and constructs a
dichotomy between Marxism and nationalism. By interpreting the spread
of Marxist ideas before the revolution in this light, he creates the impression that the Bolsheviks imposed the revolution on the masses of the
population.

Moreover, several aspects of interethnic tension remain unclear, especially the measures taken to alleviate it. The complexity of the nationality problem in the USSR is indicated by the fact that more than
60 million people (one fifth of the total population) currently live beyond
the boundaries of "their" republics—more, that is, than the entire pop-

ulation of France. How these groups interact with the indigenous populations helps explain the actual relations of the various ethno-national groups in the republics.

It is in this connection that the question of creating national regions and rural soviets—more than five thousand of which existed until the mid-1930s—has now arisen. One proposal involves rethinking the constitutional status of national groups so as to include their representation in legal and executive bodies, their right to native-language instruction, the development of their national culture, and so on. Special cultural centers for dispersed national groups, especially in large cities, have already been established.

The complex ethno-demographic situation in the country also bears on interethnic relations. In recent decades the rate of growth of certain nationalities in Central Asia, as well as the Kazakhs and Azeris, contributed to the growth of the Soviet population.[1] The rate of growth of these groups is three times higher than that of the population as a whole. The percentage of Slavic-language groups fell from 77.1 percent in 1959 to 72.8 percent in 1979, while Turkic-language groups rose from 11.1 percent to 15.2 percent. An active demographic policy is needed to stimulate population growth in regions with low birth rates, and to discourage large families in overpopulated regions.

The use of labor resources is affected by these regional national characteristics. In some regions, for the most part in the north, there is a labor shortage; in others, mainly in the south, a labor surplus. The combination of ethno-demographic imbalances and varying rates of growth in labor productivity has led to the differentiated development of social infrastructures within the republics, a differentiation visible in such areas as housing, living conditions, medical facilities, and the like. All of these factors point to the violation of the principle of equality among the republics.

In this connection one must bear in mind that policies of budget and tax privileges played an important role in the development of backward republics in the past. In the 1930s, for instance, subsidies from centralized reserves covered more than sixty percent of budgetary expenditures in the majority of republics. Via budgetary channels the state redistributed national income in the interests of individual nationalities. Thanks to such policies a rough parity among national groups existed by the end of the 1940s. There should, then, have been no further need for many benefits and privileges.

For various reasons, however, these privileges and benefits were preserved, and to a significant degree they continue to this day. On the one hand this situation—exacerbated by the silence which reigned on this issue until recently—created a sense of dependence among local leaders; on the other it contributed to the widespread conviction among local populations that their republics had contributed a disproportionately large share to the general coffers. The leadership of various republics encouraged this attitude, as did part of the local *intelligentsia*. The latter, anticipating the wishes of the former, often bred and—with the help of the mass media—disseminated myths about the "special" role played by their own republics.

Professor Suny's thesis about Stalin's chauvinistic policies and the russification policy of subsequent regimes needs clarification. Stalin's policy on the nationalities question can hardly be called chauvinist in the strict sense of the word. It guaranteed advantages neither to the Russian people nor to Russian culture. The former were cruelly repressed, the latter ruthlessly destroyed. Stalinist "chauvinism" was essentially part of a broader policy of total unification, regimentation, suppression of dissent, and centralization. In those circumstances the natural "mold" or instrument could only be the Russian language and the Russian historical tradition. The policy of "forced russification" implemented after Stalin's death can be explained the same way.

In Stalin's nationality policy no less than in other spheres of activity, hypocrisy was the norm. Thus, answering the opponents of assimilation, Stalin simplified the ethnic and national structure of the country and displayed a hostile attitude toward the very existence of national groups. In his revealing report on the 1936 constitution, for instance, he asserted that there were sixty national groups in the country, when in fact there were at least twice that number. Not surprisingly, it was precisely at this time that national administrative units—the national regions and rural Soviets referred to above—were liquidated.

The census reveals this same tendency toward simplification—which is to say, distortion. One hundred ninety four nationalities were specified in the 1926 census, while fewer than one hundred were counted in the 1939 census. This reduction was in part connected with the change in criteria used to define national groups, as well as with consolidation processes occurring in that period. Nevertheless, a decrease of nearly fifty percent in a thirteen-year period strongly suggests that the existence of a number of nationalities, especially smaller ones, was simply ignored.

THE RISE OF ETHNIC ASSERTIVENESS
★
JULIAN BROMLEI

Professor Suny leans—mistakenly, in my view—towards the notion that democratization in the area of ethnic relations inevitably involves decentralization. True, he recognizes that the task of broadening republican rights, especially economic rights, is far from simple. Greater economy autonomy, to the point of creating a market mechanism in the means of production, may well encourage regionalism—giving priority to local interests—and could turn into autarky and a strengthening of centrifugal tendencies. At the same time, the expansion of autonomy presupposes market relations, territorial specialization, barter between republics—all factors which foster the development of centripetal, integrative forces. In such a system the self-supporting enterprise is the basic unit of self-government. In current conditions nearly every such enterprise has economic ties extending far beyond republican boundaries. The danger of conflict between republican interests and the interests of the self-supporting enterprises arises from this paradox. All attempts to substitute a republican administrative system for the well-established departmental administrative system are wrong. Regional nationalism has been clearly linked with attempts on the part of administrative authorities to preserve their position within the republics. A great deal will depend on the concrete steps taken to realize economic reforms.

Professor Suny is, I believe, unduly pessimistic in assessing the consequences of democratization in general and in national relations specifically. Genuine democratization is more likely to stabilize the situation, to strengthen unity rather than to weaken it. I am of course speaking of true democracy, and not of the pseudodemocratic ideas championed by some nationalists. Genuine democratization and glasnost are bound to become active tools in preventing any violations of the principles of social equality and justice in interethnic relations in our country. The Supreme Soviet has been debating an array of laws that would guarantee the democratization of economic, social, and cultural-linguistic life in the republics and autonomous regions, including the bases of their economic independence, language, citizenship, national minorities, etc. This is particularly important insofar as the unresolved status of these issues is one of the main reasons for the continuing conflicts in the Transcaucasus, Baltics, and Central Asia. Inevitably, the nature of the Soviet state will have to be examined as well: will it remain a federation, or will it become a confederation?

In my view history suggests that becoming a confederation would be a step backwards. Attempts at such negotiated relationships were made during the Civil War (1918–20), when they certainly helped unify the young Soviet republics against counterrevolutionary forces, but they were quickly seen to be ineffective and faulty. Closer ties of interdependence were needed; the creation of the Union of Soviet Socialist Republics in 1922 provided them. A single national government was better equipped to maintain national defense and support socioeconomic progress and national development on a basis of equality. As a result national strength was not just concentrated, but was enhanced as well.

Many difficulties lie ahead, but the party platform on nationalities, adopted in September 1989, creates a basis for resolving them: Every republic must, ultimately, become more autonomous.

In conclusion, let me call attention to the global characteristics of ethno-national processes: in addition to the tendencies towards differentiation, there are also integrative tendencies. At times the first tendency predominates, and at times the other. In the United States, for instance, the integrative factors, leading to the emergence of the so-called melting pot idea, had long prevailed. In the 1960s there came the growth of what might be called ethnic revival and ethnic pluralism, which by the 1980s resulted in the repudiation of the melting pot notion and of ethnic integration in general.

In our country, the latter tendency had predominated until only recently—that is, until the mid-1980s, approximately twenty years after it had disappeared in the United States. All told, then, ethnic assertiveness is clearly on the rise in all countries. And its further development depends to a large extent on whether and how the aspirations and demands of ethnic groups are satisfied. The measures in this direction that are now being promoted in our country under the aegis of perestroika, despite the current eruption of ethnic conflicts, provide a basis for hope that the current ethno-national tensions, in large part caused by past deformations, will eventually be placed on a more stable and favorable footing.

★

AT A FATEFUL
FORK IN THE ROAD

✰

LEONID M. BATKIN

I HAVE FEW DISAGREEMENTS WITH
Professor Suny. He describes the nationality problems of the USSR with
great knowledge and insight. But I see the whole situation as being much
more painful and threatening. Hence the title of my commentary.

First of all, it is difficult for me to agree that party and state "local
elites," beginning in Khrushchev's time and despite a total lack of democracy, grew stronger in a context of "limited political autonomy."
The republic elite, now called "mafias" because of their ties to underground business, did in fact grow stronger. But no decentralization, of
even a limited nature, occurred as a result. What did happen—officially
and simplistically called "stabilization" under Brezhnev—was a substantially different process.

If after Stalin's death his apparat was freed of the nauseating fear
and terror that affected the highest-placed party figures, generals, tech-
nocrats, and NKVD officers no less than ordinary citizens, that same
apparat later managed to put an end to Khrushchev's dictatorship, with
its bureaucratic whims and reorganizations that continually disturbed
and unsettled the ranks of the apparat. After Khrushchev was ousted in
October 1964, shifts in the cadres virtually ceased except for the quiet

shake-ups in the Politburo that accompanied the confirmation of each new general secretary. Only now could the bureaucrats feel like the real masters of the country. They enjoyed the fruits of the Stalin regime without its feverish excesses. Party and other bigwigs—whether ministers or national satraps—sat back in their armchairs, relaxed and secure, seemingly forever. They put their relatives and friends into cushy jobs. Powerful groups formed, like Aliyev's "Nakhichevan" clan and Brezhnev's henchmen in Dnepropetrovsk and Kishinev.[1] Republics, oblasts, and departments were theirs for the asking.

But all threads led back to Moscow, which is to say, in the final analysis, to the Politburo. That is why, incidentally, Rashidov's "rabble" was so hard to kill off until Solomentsev and others were defeated in September 1988; Aliyev's group seems still to retain roots in Moscow.[2] No one could survive without a personal link "to the top." The shadow economy and corruption developed along parallel vertical lines. The USSR's ruling caste—which profits from its collectively held power in the government—is organized as a strict hierarchy, and the immense power and brazenness of local authorities, which increased sharply in the years of neototalitarian stagnation and which facilitated personal enrichment and arbitrary rule, in no way contradicts that hierarchical structure. Changes testify not to political autonomy, but only to an administratively useful division of influence, and to the stabilization of the imperial pyramid. The dependence of each apparatchik on people and organizations higher up at once guaranteed and corrected the uncontrollability of the apparat. The role of the center has not lessened so much as it has changed its colors. Kunayev, Aliyev, Rashidov, and others reflect merely a transformed aspect of all-union power, a type of restructuring within the one-party system.

During the events of 1986 in Alma Ata and Yakutsk, and the more complex troubles in Baku in the autumn of 1988,[3] mass social dissatisfaction and anger was directly inflamed by and combined with the reaction of anxious local higher-ups. But the more sophisticated and deep-rooted national movements unleashed by perestroika are directed equally against the central bureaucracy and their own servile bureaucrats. (Western terms are of limited use in explaining Soviet reality: "bureaucracy," "authoritarianism," "decentralization," and "mafia" are all *para*terms. Soviet reality is not outside the realm of known political rules, including "Eastern ones," but it substantially recreates them in a culturally specific way.)

The Baltic states are far ahead of the other republics in their political development. The Estonians and Lithuanians have even managed to achieve a real—if incomplete—renewal of the party leadership, so that for the first time the official national top echelons act in concert with the democratic movement and not on orders from outside. There is where some genuine steps toward local political autonomy have been made. Many Estonians, Lithuanians, and particularly Latvians try desperately, however, to avoid confronting the main difficulty: the violent dissatisfaction and fears of the Russian-speaking population of the Baltic states. It is essential that this large group *also* desire a return to national sovereignty, at least in the economic sphere, while its linguistic, cultural, and psychological rights are guaranteed. After the crises of the summer of 1989, both the supreme soviets and the national fronts in the Baltics have become much more careful, although the goal—secession from the USSR—is by now altogether clear; the Politburo's anxious fist-shaking has merely increased regional instability and intensified ethnic unity. The majority of the local national populations, "interfronts" notwithstanding, support the revival of democracy and Baltic sovereignty. In this connection the Lithuanian Communist party's decision to cease being a regional branch of the Communist party of the Soviet Union and to become independent is extremely important.

The Armenian situation is different. The Karabakh Movement, an outgrowth of specific national feelings and anxieties, began to turn into a national front, with a generally social-democratic content, in the summer of 1988. The atmosphere in Yerevan began to resemble feverish Petersburg in February 1917, an intoxicating mixture of liberation and fraternity. More important even than the overflowing crowds in Theater Square was the replacement of corrupt regional party bureaucrats with more popular and honest men in three republican regions.

This was accomplished by the public with the help of the Karabakh Committee. In later elections to Armenia's Supreme Soviet two members of the committee were chosen; they had powerful support from below. At a meeting on November 24, 1988, and under pressure from the masses, the Supreme Soviet passed resolutions objecting to the draft electoral reforms and to various constitutional amendments. A quorum of the Supreme Soviet met without its Presidium and without the Central Committee Bureau, which were meeting separately—an astonishing juxtaposition! That same night a decree was passed in Moscow giving military commanders extreme powers in case of a "special" situation—

the right, for example, to detain someone for thirty days without making any charges. Also *that same night*, precisely such a "special" situation was declared in Yerevan. The Supreme Soviet meeting adjourned and tanks rolled into the streets. Within a few days, when committee members were fully involved in organizing help to the regions worst hit by the devastating earthquake, they were suddenly arrested. The day before their arrest, agitated crowds obstructed Gorbachev and his wife. This played into the hands of Yerevan authorities, who attributed it to the work of the Karabakh committee. Thus men who had become the people's favorite leaders were too dangerous for the apparatchiks; men who had acted as a reasonable and calming influence on the masses were sent to Moscow prisons, on specious charges. In this fashion the central authorities made themselves the enemy in the eyes of most Armenians. As Talleyrand said of such situations, "It's worse than a crime, it's a mistake."

True, the members of the Karabakh Committee were finally released in May 1989. But incalculable damage had been done. Instead of turning against the Karabakh Committee, Gorbachev should have done from the beginning whatever he could to establish a dialogue with it. This would have defused the situation. Instead, the real nature and the monstrous details of the Sumgait slaughter were not disclosed, nor were the identities of those behind the crimes, the Azeri bureaucrats and the hired killers who were tried not for murder but for "hooliganism." The trial was scarcely covered by the media, and the killers got off with absurd sentences. Neither the republic nor the union authorities ever expressed condolences. All of this explains why the Armenians' traditional trust in Moscow was so radically undermined. Nor was the Armenians' anger allayed by the "symmetrical" arrests that took place in Baku, a foolish and illegal kind of *quid pro quo* in any event.[4] Moscow's December 1989 decision to return Nagorno-Karabakh to Azerbaijan will only intensify the radicalization of what is now the Armenian national movement.

The quality of life in Azerbaijan is pathetically low; almost no other place suffered as much, and for as long, at the hands of the local mafia. Its pernicious impact on social relations and individual morality has been enormous. While the ban on public discussion of this subject precludes an accurate assessment of how deeply fundamentalist Shiism has penetrated into Azerbaijan from Iran's eight million coreligionists, the green banners of Islam and signs demanding the return of Aliyev and the release of those arrested have certainly appeared at rallies. Within Azerbaijan only a few Azeris dared to condemn the Sumgait murderers, and even then only *pro forma*. The atmosphere of aggressive agitation—which may compensate for the genuine oppression of the population—and the provocative rhetoric of local mafiosi like the so-called academician Buniatov[5] threaten normal discussion and make it dangerous for democratic people in Baku to speak out publicly. A Popular Front of Azerbaijan has been formed, creating a *de facto* dual-power system much like that in the Baltics and to some extent in Armenia. There is, incidentally, an astonishing contrast between the front's fully democratic program and its practical actions, which intensify national hysteria and demonstrate not the least willingness to compromise with Armenians.

A gradualist solution of the Transcaucasus conflict, if it is to be more than a liberal dream, will require massive blows against the mafias in both Armenia and Azerbaijan and independent grassroots support of social renewal. Peace can be made only between two *democracies*, with Moscow as intermediary. Shortsighted attempts to force the more than 300,000 refugees to go back to the homes they abandoned, as if nothing were wrong, merely exacerbate national passions. And since the government cannot fight on two fronts, and is afraid of the grassroots national movements in Yerevan and Baku, the mafias' survival seems ensured.

I want to add a few words on the role Russians have to play in what is after all our common drama. Despite—or perhaps indeed because of—the "big brother" role the Russian people has played vis-à-vis other Soviet nationalities, the Russians nonetheless constitute a deprived nation. The Stalinist leadership was always afraid of the emergence of a Russian party in the RSFSR, with its own Central Committee, a republic KGB, a Russian Academy of Sciences and the like.[6] Their fear was understandable, since such a national Russian center of power and influence could present a challenge to the all-union center. (Hence, incidentally, the eternal suspicion of Leningrad, the former imperial capital, and the grim party bosses—from Zhdanov to Romanov—and ideological suffocation imposed on it.) Russian culture and Russian ecology could not even count on limited protection from its own Central Committee. The past was barbarically destroyed, regions were decimated and vandalized. The poverty, filth, drunkenness, crime, and absence of goods and roads even in Moscow, let alone outside the city, are often horrifying, on a par with circumstances in Karakalpakia or Kalmykia.

209

All along the Volga, in Siberia, and in the Urals, a mountain of grievances has piled up, needing only a spark to set off a major explosion. Thousands of people have demonstrated at rallies on local issues, most often ecological. Party functionaries try to ban or ignore them, trying to avoid honest dialogue with various "informal" groups. Yet the alternative to such independent organizations is wild, indiscriminately destructive uprisings. For the time being nationalist slogans exist only on the posters of *Pamyat* (about whose financing and organization little is known), and then in the crudest, most chauvinist and nationalist-fascist forms. But they could become detonators for explosions.

Pamyat or more respectable variants can count on a number of factors: the momentum of state anti-Semitic policies, supported by some members of the apparat, especially in Leningrad, Novosibirsk, and Minsk; a traditional and widespread popular anti-Semitism and xenophobia, which includes as its targets various national groups invidiously referred to as "southerners," "tribesmen," and "chuchmeks;" the shameful solidarity of "slavophile" writers like Valentin Rasputin, Vasili Belov, and the editorial board members of, most prominently, *Nash sovremennik* (and other little-known publications, such as *Literaturnyi Irkutsk*); and demagogic exploitation of both Russian Orthodox and official rhetoric to blame all problems and difficulties on scapegoats, specifically on the Jews. *Pamyat* is not capable of becoming a primary or constructive political force. But it is an important breeding ground for destabilization, and everyone perceived by the masses as getting in the way would fall victim. Nevertheless, the authorities show amazing tolerance of these latter-day Black Hundreds, a tolerance withheld from, for instance, such organizations as the Democratic Union, with its calls for a multiparty system.

What will happen next? Gorbachev had proclaimed the formula "Powerful republics, a powerful center." But surely "power" is not to be construed the same way for both components. How, then, is sovereignty to be divided between the center and the national "periphery?" A radical and entirely new agreement is called for, a federation of republics which would make their center no longer a center of power *over* the republics but a concentration of the republics' joint policies in the realm of foreign relations, defense, and finance. The republics would retain local military units and independent economic and cultural ties with the outside world, and would themselves resolve issues of emigration, immigration, and the like. Residents would possess dual citizenship, republican and union. The absence of internal borders and custom duties, as well as a single monetary system, would guarantee the stability of a common market. Such proposals are now being discussed in the Baltic states, but various forms and degrees of integration must be developed, since due to the variety of historic and social conditions different republics—Estonia and Turkmenia, Georgia and Kazakhstan, Lithuania and the Ukraine—have different kinds of interests in forming a federation—or a confederation.

Professor Suny is right: national strivings for sovereignty must be combined with genuine democracy in order to preserve the freely chosen unity of the USSR and to protect it from separatist tendencies. Moscow will remain a true "center" only if it manages to become a source and support for national liberation processes and a symbol of popular democracy, as it was in 1918. The focus of cooperation among republics, it would cease to be a center of domination and rule. An effective confederation of powerful republics, a center deriving from them: that is the ideal relationship—and the one, incidentally, that Lenin at one time considered the only natural and practical goal.

But back to reality. The draft law on the distribution of economic and social prerogatives between the republics and the union has been made public. Unfortunately, the most important and ecologically harmful central agricultural departments retain virtually the same degree of power, which flatly excludes the possibility of republican self-financing. The draft law suggests that the leadership of the USSR does not intend to implement radical, swift, and fundamental reform. The prognosis therefore becomes at once more nebulous and more alarming as we approach the fateful fork in the road of events my title alludes to. Popular emotions develop exponentially. If they can be checked only by force, everything (including the people at the top) will collapse.

There are many reasons that mass popular movements in our country are rooted in nationalism, and therefore develop first in regions peripheral to the center. What we face may be a historical anachronism, but it is a real and very worrying one. Seventy years ago the peoples of the Baltic states demanded independence; once again they are demanding independence. Once again we hear "All Power to the soviets" and "Land to the peasants!" Once again we are fighting for an abolition of censorship and for traditional Russian glasnost; once again we are dreaming of freeing Russia from her "centuries-old backwardness." Finally, the Kremlin leaders are once again confronting the paradox that preceded

211

Lenin's death: how an omnipotent authority (not, this time, "proletarian") can attain the unfulfilled goals of the bourgeois democratic revolution.

Like all anachronisms, the anachronism of nationalist movements at the end of the twentieth century is dangerous, however deserving of sympathy. Only if specific national interests can be subordinated to the general democratic interests of a nation, with the interests and rights of the individual superceding all collective desires, can we hope to enter the mainstream of universal progress. We could then become Europeans, not in a geographical sense but in the broadest historical and universal meaning of that concept.

—Translated by Antonina Bouis

★

POETRY IN THE AGE OF PERESTROIKA AND GLASNOST

✮

NATALYA B. IVANOVA

VERA DUNHAM'S ESSAY IS SENSITIVE AND informative, but in writing about various poets, she blends the motifs of their work in rather an impressionistic (if not arbitrary) manner. Like any unexpected foreshortening, or sidelong glance, therefore, this produces a curious effect. Because most of her examples are chosen at random, and are discussed outside of the current poetic context, she can write at the same time about superior and mediocre talents, about serious poets and about those who are—not to put too fine a point on it—not poets at all.

The complexities and contradictions of the present poetic process are therefore not reflected in Professor Dunham's essay, the more so since she has not focused on the poetry published in the last few years, by far the "freest" years. For the purposes of her analysis, poets of the Brezhnev "establishment" and those of the war generation (who to this day focus on the central trauma of their peers, the Second World War) are equally significant, but the most brilliant and representative poets of the younger generation are scanted. The result of this approach is, therefore, a rather skewed map of contemporary Russian poetry.

Poetry has long occupied an unusual position in Soviet life. In the

1920s, the works of Mayakovsky or Yesenin appeared regularly in newspapers and on billboards, and poets declaimed their verses at large public gatherings. Under Stalin, poetry fell silent, as did nearly every creative genre. It enjoyed a brief popularity during and immediately after the war, and then again twenty years later, during Khrushchev's "thaw."

Today, in the age of perestroika and glasnost, poetry has come to play a different role than in the days of Khrushchev. It does not arouse the same excitement as it did two decades ago. The contemporary literary stars are works of fiction, criticism, and politically oriented essays, appearing in huge editions and in mass-circulation journals. Whereas during the "thaw" it was precisely the poets—Yevgeni Yevtushenko, Andrei Voznesensky, Bulat Okudzhava, Bella Akhmadulina—who drew vast audiences, today only a few dozen people gather to hear the former poet-dissidents in Moscow and Leningrad, while thousands of people turn out to listen to prominent journalists and historians. This in no way reflects on the *quality* of today's poetry, some of which is exceptional. Rather, it suggests that in this period of turmoil and change it is history, economics, politics—in the raw or in literary garb—that the public craves above all else. Nonetheless, poetry still claims a large and devoted readership, and its themes and permutations provide an important clue to the spirit of the times.

The most striking event in contemporary poetry is the return to print of formerly forbidden authors, including emigres, the appearance of poems about the Stalin era, and about the terror-ridden years of the Civil War. The poems of such relatively recent emigres as Joseph Brodsky, Yuri Kublanovsky, and Naum Korzhavin, of "second wave" emigres (i.e., those who left the Soviet Union in the wake of the Second World War) like Ivan Yelagin (1918–87), and even of those who had left soon after the Revolution, such as Georgi Ivanov (1894–1958), play an enormous role in the emancipation of public consciousness. When Brodsky's poems first appeared, it was the Leningrad poet Aleksandr Kushner who wrote the afterward.[1]

The result of this process is extraordinary: readers are pelted with a multitude of poetic languages, trends, and schools dating from different historical periods, yet unified by a thread that is distinctly Russian. Anna Akhmatova's "Requiem," the tragic lament of Mother Russia for her sons murdered in the concentration camps, and Aleksandr Tvardovsky's "By Right of Memory," a long poem about the fate of repressed peasants (among them the poet's family), were both published in two journals simultaneously—indeed, the journals competed for the honor of first publication of these works in their own country. The appearance of Maksimilian Voloshin's "Russia" as well as of some of his other, previously banned poems, was also of major significance.[2] A full volume of Osip Mandelstam's lyrics finally came out, including the piercingly prophetic "Poem on an Unknown Soldier." Nikolai Klyuyev's famous poem "The Holocaust" (*Pogorelshchina*) was at long last published in the Soviet Union, as were letters and documents from the last and most difficult years of his life.[3] The "Oberyut" poets Daniil Kharms and Aleksandr Vvedensky have been published, as has Velimir Khlebnikov's ballad "Boss of the Cheka" and portions of Varlam Shalamov's poem-cycles.[4]

What emerges from this poetry is an arresting picture of the losses borne by the nation and its culture. Apart from its poetic value, it serves as a catalyst in the effort to change popular stereotypes and to restore historical truth. Its impact on the moral sensibility of the public cannot be overestimated. To borrow a phrase from the great (and formerly banned) philosopher Nikolai Fyodorov, who strongly influenced Dostoevsky and Tolstoy, a "resurrection of the fathers" is taking place in poetry today. What had been forcibly scored out, ripped from the fabric of society, is being returned to it. (The publication in mass-circulation journals of Russian religious and philosophic thought—the work of such diverse thinkers as V. Solovyov, P. Florensky, S. Bulgakov, L. Karsavin, A. Losev, and other—plays no small part in this process.) Along with the most famous names, virtually unknown poets are being brought back to life—the mystic Daniil Andreyev, whose poem-treatise "Rose of Peace" has so far been published only partially, Gleb Semyonov, Anatoli Kleshchenko, and Nikolai Stefanovich.

Finally, readers are discovering new, unexpected sides of the poets they already know. Thus, for instance, the posthumous publication of Boris Slutsky's work came as a revelation: after his death more than two thousand poems were found in his archives, none of which had been published, for political reasons.[5] The "camp" poems of Yaroslav Smelyakov, a talented poet whose reputation was tainted by conformism, have also appeared. (Sadly, Smelyakov and even Slutsky lent their names to the vile campaign against Boris Pasternak in October 1958.)

These works are not merely of academic or historical importance. They are part of the current social and political landscape. Lines of poetry find their way into political debate. They touch upon agonizing subjects: the repressions of the late 1930s, the "Red Terror," the Civil War, collectivization, the collapse of peasant culture, the violence done to spiritual and physical freedom. They serve a social function, shedding a light on current reality, and they serve an aesthetic function, reanimating a poetic culture lost for decades to the domination of insipid, "gray" versification.

Against the background of brilliant stars from the past, who have in this historic instant become our contemporaries and collocutors, more recent names—Voznesensky and Yevtushenko—lose their luster. Not wanting to be left out of today's social, intellectual, and political processes, they have published old poetry once banned by the censors. They exploit their private poetic discoveries of the 1960s. But these darlings of fortune (who, far from suffering during the Brezhnev years, even garnered top-level government prizes) are not—in terms of intellectual complexity and independence—the equals of many poets now appearing on the pages of literary journals.

Paradoxically, the significance and incisiveness of Voznesensky and Yevtushenko's articles, essays, and public speeches cannot be gainsaid: they are, now, far more serious as essayists and publicists than as poets. Though in their poetry, too, they speak of crucial matters—chauvinism, ecology, the consequences of Stalinism, loneliness, individual rights, pervasive mediocrity—their poetry has, sadly, become no more than illustration.

An intense reassessment of values, a "reshuffling of the deck" is taking place in all areas of social life, poetry included. Of the poets now active, a number of names stand out: Oleg Chukhontsev, Boris Chichibabin, Vladimir Kornilov, Inna Lisnyanskaya, Aleksandr Kushner, Nonna Slepakova. Their work reflects the spirit of the great classics of Russian literature and the traditional values and forms of Russian poetry.

Boris Chichibabin and Vladimir Kornilov were both expelled from the Writers Union: Chichibabin for poems in memory of Tvardovsky (poet and, as editor of the journal Novy mir, protector of Solzhenitsyn), Kornilov for dissident activity as an active participant in the human rights movement of the 1960's and 1970s. Now they are sought after by editors of literary and popular journals, as well as by publishing houses: two books by Kornilov appeared in 1988.

It comes as no surprise that the title of Kornilov's first book after nearly twenty years of silence should be Hope. He writes:

I can still drag myself along
Can't manage without a bit of hope.[6]

In another verse the poet proclaims:

I hope for glasnost,
For it and it alone . . .[7]

But glasnost has by no means assuaged his doubts and apprehensions. He writes with some bitterness about the anxieties of people unaccustomed to freedom:

I'm not ready for freedom—
I'm hardly to blame.
Since I've been at the factory
There's been nought by that name.
. . . .
What is it, then—freedom?
A pleasure-dome's bequest?
Or putting yourself last,
After all the rest?

Happiness or its lack,
Shedding envy and conceit,
Throwing open your soul,
Not wanting to cheat?

Oceans of sweat,
Workloads that kill—
But lack of freedom is
Heavier still.

For years I have waited,
Waited aching and scared.
Freedom's finally come—
And I'm not prepared.[8]

Time and again Kornilov recalls the dread years of Stalinism, linking it
with German fascism and invoking what he hopes will be irreversible
change:

> You alone please me, my age!
> I begrudge you neither strength nor zeal.
> Only give me once more your pledge and seal:
> You'll find no roads back.[9]

He demands that the reader immerse himself into the nightmarish phan-
tasmagoria of Stalinist Russia,

> . . . where no light gleams, and
> Only one freedom is given—
> To watch the naked Marika Rokk.[10]

In "The Phenomenon of Voznesensky," a delicate and skillful debunking of the former favorite of the public, the critic L. Timofeyev
demonstrates that the most important theme in Voznesensky's work,
carefully concealed behind his verbal acrobatics, is the poet's complicity
in his own inner enslavement (what Arkadi Belinkov in his book about
Yuri Olesha, called "the surrender of the intellectual").[11] In contrast to
Voznesensky, Kornilov and the other poets mentioned above are perhaps
not blessed with such linguistic brilliance, with such opulent rhythmic
talent, but in the final analysis they are superior because of the profound
moral quality of their creative work as well as their behavior.

Boris Chichibabin is over sixty, lives in the Ukrainian city of Kharkov
and to this day, despite his growing fame and readmission to the Writers
Union, continues to work as a bookkeeper in a trolley depot. A verse
of Kornilov's can serve as epigraph to his lyrics:

> Journalism pulls down the palings,
> Spreads out a roadway of brush.
> But poetry must think of eternity,
> How not to lose touch.

"Eternal" themes, "accursed" questions fill Chichibabin's lyrics; they combine an acute political sensibility with broader philosophical concerns. After nearly twenty years of enforced silence, Chichibabin reaches out (as do many others) for Christian motifs:

And thanks to the beasts, the trees, the flowers and spikes of grain,
And to humble Bach, whom we follow through tears.
And pardon to foes—not for the sake of their sweet sleep,
But for us, to be for a moment easier and free.[12]

But Chichibabin's muse rages, and his voice acquires an oratorical power, when he writes about the behavior of the vast majority of people during the Stalinist terror. The Russian literary tradition is marked by a special, almost worshipful attitude toward "the people," *narod*. (Pushkin, with his "What do the herds need with gifts of freedom?" is an exception). For Chichibabin, their silent connivance merits anger and contempt:

If the nation is still alive,
Why does it falter?
Why is it mute at the lies,
Its mouth full of water?[13]

Chichibabin's poetry is morally demanding—of itself, of "the people," of Russian writers. He accepts the mantle of his predecessors, and the traditional obligation of the Russian poet:

Fair knight and faithful prophet,
I am pierced by rays of silence.
Pushkin and Blok buttress me.
Equate me not with rhymesters.

Let me be fickle and shy in the world.
My body weak, my mind foolish.
But when I die of grief I will
Be counted in the holy assemblage.

I am a poet. That says it all.
I am released from time into eternity. . . .[14]

Chichibabin has another theme: our history, apart from and without which one cannot be a poet in Russia:

I have breathed the history of Russia.
Its pages all in blood—wherever you look . . .
The timid light of prophets and madmen
Falls quietly from gallows and block. . . .[15]

Chichibabin shares motifs of national suffering, of historical guilt and repentance with another poet, Inna Lisnyanskaya, who is of the same generation as Vladimir Kornilov. Lisnyanskaya left the Writers' Union in 1979 to protest the official campaign against the uncensored almanac *Metropol.*[16] After an involuntary interruption of seven years (from 1979 to 1986 two collections of her poetry were published abroad), her poetry finally appeared in the Soviet Union, first in the journal *Znamya*, and then in *Novy mir* and *Druzhba narodov*. Lisnyanskaya, who commands great technical virtuosity, wrote several brilliant "wreaths of sonnets," one of which is threaded with verse-epigraphs from other poets that she weaves into her own poetic weft with remarkable subtlety.[17]

As early as 1981 Lisnyanskaya wrote a poem entitled "Fire in the Swamp," anticipating Valentin Rasputin's 1985 novella *The Fire.*[18] Lisnyanskaya was one of the first to call the Brezhnev years "stifling" and "swamplike"; she understood the physical and moral damage wrought by those years before glasnost gave them an official label. In the tradition of the Golden Age of the nineteenth-century Russian intelligentsia, the symbol of whose atonement might be Ostrovsky's famous play "Guilty without Guilt,"[19] Lisnyanskaya does not absolve herself from responsibility for the horrors of the past. A historically guilty "we" reverberates in her poetry:

I will ask forgiveness in the hellish heat,
Even if God forgives me.

220

White ash on the matte raspberry-bush,
And the peatbog flushed.

In a stifling time, in a swampy flame
Long did we burn Truth's name
And burned ourselves up.
And, like a sign portended,
Cloudbursts of mercy descended.

I, a burned-out apostate,
Repent on the boggy waste,
My low voice spreading over Russia entire,
Like smoke, that once was fire.[20]

A question and a temptation confronted many creative artists in the "years of stagnation:" what to do? Remain, in the face of slander and enforced silence? Or leave the country, emigrate? For Lisnyanskaya, as in her time for Anna Akhmatova ("I closed my ears with my hands, so that a proud spirit would not be offended by such unworthy speech"), only one decision was possible:

I sneak a look around my own home.
Everything—even the pillow—threatens me with alien ways. . . .
How can I, alive, come unstuck from the place where once I sang?

Abandonment, loneliness, social exile, loss of status, all characteristic of Lisnyanskaya's verse in her "unpublished" period, move her to invoke the fate of banished nations, such as the Crimean Tatars:

Along with the mountains, the sea and the heavens I grieve:
Where are they, the people who for centuries lived here?
. . . Here only the stream murmurs in Tatar without fear,
The roof-shadows of punts float down the river bed,
Stones on the bottom, like fezzes of a coffee shade. . . .

The poetry of Lisnyanskaya, Chichibabin (who dedicates one long cycle of verse to the national cultures of Lithuania, Estonia, Latvia,

Moldavia, and the Ukraine[21]), Kornilov, and Chukhontsev, so deeply rooted in the Russian land and culture, has no taint or tinge of chauvinism: indeed, it is strikingly "universalist." As such, it belongs firmly in that humanist tradition of Russian literature of defending the weak and the victims. Lisnyanskaya takes her own pain, her personal experience of ostracism, and creates from it a "length of sorrow," a plaint for the fate of an entire people.

Inna Lisnyanskaya is a unique mediator between Old and New Testament worldviews: pride is tamed by repentance, spiritual arrogance by humility. Lisnyanskaya's rebellious nature demands action, but conscience, delicate yet strong, tempers her consciousness:

> Everywhere I look—sadness all around.
> I strike out at the glass.
> My eyes are frozen, duty-bound
> To tell the truth—no more no less.
> My heart alone is bloodied.
> My heart alone—but not my fist.

The best poets who are at long last appearing in print usually note at the end of each poem the year of its composition. Nearly every important selection of poetry therefore acquires a temporal longevity, an historical meaning. Even those poets who—unlike Kornilov, Lisnyanskaya, and Chichibabin—continued to publish during the "stagnant" years kept many works locked in their desk drawers, unable to get them past the censors. Because of the poetry now appearing from under the censors' mute, these poets are receiving new and more discerning critical attention. Thus one of the most interesting contemporary poets, Oleg Chukhontsev, managed in the course of twenty-five years of intensive work to publish only two small collections of poetry, *From Three Notebooks* and *Dormer Window*. Now each new publication of Chukhontsev's verse is an event. It was an event when his small ironic lyric "Namesake" appeared, after ten years in the drawer—a poem about a middle-aged intellectual, ruined by the suffocation of the Brezhnev years. Stifled by that "swampy fire" Lisnyanskaya describes, he has lost his moral compass, taken to drink, and hit bottom. It was an event when his poem-cycle "Common Walls" was published, containing early and unfamiliar verse as well as poems unpublished for twenty-five years. In an afterward Chukhontsev writes:

> The poet always finds himself in conflict with his times. . . . The theme of the homeland is at once the theme of time. From Lermontov's "strange love," to Nekrasov and Blok, this feeling—"of passion and of hatred for the fatherland"—is one of the most fundamental testimonies to the living dialogue of Russian poets with their times.[22]

In a poem from 1968, the year of the Prague Spring, Chukhontsev, describing the military parade drill on Red Square in the fall, hurls an angry challenge at the men in power—and not only at them. The celebrated "Just you wait!" of Pushkin's "Bronze Horseman" sounds, in the lines of this contemporary poet, like a call to the entire country:

> Who is playing with you,
> Brigandage of the new,
> Could it possibly only be Fear?
> . . . Is it not Judgment Day
> That they march all the way—
> Checkered tractors and tools disappear?
> . . . O my motherland hymned! How your glory is dimmed!
> At least give mankind half a chance.
> As He sees, in His name,
> Your imperial shame
> Stinks to Warsaw's suburban advance.
> And what now? To what strands,
> To what languages, lands,
> Will stretch out the giant that's lame?
> From the war-coffers filled
> To posterity willed—
> Could it possibly only be Shame?

From previously unpublishable poetry Chukhontsev has put together a cycle which reflects the most painful moments of recent history. Lisnyanskaya's sultry air of stagnation is, in Chukhontsev's work, not merely intolerable, but dangerous:

And the day takes aim at the temple.
And speech takes breath in the skull.
And the age turns, stuck
Like a top blundered into a funnel.
From weak-sighted Butyrki[23]
Peers a pointer's keen gaze.
And the blood-washed pupil
With malice watches the shades.

In his poetry from the late 1960s Chukhontsev underscores the desolation of that era, "a dead end, squeezed in a deadly knot," "a leaf [falling] ghostlike" (from poems dated 1967).

This poet of the "middle" generation feels himself to be a part of, and the voice for, the annihilated millions. It is in their name that he speaks, in his extraordinary 1970 "Voice Behind the Photograph," published only in 1989:

I am ash, and if I speak
I speak by right of the dead,
The flesh of those fed to the beast,
The cement grains of those worn down.
I am the dust of factories and fields,[24]
Sown through sieves
Of articles,[25] transport stops, camps,
Barracks and graves without number.

I am the earth's dust, and if dust
Stings tearless eyes,
Do not say: this is a place.
Say rather: the dead are speaking!

And don't be scared! What's a convoy
If the earth itself stands guard!
I breathe in as one. But I breathe out
From Solovki to Magadan.[26]

Politics in the most general sense impinges even on those poets considered "pure" lyricists, such as the Leningrad poet Aleksandr Kushner.

In his new collection, about a third of the poems are devoted to urgent contemporary problems. In one of them Kushner thus defines our present scene:

> Suddenly a clear day, a sudden unexpected ray,
> Like a tender word in a dark quarrel.
> Nowhere, nowhere such a sun,
> So longed for midst the gloom and sleep!
> . . . Suddenly, a bright hour in history, so sparing
> Of gentle glance and long indulgences.
> Suddenly—a loud laugh in an empty square
> And a shaft of light, playing tag.[27]

The semiofficial critics of the 1970s called Kushner's poetry "a-social," with its landscapes and lyricism (poems about butterflies and birds, flowers and trees) and his deliberate exit from the public scene. In point of fact, it was a protest against pseudocitizenship, a rejection of a meaningless if vaunted relationship between the citizen and the state. Today the most complex topical questions appear in some of Kushner's poetry, if in an essentially philosophical vein.

Thus he considers the sensitive question of judgment of the past, currently the subject of considerable debate in Soviet society. He distinguishes it from repentance, which is an inner and personal form of purification. What is needed above all, says Kushner, is the difficult kind of judgment which flows from an effort to understand how all this came to pass in our history, when people were living with the constant fear of arrest and execution:

> Easy to be an angel. Angels are not sent
> Instructors with the latest directives.
> They aren't inspired, with word or gun,
> To life, to exploits and to work.
>
> . . . I am not looking for saints.[28]

In Kushner's poetry restraint and the serenity of a kind of stoicism (for years the only possible and legal means of opposing the system) are today joined with an almost frisky, sensual joy in the times, in the flooding light of unexpected possibility.

> Like an excited boy reads a note from his girl,
> That's how we read the papers today—
> As if time itself
> Were airing out cupboards and rooms.
>
> Moscow news. . . .[29] If you only knew
> How tensely Leningrad waits for you.
> Oh rustle of pages, you eclipse the rustle of leaves,
>
> Make noise for God's sake![30]

If joy comes to so refined, subtle, and independent a poet as Kushner, adding a political cast to his lyrics, one can well imagine the state of mind of more consistently *engagé* intellectuals. Another Leningrad poet, Nonna Slepakova, takes caustic exception to Kushner, however. She replies—to the Kushner who once prided himself on his noninvolvement—that the short-lived rustle of newsprint should not be preferred to the sound of leaves:

> Everybody's interested.
> And the poet, at first
> Eager to burst with optimism, grows mute
> When the rustle of newsprint
> Is louder than the swish of falling leaves.

Nonna Slepakova takes the most rigorous, sober, and even pessimistic view of the new situation, full as it is of nearly insoluble problems and daily difficulties for the ordinary person, if not the intellectual caught up in the "newspaper" euphoria. In her poem "Rush Hour" she writes:

> Everywhere, in half-cities and towns,
> A dull droning, a rage, a madness goes down.

POETRY IN THE AGE OF PERESTROIKA AND GLASNOST
★
NATALYA B. IVANOVA

What's falling isn't snow, isn't rain,
Easier to die by rope than a bullet in the brain.

Dank greed, sweat, shaking . . .
And life squeezed out through a dropper
Between mealy spuds costing a copper
And costly private baking.

We make our slippery and crooked way
Through the meager joys of NEP's new day
Whatever we dream is just dumb,
Freedom's forced on us, newness won't come.[31]

We rage at each sign that we're right,
Hear our own words with familiar fright . . .
Pushed into heaven itself with the shove
That we know from the coppers we love.[32]

The younger generation of the poetic avant-garde—two groups called by the critics "Meta-metaphorists" (A. Yeremeyenko, A. Parshchikov, D. Prigov, I. Kutik) and "Conceptualists" (O. Sedakova, I. Zhdanov)—have also reached the public. Their poetry avoids political themes on principle, and their complex associative style has yet to win much reader interest. Mainly they interest one another; and in their hermetic self-sufficiency they have more in common with postmodernist artists than with their poetic colleagues.

There are more traditional younger poets (O. Khlebnikov, O. Nikolayeva, T. Bek, O. Yermolayeva, M. Pozdnyayev) who join the avant-gardists in rejecting both the "big" and "small" lies of the older generation but whose vision of the world and poetic style is different. Dispassionate, even cruel in their assessment of the realities of life, their work is illuminated by traditional spiritual values and hopes for the revival of humanitarian concerns. Together with the other poets mentioned in this essay, they contribute to making the current era the richest and most exciting chapter in the history of Russian poetry since the "Silver Age" of the 1920s.

—Translated by Josephine Woll

★

OLD PROBLEMS, NEW THINKING

✯

YURI DAVYDOV

I WELCOME DAVID HOLLOWAY'S ESSAY, though I may not entirely subscribe to his assessment of the reasons for changes in the Soviet vision of the world and their consequences for Soviet policy. This is in no sense to question any of the author's particular views, because in general I find his analysis highly professional, balanced, objective, and, most important, devoid of ideological prejudice. As such, it paves the way towards a better understanding of current developments in the USSR, and of how these developments may affect the course of Soviet-American relations and East-West relations in general. What I propose to do is to concentrate on those subjects that are not fully explored in Professor Holloway's essay.

First, it must be stressed that the principal points of departure for new Soviet foreign-policy thinking are—and have been from the outset—the domestic changes in the USSR itself, and that there is a causal relationship between Soviet domestic and foreign policies. Indeed, the construction of a new model of socialism, with its emphasis on humanitarian values, almost automatically leads to the elaboration of a new model of Soviet—which is to say socialist—foreign policy. The democ-

228

ratization of political life in the Soviet Union provides the basis for democratization in the area of international relations as well.

We are striving toward a socialist pluralism that has much in common with political pluralism in the West. The two are not identical, but increasingly they are linked by bridges of perception and understanding. The development of pluralism in our country has made it possible to view the political structures and decision-making processes in other countries with far greater objectivity. We are able to understand more clearly the national interests of Western countries—for instance, that they are shaped not only by monopolistic capital but by the views and interests of a wide variety of social groups.

Moreover, as Mikhail Gorbachev noted in his United Nations speech in December 1988, socialist pluralism dictates the principle of freedom of choice for all countries. This has profound implications for Soviet policy towards Eastern Europe, the West, and the Third World. Above all, it impels us to examine world developments in a historical context, and to consider socialist and capitalist societies not as adversarial, but as alternative systems, both with legitimate rights to exist, evolve, and influence each other.

Glasnost cannot be confined to the domestic sphere: there must be glasnost in foreign policy, too. Access to data on Soviet military spending, for instance, is a matter of concern not only to other countries, but to Soviet citizens as well. You cannot analyze the economic situation of a country without knowing the level of defense expenditures. You cannot reform an economy without devising a way of redistributing material resources between civilian and military production. The same is true in international relations. The policy of openness has produced a change in the Soviet approach to verification of international agreements, especially in the area of arms control, and to proposals for measures that cannot help but increase confidence and trust. The Soviet Union is far from being an altogether open country, but the imperatives of glasnost propel it in that direction.

The issue of human rights is affected in much the same way. We recognize that in spite of our very considerable achievements in the socioeconomic sphere of human rights, we still have a long way to go to improve our performance on the political level. It would be a mistake to see it only in terms of our emigration policy. It also impinges on judicial matters, on our criminal and civil legal codes. In the last analysis, our goal is to build a state based on the rule of law. Of course the Soviet

Union is far from having reached this goal, but there is widespread confidence that we are coming closer to it. And it is precisely this confidence, as well as some concrete achievements, that has cleared the way to greater cooperation between the USSR and the West during the Vienna conference on human rights, held in 1988.

The interrelationship between Soviet domestic and external policy manifests itself on the methodological level, too. As in our economy, so in our international relations quantity had far too long been one of our main criteria for success. Our foreign-policy bureaucracy took pride in having launched more international or disarmament initiatives than any country in the world—much as our ministers boasted of producing more steel, shoes, or whatever than other countries. The problem of whether their proposals were realistic or whether they could be accepted by the international community was of little concern to them. Now the Soviet Union is trying to create an economic system based on quality and satisfaction of consumer needs. Much the same is true for our foreign policy.

The point to be emphasized is that changes in our foreign policy did not come about because of the toughness of the Reagan Administration, and not only because we created difficulties for ourselves by engaging in misguided activities. They came about primarily because of the policy of perestroika, which enabled us to understand our own mistakes, to revise many of our traditional assumptions about international relations, and to set our foreign policy on a more realistic course. To repeat, our new political thinking is firmly linked to domestic changes in our country. This, above all, is what our Western partners must realize, especially when they attempt to assess the implications of perestroika for themselves.

Our new political thinking rests squarely on the premise that we live in an interconnected and interdependent world. The global problems affecting all mankind cannot be solved either by a single state or even by several states in alliance. This is true for ecology no less than for the search for security. It means that in addition to class interests and contradictions, or to national and regional interests, there are universal interests—which is to say, the interests of human beings.

The consequences of this new Soviet approach to international relations have already been enormous. Not long ago the prevailing Soviet view of the world divided it into two hostile groups—"us" and "them": *we* were the righteous ones, *they* were the villains. Once you accept this simplistic dichotomy, it is easy to accept corollary notions of confrontation, arms race, psychological warfare, and so on. But in an interconnected and interdependent world such a "black and white" vision is nothing but the enemy of international relations.

This is true for both sides. The economic crisis in the West at the beginning of the 1980s was one of the obstacles to the development of East-West trade at a time when the East was so interested in expanding it. And many Western analysts understand that the destabilization of Eastern Europe may, under certain circumstances, not be advantageous to the West. World equilibrium is very fragile, and it rests not only on military balances but on a host of political, economic, ideological, and moral factors.

The recognition of interdependence has led Soviet experts and the leadership to some ineluctable conclusions. The first is that the West and the East, facing common problems, are more partners than enemies. Both agree that it is impossible to win a nuclear war, that the drive for superiority is counterproductive, and that the arms race will in the end weaken both sides. Both agree that their common goal must be to prevent war, nuclear and conventional alike. They may disagree about how best to solve these problems, but in the last analysis this is a technical question. All this impels both sides to curb the traditional "enemy image" of each other, on the level of public opinion as well as in their actual relations. This is certainly true for the Soviet Union: we try to listen to and understand what the other side is speaking about and what it proposes. Above all, we now reject the idea that our decisions in the area of foreign policy must be based on "zero-sum-game" notions.

Having accepted the principle that not only our own but also the other side's interests must be taken into account, we have arrived at another basic conclusion—namely, that international relations should be based not on a "balance of power" but on a "balance of interests." This means that each country is obliged to consider the security of other countries no less than its own. For instance, security cannot be achieved through the unilateral accumulation of strength. In order to be lasting, it must be mutual, and in order to be mutual, it must be arrived at through common effort and a common realization of what is desirable for all parties concerned.

The same applies to the political arena. Disagreements between capitalist and socialist countries can be solved through compromise rather than by the "victory" of one's policy over the other's. The principle of "reasonable sufficiency" can be applied to international relations, too. We cannot expect that our foreign-policy aspirations will be realized in full measure—this is impossible in an interdependent world, a world that reflects and is guided by a multiplicity of interests. Our goal is not to change the other side but to arrive at mutual accommodation. We have no monopoly on truth; and neither does anyone else.

The new Soviet political thinking proceeds from common sense. The Soviet Union is prepared to use traditional foreign-policy instruments to improve international relations, while fully aware that the old spirit of confrontation and mistrust is still very much alive. To change this we need some kind of a breakthrough, one that requires the deployment not only of ordinary foreign-policy tools, but of new ones as well. Radical changes cannot be achieved without radical ideas and radical steps. And it seems that the new Soviet political thinking is predicated on the need for such steps.

This may be difficult under present conditions, especially in the light of the conservatism that now prevails in the West. Nevertheless, the measures taken by the Soviet Union can accelerate the general move towards a new system of international relations based more on cooperation than confrontation. The Soviet moratorium on nuclear weapon tests did not result in similar bans in other countries. But it helped to rekindle negotiations on this matter. The Soviet Union was absolutely sincere in Rekjavik when it proposed eliminating strategic nuclear weapons within ten years. Both sides were close to a final decision. They failed, but the world realized that we could eliminate nuclear weapons from our arsenals. And future East-West relations are bound to be affected by this possibility.

New Soviet political thinking, then, is a reality. No doubt it still faces considerable resistance both in the USSR and abroad. Yet I am convinced that it can only go forward, gradually but inexorably.

★

THE USSR AND
THE THIRD WORLD

✦

SERGO A. MIKOYAN

I HAVE BEEN ASKED BY THE EDITOR
to respond to David Holloway's chapter by addressing the question of
the new political thinking and Soviet foreign policy in the Third World.
This is a complex question, and it is not surprising that both the countries
of the Third World and the West are trying to cope with it. Many
answers, often wildly different from one another, have been offered.

Let's look at the most extreme interpretations. One is that rap-
prochement between the USSR and the United States and Moscow's
intention to deideologize its foreign interstate relations amount to a
betrayal of the interests of the developing countries. The diametrically
opposite view holds that the new political thinking disguises the same
old policies, that it is simply an attempt to deceive the West and to
continue the expansion of Soviet ideology and practice in the countries
of the Third World.

An allegorical comparison may illuminate the first point of view.
When two elephants do battle, they trample all the grass in the glade
around them. But when they make love, they trample it not one whit
less. Hence the notion that the very existence of elephants is evil, and
that no good can come from them. Similarly the popular thesis, not

exactly buttressed by either serious argument or compelling evidence, about the struggle between "two forms of imperialism." Hence too Mao's fanciful notion to set the two elephants against each other, so that afterwards a single, new elephant will come out onto the emptied glade. . . .

At the same time, how can one put together the deideologization and new political thinking with the indubitable differences in foreign policies between socialist countries and other countries? Or do such differences no longer exist?

Let us first of all recall the wisdom of the ancients: any truth can become absurd if carried too far. Deideologizing pertains to relations between governments, and not to international life as a whole. It applies to legitimate regimes—that is, regimes that are free to determine their foreign policies.

Moreover, a close look at the genealogy of the new political thinking will reveal that it represents *au fond* a coherent effort at dealing with everything that has grown up on the plot of ground cohabited by our two elephants. What has now become crystal clear is that as they clarify their relationship the elephants must think first and foremost of the ecology of that plot, that is to say our small planet.

The anecdote itself, of course, is hopelessly out of date—a product of a bipolar world. Now the elephants share the glade with a large cast of characters. A new *modus vivendi* embracing all regimes—or all except the illegitimate ones—and certainly all nations must be worked out. Moreover, the new political thinking that informs the foreign policy aspect of perestroika is a process that gradually leads to the emergence of something new, and not something that produces miracles out of the blue. We are moving step by step, the speed of the advance depending on our foreign partners. If the pace of perestroika is arduous and obstructed by considerable resistance inside the country, how much more true is it on the international arena! Yet given its significance for the survival of all of mankind, it is also the inevitable path for the foreign policies of all countries. It is a path that had in effect been chosen by many countries in the past, though not always consciously or consistently.

For understandable reasons, the process of deideologizing policies in the Third World lags behind the pace of the process in Europe, and even behind that of Soviet-US relations. But it is one that must be obligatory for all big powers. That means an end to exporting revolution—

but no less an end to exporting counterrevolution, something that is occasionally forgotten.

Does an end to ideology imply betrayal? I think not. Based as it is on a shared agreement between the superpowers, it implies the triumph of noninterventionism and respect for the sovereignty of nations. Of course skepticism comes easy: how often have we heard just such declamations, and how often have we seen illusions crumbling in the face of ugly reality. Yet there is no other way. Skeptics should keep in mind that certain things have already been accomplished. I will not rely on parallels, analogies, or "mirror-image" theories. Instead, let me offer a few randomly chosen examples:

1. Soviet troops left Afghanistan. Now it is the turn of Pakistan and the United States to fulfill the terms of the Geneva agreement.
2. South Africa obtained a judicious compromise, formalized in an agreement. It now remains to be strictly enforced.
3. The United States did not invade Nicaragua, but neither has it stopped aiding the contras. Nor did it succeed in undoing the agreements launched by President Arias of Costa Rica—in fact, it has even been forced to speak out in favor of them.
4. In Indochina there is finally some light at the end of the tunnel.

The Soviet Union is sometimes accused of sticking to its old ways whenever it is profitable for it to do so. What some who level this charge seem unable to grasp is the factor of gradual progress which I mentioned earlier. You simply don't go directly from fourth gear into reverse—it doesn't work that way. Actual policy depends not only on theory. It is the result of various forces acting on one another—in its own way a vector. One of those forces is certainly the establishment of international ties, trust in one's friends, trust in signed accords. Public opinion, especially within the USSR (though also in the world at large), is relevant as well, and tends in another direction. In the Soviet Union it has developed over many years and has become part of people's mentalities. And individual psychology is the most serious obstacle to any kind of radical change, in part because it is the preserver of tradition. Naturally some of these traditions must be preserved and some not.

It is possible that those who speak of "camouflage" would like to see in the Soviet Union's new political thinking a return to some kind of political isolationism, but this is out of the question.

The essence of the new political thinking is the priority of universal values. Such values are in no way alien to the Third World, as some suggest. Who if not the peoples of the Third World bears the brunt of such universal afflictions as hunger, disease, dearth of social services, lack of adequate educational facilities, and the like? The developed countries, including the United States to some extent, underestimate the meaning of such universal values. There are those who assume that their own values are in and of themselves universal. This is due to the persistence of certain psychological attitudes, an inability to understand the need for a global approach to certain problems, a belief in one's eternal God-given superiority and messianic mission.

Others prefer their own sort of camouflage, accepting only those elements of the new political thinking which contribute to their own security. As for the security of others or, for instance, regional conflicts, they tend to adhere to a rigid ideological stance, refusing to acknowledge the Third World's legitimate struggle for survival, and to favor the use of force. To them the concept of "revolution" is incompatible with the new political thinking and with universal values. But such an approach is out of touch with reality. Revolution does not become a universal value only when it takes place in France and America in the eighteenth century. The value of revolution as a spur to progress is not confined to specific nations and historical periods. All nations have the right to choose their own path of development. Many in the Third World are still in search of it.

Naturally the character of revolution is shaped by historical circumstances and is distinguished perhaps most of all by the degree of violence it employs. The new political thinking is clearly partial to the least amount of violence possible, if not to avoiding it altogether. Neither does it ignore the forces of history. Quite the contrary: it must count on them as much as possible precisely in order to enable universal values to prevail, to prevent the "strong" from dominating the "weak." It must not pretend to have a monopoly on the truth and must not prevent other nations from making their own choices.

There is still one more question raised by many people in various countries: how does the difficult, even critical economic situation of the Soviet Union affect its relationship with the Third World? Will it not force a radical curtailment or even cessation of support for traditional allies and friends? I am reminded of Mark Twain's famous remark, "The reports of my death are greatly exaggerated." The critical situation that exists in the USSR does not mean that this enormous country, occupying one-sixth of the earth's territory, with vast resources and potential, has become a paralytic or even an invalid.

Moreover, fundamental reform has already begun. Of course right now the regime must economize and steer clear of needless expenses. It must reexamine the question of how much money is to be spent on foreign aid. But the leadership of the country, including the parliament created in May–June 1989, will hardly consider all such outlays pointless, especially since only a small portion of that aid uses up hard-currency reserves. Most of it is spent in rubles. Whatever the figures are, they cannot compare with the waste within the country because of the absence of a self-regulating economy. The fundamental reserves and economic means lie within the country—and they substantially exceed money spent on foreign aid, which is also in many cases justified both from a moral and from a political point of view.

★

NOTES

INTRODUCTION: LEAP INTO THE UNKNOWN
ABRAHAM BRUMBERG

1. Natan Eidelman (interviewed by Vladimir Glotov), "The Optimism of Historical Knowledge," *Ogonyok*, 1988, no. 44.
2. For the "psyche" model, see, for instance, Geoffrey Gorer and John Rickman, *The People of Great Russia: A Psychological Study* (New York: Chanticleer, 1950), especially the contribution by Gorer, a British anthropologist, who traces the behavior of Soviet adults and the character of Soviet institutions to the custom of swaddling infants. Margaret Mead and Rhoda Metraux, eds. *The Study of Culture at a Distance* (Chicago: University of Chicago Press, 1953), develops the same hypothesis through an analysis of Russian culture. The "Asiatic mode of production" theory was propounded by the late historian Karl Wittfogel. See his *Oriental Despotism* (New Haven: Yale, 1957). On the "patrimonial" model, see Richard Pipes, *Russia under the Old Regime* (New York: Scribner's, 1974).
3. One of the by-products of the Hitler-Stalin Pact of 1939, for instance, was the transfer of a number of prominent German Communists into the hands of the Gestapo. See Margarete Buber, *Under Two Dictators* (London: Gollancz, 1949). Buber was a German Communist who was arrested by the Soviet secret police in 1937, together with her husband, Franz Neumann. Neumann perished in a Soviet camp, and his wife was handed over to the Gestapo in 1939. For a discussion of Soviet efforts to woo certain Latin American *caudillos*, often at the expense of local Communist parties, see Victor Alba, "Friends of the Communists: Some Curious Examples," *Problems of Communism*, 1961, no. 1, pp. 19–28.
4. For a contemporary account of labor unrest in the USSR in the 1960s, see Albert Boiter, "When the Kettle Boils Over . . . ," *Problems of Communism*, 1964, no. 1, pp. 33–43. The details of the strikes that took place at that time have now been fully disclosed in the Soviet press.
5. The attitude persists to this day. In an interview in the Paris weekly *Paris-Match*, 1 and 3 July 1989, the former Soviet philosopher and, since his emigration to the West, prolific novelist and satirist Alexander Zinoviev, asserts that Gorbachev is "not to be trusted," and that his flexibility merely disguises his thirst for absolute power and his determination to follow the same policies as Brezhnev. The Soviet system, says Zinoviev, "remains immutable."
6. Robert Byrnes, ed., *After Brezhnev* (Bloomington: Indiana University Press, 1983). The book was the product of an eighteen-month "Project on the Soviet Union in the 1980s," sponsored by the Center for Strategic and International Studies (CSIS), Washington, D.C. Thirty-five scholars—almost all of them

239

Americans—participated in it, and eight contributed essays on subjects ranging from "The Economy" to "Eastern Europe."

7. Ibid., p. 439.
8. Here are some typical examples in Byrnes's collection: "Stress on law and order, social discipline, unswerving loyalty and punitive and restrictive measures will almost certainly become more pronounced" (Seweryn Bialer, "The Political System," p. 44). "The West will face an active and expansionist foreign policy" (ibid., p. 66). "This, after all, is what is meant by 'muddling through'—little adjustment here, some trimming of aspirations there, palliative measures to defuse a few of the most threatening situations" (Robert W. Campbell, "The Economy," p. 121). "It is therefore likely that the Soviet system will evolve in more authoritarian directions and will rely on a greater degree of repression" (Gail Warshofsky Lapidus, "Social Trends," p. 245). "I foresee little likelihood of significant relaxation in political controls over cultural and intellectual life," (Maurice Friedberg, "Cultural and Intellectual Life," p. 288).
9. From the Foreword by David Abshire, head of CSIS, ibid., p. 1.
10. See the chapter by Archie Brown and the commentary by Aleksandr Vaksberg.
11. In addition to the "'interregional Group of Deputies" that emerged in the summer of 1989, the Baltic popular fronts have also made it clear that they consider themselves de facto political parties, and in December 1989 the Lithuanian parliament formally abolished the constitutional provision for the "leading role of the Communist party" and established a multiparty state. As this book goes to press, similar attempts are being launched in other republics, as well as in the USSR Supreme Soviet.
12. The tendency is displayed even by such serious historians as Walter Laqueur, who in his The Long Road to Freedom (New York: Scribners, 1989), observes that the Soviet Union is "no longer" so "predictable"—but that glasnost had passed its "heyday" (p. 281). Another scholar, Stephen Sestanovich, goes farther: Gorbachev's policies, he writes, are based on the "strategy Lenin called 'the worse, the better.' " According to Mr. Stefanovich's curious reasoning (and rather cavalier disregard for the facts), Gorbachev does indeed want to "overthrow the [old] system," but to do so by deliberately encouraging "upheaval" and "disorder . . . at home and abroad" ("Gorbachev: Beyond Our Help," New York Times, 20 Sept. 1989, p. A27). Visceral impulses play havoc with a sense for the dynamics of history: In 1987, the Russian writer Vassily Aksyonov belittled the idea that he would soon be able to return to his native land, whose "newspapers still make me nauseous" ("Through the Glasnost, Darkly," Harper's, April 1987, p. 66). Two years later, he was in Moscow for the production of two of his plays, and to be interviewed by (no longer so nauseous) Soviet papers.
13. One of the inveterate doomsayers is the British scholar Peter Reddaway (now at George Washington University, Washington, D.C.), who in his well but selectively documented essays always manages to conjure up an image of impending disaster, especially of a Gorbachev about to be unseated through the machinations of his conservative adversaries. Still wedded to the maxims of "Kremlinology," Reddaway quotes the bitter comments of some of Gorbachev's critics as "evidence" of general disillusionment on the one hand, and of a strong cabal against the general secretary on the other, without considering that disillusioned intellectuals do not represent public opinion at large and that "conservatives" do not comprise a coherent or well organized force, but rather a motley collection of russophile writers, bureaucrats loth to give up their perks

and privileges, and soi-disant *intelligenty* hankering after the good old days of Stalinist discipline. As for the danger of a "military coup," which Reddaway repeatedly stresses, all the available evidence (see, for instance, Victor Yasman, "The Internal Security Situation in the USSR," *Report on the USSR*, Radio Liberty, Munich, 18 Aug. 1989) suggests that this is an unlikely possibility, Gorbachev having carefully and firmly consolidated his power over the military and the KGB. (See Peter Reddaway, "The Threat to Gorbachev," *New York Review of Books*, 17 Aug. 1989, pp. 19–25).

THE ROAD TO REFORM
S. FREDERICK STARR

1. For instance, the famous "Novosibirsk Report" by Tatyana Zaslavskaya. (See "An Economy in Transition," by Alec Nove, in this volume. —*Ed.*)
2. "Distsiplina truda v dinamike" (The dynamism of labor discipline), *Ekonomika i organizatsia promyshlennovo proizvodstva*, 1981, no. 9, pp. 18–45.
3. Donnella H. Meadows et al. eds., *The Limits to Growth* (New York: Universe Books, 1972).
4. See review by V. Motylyov, *Voprosy ekonomiki*, 1977, no. 4, pp. 132–41.
5. V. G. Kostakov, ed., *Trudovye resursy. Sotsialno-ekonomicheski analiz* (Moscow: Ekonomika, 1976).
6. This is discussed by Myron Rush, "The Soviet Policy Favoring Arms Over Investments Since 1975," *Soviet Economy in the 1980s: Problems and Prospects* (Washington D.C.: Joint Economic Committee, 1982), pp. 319ff.
7. *Izvestia*, 5 Mar. 1977, p. 1.
8. N. Ya. Petrakov, *Kiberneticheskye problemy upravlenia ekonomiki* (Moscow: Nauka, 1974).
9. K. N. Plotnikov and A. S. Gusarev, *Metodika i praktika tsenoobrazovania* (Moscow: Finansy, 1975), pp. 189ff. See also Morris Bornstein, "Soviet Price Policy in the 1970s," *Soviet Economy in a New Perspective* (Washington D.C.: Joint Economic Committee, 1976), p. 17.
10. "Diskussiony klub" (Discussion club), *Literaturnaya gazeta*, 22 Mar. 1978, p. 10.
11. See Alice C. Gorlin, "The Power of Soviet Industrial Ministries in the 1980s," *Soviet Studies* (Glasgow), July 1985, pp. 364ff.
12. Gertrude E. Schroeder, "The Soviet Economy on a 'Treadmill of Reforms,' " *The Soviet Economy in a Time of Change*, vol. I (Washington D.C.: Joint Economic Committee, 1979), p. 312.
13. See, for instance, N. N. Diomochkin, *Vlast naroda. Formirovaniye, sostav, i deyatelnost sovetov v usloviakh razvitovo sotsializma* (Moscow: Nauka, 1978); also Diomochkin, *Sovershenstvovat rabotu sovetov* (Moscow: Nauka, 1978).
14. Anne Lane, "USSR: Private Agriculture on Center Stage," *The Soviet Economy in the 1980s: Problems and Prospects*, vol. II (Washington, D.C.: Joint Economic Committee, 1982), p. 23ff.
15. See, e.g., N. Kozlov, "Ekonomicheski mekhanizm i brigady novovo tipa," *Ekonomicheskaya gazeta*, 1980, no. 45, p. 6.
16. "Statya 17: spektrum mneni," *Pravda*, 23 Aug. 1977, p. 3.
17. E. Vostrukhov, "Kafe bez bukhgaltera," *Izvestia*, 3 Feb. 1980, p. 3.
18. See Marshall I. Goldman, "Autarky or Integration—The USSR in the World Economy," *The Soviet Economy in the 1980s: Problems and Prospects*, vol. I (Washington D.C.: Joint Economic Committee, 1982), pp. 81ff.
19. Robert V. Daniels, "Soviet Politics Since Khrushchev," *The Soviet Union Under*

Brezhnev and Kosygin, John W. Strong, ed. (New York: Van Nostrand, 1971, pp. 16–25.

20. Andrei Sakharov, *My Country and the World,* transl. Guy V. Daniels (New York: Knopf, 1975), p. 13.
21. For more on the pre-Gorbachev discussions on legal reform, see essay by William E. Butler in this volume. —*Ed.*
22. *Pravda,* 5 Oct. 1977, p. 3.
23. R. A. Safarov, "Politicheski status obshchestvennovo mnenia," *Sotsiologicheskye issledovania,* 1979, no. 4, pp. 11ff.
24. For a comprehensive review of this discussion, see Robert S. Sharlet, *The New Soviet Constitution of 1977: Analysis and Text* (Brunswick, Ohio: King's Court Communications, 1978).
25. "Partinaya rabota," *Partinaya zhizn,* 1977, no. 7, pp. 17ff.
26. See, for example, the many articles on alchoholism and its social roots in *Zaria vostoka,* beginning on 16 Oct. 1979, or the articles attacking nationalism, but at the same time explaining it, in *Sovietskaia Litva,* beginning on 16 Apr. 1978.
27. Yevgeni Fastovets, *Zhurnalist,* 1977, no. 6, pp. 34–35.
28. S. Tsukasov, "Sovetskaya pechat," *Kommunist,* 1977, no. 7.
29. This flowered into an illegal movement for free trade unions. See Kevin Klose, *Russia and the Russians: Inside the Closed Society* (New York: Norton, 1984), pp. 53–91. More current is Elizabeth Teague, *Solidarity and the Soviet Worker,* (London: Croom Helm, 1988).
30. S. Frederick Starr, *Red and Hot: The Fate of Jazz in the Soviet Union* (New York: Oxford, 1983), pp. 275–88.
31. Schroeder, "Soviet Economy on Treadmill."

RECONSTRUCTING THE SOVIET POLITICAL SYSTEM
ARCHIE BROWN

1. See, for example, Ronald J. Hill, *Political Science, Soviet Politics and Reform* (London: Martin Robinson, 1980), esp. Ch. 2. (See also essay by S. Frederick Starr. —*Ed.*)
2. See Giovanni Sartori, "Concept Misformation in Comparative Politics," *American Political Science Review,* 1970, no. 4; and Valerie Bunce, "The Political Economy of the Brezhnev Era: The Rise and Fall of Corporatism," *British Journal of Political Science,* Vol. 13, pt. 2, April 1983.
3. Following the Brezhnev years in which Khrushchev was rarely mentioned, and never positively, a number of sympathetic reappraisals of the part played by Khrushchev in Soviet history have appeared in Soviet publications. For a notable example see Fyodor Burlatsky, "Khrushchev," in Yuri Afanasev, ed., *Inovo ne dano* (Moscow: Progress, 1988). The first meeting in the Soviet Union entirely devoted to a consideration of Khrushchev's virtues and achievements as well as his faults was held in the auditorium of the Cinematographers' Union on 16 Apr. 1989. It was attended by almost a thousand people and addressed by writers, historians, and survivors of Stalin's prison camps.
4. For an account of the crosscurrents, see Abraham Brumberg, "Moscow: The Struggle for Reform," *New York Review of Books,* 30 Mar. 1989, pp. 37–42.
5. Bogomolov at a press conference reported in BBC Summary of World Broadcasts, 10 Feb. 1989; Burlatsky in "Problemy razrabotki kontseptsii sovremennovo sotsializma," *Voprosy filosofii,* 1988, no. 11, pp. 31–71.
6. Medvedev in *Pravda,* 5 Oct. 1988, p. 4; and Gorbachev in *Pravda,* 26 Nov. 1989, pp. 1–3.

7. Gennadi Lisichkin, in a Soviet television broadcast on 3 July 1987, as reported in BBC SWB, 11 July 1987.
8. Ye. A. Ambartsumov, in "Problemy razrabotki kontseptsii sovremennovo sotsializma," *Voprosy filosofii*, 1988, no. 11, pp. 31–71.
9. See chapter by David Holloway. —*Ed.*
10. Ambartsumov, "Problemy razrabotki kontseptsii."
11. G. Shakhnazarov, "Nauka o politike," *Pravda*, 26 Sept. 1988, p. 6.
12. See my chapter, "Ideology and Political Culture," in Seweryn Bialer, ed., *Politics, Society and Nationality Inside Gorbachev's Russia* (Boulder: Westview, 1989) for a discussion of the first of these. I deal with the second somewhat more fully in "Political Change in the Soviet Union," *World Policy Journal*, 1989, no. 3.
13. S. Ye. Deitsev and I. G. Shablinsky, "Rol politicheskikh institutov v uskorenii sotsialno-ekonomicheskovo razvitia," *Sovetskoye gosudarstvo i pravo*, 1987, no. 7, p. 120.
14. Communist party members number about 20 million, out of a total Soviet population of around 286 million.
15. Sergei Andreyev, "Struktura vlasti i zadachi obshchestva," *Neva*, 1989, no. 1, pp. 144–73. Andreyev's views were echoed by a number of speakers at the First Congress of People's Deputies.
16. Ibid., p. 159.
17. See *Izvestia TsK KPSS*, 1989, no. 1, pp. 81–88, esp. p. 87. The appearance of this journal (News of the Central Committee of the CPSU) is in itself a remarkable event.
18. Vladimir Lakshin, "From Glasnost to Freedom of Speech," *Moscow News*, 1989, no. 15, p. 4.
19. Ibid.
20. See essay by Ronald Suny and commentaries by Julian Bromley and Leonid Batkin in this volume. —*Ed.*
21. See essay by Alec Nove and commentary by Otto Latsis in this volume. —*Ed.*
22. Tatyana Zaslavskaya, "O strategii sotsialnovo upravlenia perestroikoi," in Afanasev, *Inovo ne dano*, 9–50, on p. 10.
23. See essay by Jutta Scherrer in this volume. —*Ed.*
24. *Literaturnaya gazeta*, 25 Jan. 1989, p. 2.
25. Ibid. The *veche* was a town assembly in medieval Russia which in some places shared power with a local prince, but which in Novgorod and Pskov enjoyed full sovereignty.
26. Ibid.

AN ECONOMY IN TRANSITION
ALEC NOVE

1. Nikolai Shmelyov, "Avansy i dolgi," *Novy mir*, 1987, no. 6.
2. E. Gaidar, in *Kommunist*, 1989, no. 2.
3. Gavriil Popov, "The Administrative System," *Nauka i zhizn* (Science and life), Moscow, 1987, no. 4.
4. Shmelyov, "Novye trevogi," *Novy mir*, 1988, no. 4, p. 167.
5. E. Gaidar, *Kommunist*, 1989, no. 2.
6. See my *Soviet Agriculture: The Brezhnev Legacy and Gorbachev's Cure* (Los Angeles: Rand/UCLA, 1988).
7. Alec Nove, "On Success Indicators in Soviet Industry," *Economica* (London), Jan. 1958.

8. For detailed surveys, see my "Soviet Industrial Reorganization," and Gregory Grossman, "Communism in a Hurry: The 'Time Factor' in Soviet Economics," in A. Brumberg, ed., *Russia Under Khrushchev* (New York: Praeger, 1962), pp. 189–218; also my article "Problems of Economic Destalinization," *Problems of Communism*, 1957, no. 2, pp. 15–22.

9. Indeed, this author did so in an article called "The Economic Problems of Brezhnev's Successors," *Washington Papers* (Washington, D.C.: Center for Strategic and International Studies, 1978).

10. For more on the discussions about the Soviet economy during the Brezhnev period, see essay by Frederick S. Starr. —Ed.

11. Leonid Abalkin, *Moscow News*, 26 June 1988, p. 9. Since that time, incidentally, numerous other articles by prominent Soviet economists, such as Gavriil Popov, Otto Latsis, Vasili Selyunin, have voiced grave concern about lack of progress.

12. See, for example, *Voprosy ekonomiki*, 1987, no. 6.

13. *Ogonyok*, 1987, no. 25.

14. The minister of finance has finally admitted that the budget has been in deficit for years, and that no less than 100 billion rubles of expenditure in 1989 is to be covered by advances from the State Bank. As a percentage of GNP, this is over three times the US deficit.

15. *Literaturnaya gazeta*, 1988, no. 18.

16. See, for example, the interview with Vasily Seliunin, *Sovetskaya Estonia*, 27 March 1989.

17. Gavriil Popov and Nikolai Shmelyov, *"Anatomia defitsita"* (The Anatomy of the Deficit), *Znamya*, May 1988, p. 180.

18. A. Rakitsky, in *Voprosy ekonomiki*, 1988, no. 10.

19. A. Sergeyev, in *Voprosy ekonomiki*, 1988, no. 7.

20. Aleksandr Bovin, "More Consistency," *Moscow News*, 1989, no. 1, p. 3.

TOWARDS THE RULE OF LAW
WILLIAM E. BUTLER

1. S. A. Kotlyarevsky, *Pravovoye gosudarstvo i vneshnyaya politika*, 1909, p. 338. Also see N. Khlebnikov, *Pravo i gosudarstvo v ikh oboyudnykh otnosheniakh*, 1874.

2. M. Baglai, "Tolko zakon," *Izvestia*, 1 Sept. 1988, p. 3.

3. V. Nersesyants, a participant in the roundtable "Vlast i pravo," *Chelovek i zakon*, 1988, no. 10, p. 12. Andrei Vyshinsky, who earned his spurs as the ruthless and vituperative prosecutor at the trials of Old Bolsheviks in the mid-1930s, was later bestowed with sundry honors, including the Order of Lenin and the Stalin Prize, and held several important government jobs until his death in 1954. In his book *Teoria sudebnykh dokazatelstv v sovetskom prave* (The Theory of Legal Evidence in Soviet Law), he decried the concept of "presumption of innocence" as "bourgeois," and asserted that confessions by the accused "inevitably assume the nature and significance of basic evidence." See Arkadi Vaksberg, "Morality and the Law: The Queen of Evidence," *Literaturnaya gazeta*, 27 Jan. 1989, p. 13.

4. See the amendments published in *Izvestia*, 3 Dec. 1988 and 23, 26, and 28 Dec. 1989.

5. Roundtable, note 3 above. Presumably the resistance originated in senior party circles.

6. V. M. Savitsky in the roundtable, note 3 above, p. 69.

7. Ibid.

8. V. Yakovlev in the roundtable, note 3 above, pp. 11, 24.
9. Note 2 above, col. 1.
10. Ibid., cols. 1–2.
11. Ibid., col. 2.
12. O. Kutafin in the roundtable, note 3 above, p. 12.
13. Ibid., p. 16.
14. V. A. Tumanov, quoted in "Pravovoye gosudarstvo—kak dolzhno byt," *Pravda*, 2 August 1988, p. 1.
15. Ibid., p. 2.
16. V. N. Kudryavtsev, quoted in "Pravovoye gosudartsvo," p. 2.
17. The law is translated in W. E. Butler, "Soviet Legislation on Judicial Review of Unlawful Actions by Officials," *Coexistence*, 1988, pp. 129–33.
18. V. Perevalov in the roundtable, note 3 above, p. 15.
19. Savitsky in the roundtable, note 3 above, p. 70.
20. Ibid., p. 71.
21. V. Sirenko in the roundtable, note 3 above, p. 71.
22. Perevalov in the roundtable, note 3 above, p. 73.
23. Nersesyants in the roundtable, note 3 above, p. 73.
24. See P. Lebedev, "Konstitutsionny nadzor: Kakim yemu byt," *Izvestia*, 13 November 1988, p. 2.
25. Savitsky in the roundtable, note 3 above, p. 77.
26. M. S. Strogovich, *Kurs sovetskovo ugolovnovo protsessa*, vol I (1968), p. 331.
27. See H. J. Berman, *Justice in the U.S.S.R.*, rev. ed., 1963, p. 71.
28. On the numerous ways that the presumption of innocence can affect the model of criminal justice, depending on the role the presumption is deemed to perform, see G. Fletcher, "The Presumption of Innocence in the Soviet Union," *UCLA Law Review*, vol. 15, pp. 1203–25.
29. Yu. Feofanov "Vlast i pravo," *Izvestia*, 21 June 1988, p. 3.
30. See commentary by Arkadi Vaksberg. —*Ed.*

HISTORY RECLAIMED
JUTTA SCHERRER

1. *Pravda*, 14 Feb. 1987.
2. Aleksandr Nekrich, *22 June 1941* (Moscow: Nauka, 1965).
3. *New York Times*, 21 Mar. 1966; p. 2. The letter appeared in 1988 in *Ogonyok*.
4. See Leopold Labedz and Max Hayward, "Writers in Prison," and Abraham Brumberg, " 'Traitors in the Dock,' " *Problems of Communism*, 1966, no. 2, pp. 65–78.
5. *Voprosy istorii KPSS*, 1987, no. 7, pp. 137–52.
6. See the excellent article by Thomas Sherlock, "Politics and History under Gorbachev" (*Problems of Communism*, July–August 1988), for other reasons why historical revisionism is necessary for Gorbachev.
7. At its first session in June 1989, the Congress of People's Deputies created a commission to examine the Stalin-Hitler Pact and the incorporation of the Baltic republics into the USSR, headed by Aleksandr Yakovlev, and including, among others, the historian Roy Medvedev. (In December 1989, the USSR Supreme Soviet formally condemned the pact and declared it null and void.)
8. *Znamya*, 1987, no. 12.
9. *Teatr*, 1986, no. 6.
10. *Novy mir*, 1987, no. 4.
11. See David Joravsky's excellent review of Shatrov's plays and their particular

genre in "Glasnost Theater," *New York Review of Books*, 10 Nov. 1988, pp. 34–39.

12. Shatrov was reproached for "defeatism" by three historians who sharply attacked his play in *Pravda*, 15 Feb. 1987.

13. See note 11 above.

14. Alexis Berelowitch, "Mikhail Chatrov," *Quinzaine litteraire*, Dec. 1987, pp. 27–28.

15. *Druzhba narodov*, 1987, nos. 4–6.

16. *Neva*, Leningrad, 1987, nos. 1–4.

17. *Novy mir*, 1987, nos. 1–3.

18. *Don*, 1987, nos. 1–3.

19. *Znamya*, 1986, nos. 10–11.

20. *Oktyabr*, 1988, nos. 1–3; published in English in 1988.

21. By the second half of 1989, *Gulag Archipelago* and other Solzhenitsyn works were appearing serially in Soviet journals. —Ed.

22. *Nedelya*, 1989, no. 16.

23. See the summary of Afanasev's speech at the Harriman Institute, 17 Oct. 1988, "The Revolution in Soviet Historiography," *At the Harriman Institute* (Columbia University), 1988, no. 4.

24. "Osnovnye etapy raskrytia sovetskovo obshchestva," *Kommunist*, 1987, no. 10, pp. 66–79.

25. "Krugly stol: Sovetski soyuz v 20-ye gody," *Voprosy istorii*, 1988, no. 9, pp. 3–115.

26. See essay by Alec Nove in this volume. —Ed.

27. See commentary by Otto Latsis in this volume. —Ed.

28. For two first versions see *Vek XX i mir*, 1987, no. 8; and *Rabochi klass i sovremenny mir*, 1988, no. 1. The third version, cited here, appeared in Afanasev, *Inovo ne dano*, 1988, pp. 297–323.

29. V. I. Lenin, *Polnoye sobraniye sochineni*, 5th ed., vol. 45, p. 356. The topic of Lenin's last notes was taken up by Yegor Yakovlev in *Moscow News*, 1989, no. 4.

30. "Istoki," *Novy mir*, 1988, no. 5, pp. 162–89.

31. Nikolai Popov, "Is Anyone Above the Law?" *Sovetskaya kultura*, 26 Apr. 1988.

32. *Voprosy filosofii*, 1987, no. 11, pp. 31–71.

33. *Nauka i zhizn*, 1988, nos. 11 and 12, and 1988, nos. 1 and 2. In an interview published in the popular weekly *Nedelya* (1989, no. 11), Tsipko repeated and elaborated upon his views.

34. *Izvestia*, 4 June 1989.

35. Another example of the steadily exanding criticism of Lenin and his policies is found in Vyacheslav Kostikov, *Ogonyok*, 19 June 1989, no. 22, which, in criticizing Soviet press censorship in general, singles out Lenin's decree of 27 October 1917, on the suppression of "bourgeois periodicals," showing that it led to the eventual suppression of all non-Bolshevik publications. The NEP under Lenin also comes in for its share of criticism. Kostikov mentions in particular the expulsion without trial of a group of leading Russian philosophers in 1922, among them Nikolai Berdyaev, Father Sergei Bulgakov, and Semyon Frank. —Ed.

36. *Literaturnaya gazeta*, 17 May 1989, finally published the figures on the deportations of national groups in 1943–44. According to the article, about 200,000 Chechen and Ingush, more than 120,000 Kalmyks (nearly half of the total Kalmyk population), 40,000 Karachais (more than one-third of the total

NOTES
★

number of Karachais), and more than 20,000 Balkars (nearly half of the total) died either in transit or in exile. The article does not provide any statistics on the Crimean Tatars and the Meskhetians, nationalities that were uprooted in their entirety in 1943–44, or on the approximately 800,000 Volga Germans deported in 1941–42, but it is safe to assume that eventually these figures, too, will be disclosed. —*Ed.*

37. Yurasov's speech was reported in the Western press, and later cited and commented upon in an article by V. Chalikova in *Neva*, 1988, no. 10.
38. See, for instance, the article "The Murderers Wore NKVD Uniforms," *Moscow News*, 1988, no. 48.
39. Danilov, in *Voprosy istorii*, 1988, no. 3.
40. For Shmelyov, see his "Avansy i dolgi," *Novy mir*, 1987, no. 6. Figures not even any Western historians had ever cited were produced in Oct. 1988 by Fyodor Volkov, a professor at the Moscow Institute for International Relations: 18 million died during the Civil War, 22 million during collectivization, 33– 35 million in World War II, 6 million during the Stalinist terror after the war (see *Die Zeit*, 4 Nov. 1988, no. 45).
41. See *Moscow News*, 1988, no. 48, pp. 8–9.
42. Ibid., p. 11.
43. For the exchange between Afanasev and his critics, see *Moscow News*, 1987, no. 2.
44. Since that time, Stalin's role as Trotsky's assassin has been disclosed, first by *Literaturnaya gazeta*, 1989, no. 1, which named the Soviet secret police agent who provided the assassin with $5000 and a false passport. In addition, Trotsky's works are gradually being republished, often with laudatory comments. Thus in his preface to excerpts from Trotsky's biography of Stalin, the historian Nikolai Vasetsky praised Trotsky for his "undeviating struggle against Stalin's tyranny" (*Argumenty i fakty*, 1989, no. 34); and in an introduction to one of Trotsky's articles on Lenin, the historian Vitali Startsev denounced the anti-Semitic attacks on Trotsky that appear in various nationalist journals, noting that "Trotsky belongs entirely to Russian culture and Russian literature." Furthermore, he said, it was Lenin far more than Trotsky who was responsible for the terror of the Civil War (*Rodina*, 1989, no. 7). —*Ed.*
45. See Afanasev's contribution to a round-table discussion held in 1987 under the auspices of the journal *Istoria SSSR* (1988, no. 1), on the subject of "Soviet non-Marxist Historiography and Soviet historical science." See also Afanasev's contribution to *Inovo ne dano*, note 28 above, p. 506.
46. See *Knizhnoye obozreniye* (Review of books), 1988, no. 38, pp. 7–10.
47. L. G. Yonin, in an essay on the film "Repentance," *Sotsiologicheskoye issledovania*, 1987, nos. 5–6, pp. 62–72.
48. See note 7 above.
49. Mikhail Gorbachev, *Oktyabr i perestroika*, Moscow, 1987, pp. 31–32.

NATIONALITIES AND NATIONALISM
RONALD SUNY

1. This point about Armenians viewing Sumgait through the lens of genocide has been made by several observers and journalists, most persuasively by Nora Dudwick, an American anthropologist who spent much of 1987–88 in Yerevan, in "The Karabakh Movement—An Old Scenario Gets Rewritten," a paper presented to a conference on Soviet Armenia at the University of Pennsylvania, 8 Oct. 1988.

2. Armenians had lived in eastern Anatolia, now the eastern part of the Republic of Turkey, since the sixth century B.C. In ancient and medieval times this mountainous plateau was home to numerous Armenian principalities and kingdoms. The last independent Armenian kingdom fell in 1375, after which the entire plateau became part of the Ottoman Empire. Over the next few centuries the Christian population was Turkicized, and by the nineteenth century Armenians were a minority in the territory that had once been the center of their political existence. Current-day Soviet Armenia had formerly been an Armenian enclave in the Iranian empire, annexed by Russia in the early nineteenth century. After the genocidal massacres and deportations of 1915, Russian Armenia was the only area that possessed a compact Armenian population. In 1918 it became an independent republic; in 1920 it became the Armenian Soviet Socialist Republic. (For a brief history of modern Armenia, see Ronald Grigor Suny, *Armenia in the Twentieth Century* [Chico, Cal.: Scholars Press, 1983].)

3. For a detailed chronology and documents on the first phase of the Karabakh crisis, see Gerard J. Libaridian, ed., *The Karabakh File: Documents and Facts on the Question of Mountainous Karabakh, 1918–88* (Toronto: Zoryan Institute, 1988).

4. James E. Mace, "Famine and Nationalism in Soviet Ukraine," *Problems of Communism*, 1984, no. 3, pp. 37–50; Robert Conquest, *The Harvest of Sorrow: Soviet Collectivization and the Terror-Famine* (New York: Oxford University Press, 1986). For revisions of earlier estimates of the numbers of victims, see Barbara A. Anderson and Brian D. Silver, "Demographic Analysis and Population Catastrophes in the USSR," *Slavic Review*, 1985, no. 3, pp. 517–36.

5. *Vechernyaya Kazan*, 5 Sept. 1988, p. 2.

6. For a fuller discussion of the low level of development of nationalism during the revolution and civil war, see Ronald Grigor Suny, "Nationalism and Class as Factors in the Revolution of 1917," in Edith Rogovin Frankel and Jonathan Frankel, eds., *From February to October: A Reassessment of the Russian Revolution of 1917* (forthcoming).

7. Moshe Lewin, *Lenin's Last Struggle* (New York: Pantheon Books, 1968).

8. James E. Mace, *Communism and the Dilemmas of National Liberation: National Communism in Soviet Ukraine, 1918–33* (Cambridge, Mass.: Ukrainian Research Institute, 1983).

9. Zvi Y. Gitelman, *Jewish Nationality and Soviet Politics: The Jewish Sections of the CPSU, 1917–30* (Princeton: Princeton University Press, 1974). It must be noted, however, that the encouragement of Jewish culture excluded the Hebrew language and all other aspects considered to be "clerical" or "nationalistic."

10. Aleksandr M. Nekrich, *The Punished Peoples: The Deportation and Tragic Fate of Soviet Minorities at the End of the Second World War*, trans. George Saunders (New York: Norton, 1978).

11. *Moscow News*, 1988, no. 14; *Pravda*, 23 Jan. 1988.

12. The long tenure of first secretaries in the Central Asian republics encouraged illegal activity and cronyism. In Uzbekistan, Sharaf Rashidov ruled from 1959 until his death in 1983; in Tajikistan, Jabar Rasulov ran the party from 1961 until his death in 1982; Turdakun Usubaliev was party chief in Kirgizia from 1961 to 1985; Dinmukhammed Kunayev headed the Kazakh party from 1964 until his removal by Gorbachev in December 1986; and Mukhamednazar Gapurov headed the Turkmen Communist party from 1969 to 1985. In the Soviet west the situation was not dissimilar: Pyotr Masherov in Belorussia (1965–

83), Ivan Bodyul in Moldavia (1961–80), I. G. Kebin in Estonia (1950–78), August Voss in Latvia (1966–84), and P. P. Grishkiavichius in Lithuania (1974–87).

13. Gerald Mars and Yochanan Altman, "The Cultural Bases of Soviet Georgia's Second Economy," *Soviet Studies*, 1983, no. 4, pp. 546–60.

14. On Lenin's views, see his article "O natsionalnoi gordosti velikorossov," *Polnoye sobraniye sochineni*, 5th ed. (Moscow: 1961), pp. 106–10. On Lenin's disagreements with Stalin regarding the incorporation of Georgia and other national republics into the RSFSR, see Yegor Yakolev, "The Last Act—Synopsis of Vladimir Lenin's Final Drama," *Moscow News*, 1989, no. 4, pp. 1, 8–9.

15. Since then, other nationalist groups have emerged in Russia. —*Ed.*

LYRICS: THE PAIN OF DISCOVERY
VERA DUNHAM

1. In *Penguin Book of Russian Verse* (London: Penguin, 1962), pp. 132–33. I have slightly emended Dimitri Obolensky's translation.

2. Ilya Fonyakov, untitled poem in *Den poezii* (Day of Poetry) (Leningrad: 1978). Unless otherwise specified, the translations in this essay are my own.

3. Dmitri Prigov, untitled poem, tr. Sally Baird, in *Index on Censorship*, June–July 1978, p. 11.

4. Anatoli Pristavkin, *I nochevala tuchka zolotaya* (And a Golden Cloud Spent the Night), *Znamya*, 1987, nos. 3 and 4.

5. Anatoli Pristavkin, "Let Bygones Be Bygones, but Not Dead," *Moscow News*, 1987, no. 9, p. 10.

6. Vladimir Admoni, *Iz dolgoty dnei* (From the Length of Days) (Leningrad: 1984), p. 76.

7. Yuri Voronov, *Blockada* (Blockade) (Leningrad: 1986), p. 6.

8. Yulia Drunina, untitled poem in *Den poezii* (Day of Poetry) (Moscow: 1970), p. 73.

9. Aleksandr Mezhirov, *Vremena* (Times) (Moscow: 1976), p. 66.

10. Aleksandr Mezhirov, untitled poem in *Novy mir*, 1988, no. 5, p. 6.

11. Yevgeni Yevtushenko, untitled poem in *Pochti naposledom* (Almost at the End) (Moscow: 1985), pp. 46–47.

12. Olga Berggolts, untitled poem in *Ogonyok*, 1987, no. 12.

13. The word here is *sueta*. It has an eighteenth-century flavor and is, alas, impervious to translation. One wishes it were *sham*, but it isn't.

14. Vitali Korotich, untitled poem dated 1969 in *Izbrannoye* (Selected Works) (Moscow: 1986), p. 70. This poem, like many others, was beautifully translated from the Ukrainian into Russian by the Ukrainian poet Yunna Moritz.

15. Valentin Rasputin, "Pozhar" (Fire), in *Nash sovremennik*, 1985, no. 7, p. 47.

16. Andrei Yudin, untitled poem in *Istoki* (Sources), an almanac (Moscow: 1986), p. 339. Yudin's poem echoes, almost certainly with full deliberation, a famous 1912 poem by Anna Akhmatova:

> He loved three things in this world:
> Choir chants at vespers, albino peacocks,
> And worn, weathered maps of America.
> And he did not love children crying,
> Or tea served with raspberries,
> Or women's hysteria.
> . . . And I was his wife.

17. Yuri Nesterov, "For the First Time," in *Den poezii* (Kuibyshev: 1985), p. 208.
18. Aleksandr Dorin, "To My Daughter," in *Istoki* (Moscow: 1986), pp. 368–69.
19. Irina Moiseyeva, untitled poem in the cycle "Zhizn bespodobna" (Inimitable Life), in *Debut*, an almanac (Leningrad: 1987), p. 225.
20. Maya Borisova, untitled poem in *Den poezii* (Leningrad: 1984), p. 29.
21. Lyudmila Barbas, untitled poem in *Den poezii* (Leningrad: 1984), pp. 104–5.
22. Nadezhda Polyakova, untitled poem in *Den poezii* (Leningrad: 1984), p. 71.
23. Valentina Yudina, untitled poem in *Istoki* (Moscow: 1986), pp. 308–9.
24. Natalya Babitskaya, untitled poem in *Poezia*, 1985, no. 41, p. 144.
25. Nina Ostrovskaya, untitled poem in *Subda* (Destiny) (Leningrad: 1987), p. 71.
26. Assia Veksler, untitled poem in *Den poezii* (Leningrad: 1984), p. 27.

LEARNING TO LIVE AND LET LIVE
DAVID HOLLOWAY

1. The Independent Commission on Disarmament and Security Issues, *Common Security—A Blueprint for Survival* (New York: Simon and Schuster, 1982).
2. E. A. Shevardnadze's speech to a meeting of the *aktiv* of the Diplomatic Academy, the Institute of International Relations, and the Central Apparatus of the USSR Foreign Ministry, 27 June 1987, *Vestnik Ministerstva Inostrannykh Del SSSR*, 26 Aug. 1987, p. 31.
3. The Basic Principles Agreement was signed in 1972. It committed the Soviet Union and the United States to peaceful coexistence and mutual restraint in their relations with each other.
4. Vyacheslav Dashichev, "Vostok-Zapad: Poisk novykh otnosheni" (East-West: The Search for New Relations), *Literaturnaya gazeta* 18 May 1988, p. 14.
5. A. V. Nikiforov, "Mirnoye sosushchestvovaniye i novoye myshleniye" (Peaceful Coexistence and the New Thinking), *SShA-Ekonomika, Politika, Ideologia*, 1987, no. 12; p. 8.
6. "Soveshchaniye voyenachalnikov v Kremle" (Meeting of Military leaders in the Kremlin), *Pravda*, 28 Oct. 1982, p. 1.
7. Speech of E. A. Shevardnadze to a Foreign Ministry Conference on "The Nineteenth Party Conference: Foreign Policy and Diplomacy," *Vestnik Ministerstva Inostrannykh Del SSSR*, 15 Aug. 1988, p. 33.
8. Statement by General Secretary of the Central Committee, CPSU, and Chairman of the Presidium of the Supreme Soviet of the USSR, Yu. V. Andropov, *Pravda*, 29 Sept. 1983, p. 1.
9. On this debate see Stephen Shenfield, *The Nuclear Predicament*, Chatham House Papers no. 37 (London: Royal Institute of International Affairs, 1987), pp. 23–47.
10. "Beseda M. S. Gorbacheva s gruppoi deyatelei mirovoi kultury" (Conversation of M. S. Gorbachev with a group of world cultural figures), *Pravda*, 21 Oct. 1986, p. 1.
11. Shevardnadze, p. 32.
12. "Za delo—bez raskachki" (To business without Delay), *Pravda*, 6 Aug. 1988, p. 2.
13. "Sovremennaya kontseptsia sotsializma: Mezhdunarodnaya nauchnaya konferentsia" (The Contemporary Concept of Socialism: An International Scientific Conference), *Pravda*, 5 Oct. 1988, p. 4.
14. Shevardnadze, p. 34.
15. N. V. Ogarkov, *Istoria uchit bditelnost* (History Teaches Vigilance) (Moscow: Voyenizdat, 1985), p. 47.

16. "O voyennoi doktrine gosudarstv-uchastnikov Varshavskovo Dogovora" (On the military doctrine of the member states of the Warsaw Pact), *Pravda*, 30 May 1987, p. 1.
17. For a review of these debates, see my article "Gorbachev's New Thinking," *Foreign Affairs*, Jan. 1989, pp. 66–81.
18. As Marshal S. Akhromeyev told *Moscow News* after his removal as Chief of the General Staff, "There is a limit to unilateral reductions." *Moscow News*, Feb. 1989, p. 5.
19. *Pravda*, 31 May 1989, p. 2.

TOWARDS A NEW MODEL OF SOCIALISM
BORIS KURASHVILI

This commentary is based on a longer article that appeared in the journal *Vek XX i mir*, 1989, no. 4.

1. The Luddites were English workers who in 1811–16 smashed textile machines, which they held responsible for high unemployment. —*Ed.*

PERESTROIKA AND THE PRIMACY OF POLITICS
GAVRIIL POPOV

1. Gavriil Popov coined the term "administrative system" in an essay published in *Nauka i zhizn*, 1984, no. 4. It has come to be used by many Soviet writers for the ruling machine created by Stalin and still not fully dismantled. —*Ed.*
2. For years, the kolkhoz has been used as a source for feeding the city; forced deliveries, corvées, and laws tying the peasant to the land all caused the countryside to sink into economic and social misery. Attempts to build roads and hospitals or to provide children with adequate schooling had usually come to naught. —*Ed.*
3. The *ispolkom* is the executive committee of a local soviet, the organ of state authority. —*Ed.*
4. The Law on Enterprises, enacted in 1987, is supposed to provide enterprises with the freedom to plan their own inputs and outputs on a strict cost-accounting basis, and without interference from central ministries. Most Soviet economists, as well as numerous enterprise managers, agreed that the law left enough loopholes in it to permit the ministries to impose obligatory plans upon enterprises. In 1989, the law was strengthened by the Supreme Soviet. —*Ed.*
5. The reform of 1861, which abolished serfdom, nevertheless still deprived the peasant of full civil rights (including property rights), in fact making him completely dependent on the government bureaucracy. Other and more thorough reforms were enacted between 1864 and 1874. —*Ed.*

LEGAL REFORMS AND BASIC PRINCIPLES
ARKADI VAKSBERG

1. Valeri Savitsky, of the Institute of State and Law, Moscow, has written widely about criminal law in the USSR. —*Ed.*
2. See references to Professor Baglai in the chapter by William Butler. —*Ed.*
3. *Izvestia*, 11 June 1989.

THE RISE OF ETHNIC ASSERTIVENESS
JULIAN BROMLEI

1. In the Soviet Union, Kazakhstan is not formally considered part of Central Asia. —*Ed.*

NOTES
★

AT A FATEFUL FORK IN THE ROAD
LEONID M. BATKIN

1. See Ronald Suny's essay. —*Ed.*
2. This is a reference to the concerted opposition within the highest rungs of the party apparat to the transfer of Nagorno-Karabakh to Armenia. —*Ed.*
3. Alma Ata was the scene of riots in December 1986 when a Russian was named to replace a Kazakh as republican party secretary. Ethnic disturbances also took place about the same time in Yakutsk. In the autumn of 1988 Azerbaijanis staged a protest in Baku against Armenian claims to Nagorno-Karabakh. The demonstrators also protested against inadequate housing conditions for workers in Baku. —*Ed.*
4. The Soviet media reported on the Armenian-Azerbaijani conflict in an "even-handed" manner, thus in effect distorting the nature of the massacre in Sumgait, in which thirty Armenians lost their lives. The arrest of several Azeris after the riots in Baku was also to illustrate the government's "objectivity." —*Ed.*
5. The reference here is to Zia Mustafavich Buniatov, director of the Institute of the Peoples of the Near and Middle East, known for his animus towards Armenians. —*Ed.*
6. On 17 June 1989, a Russian People's Academy of Sciences (Rossiskaya Narodnaya Akademia Nauk) was established in Moscow. According to Tass (19 June), the aim of the academy is "to reveal more fully the scientific potential of Russia." —*Ed.*

POETRY IN THE AGE OF PERESTROIKA AND GLASNOST
NATALYA B. IVANOVA

1. *Neva*, 1988, no. 3.
2. Maksimilian Voloshin (1877–1932) was an anthroposophist and poet who has been called a "poetic chronicler" of the Revolution. In his poetry the Revolution is depicted as a fratricidal conflict Russian in both its nature and its historical roots, and as a necessary stage before the final emergence of an ideal spiritually cleansed Russia. —*Tr.*
3. Klyuyev was a "peasant" writer who borrowed much of his imagery from Russian religious sects to create a poetic myth of peasant Russia. —*Tr. Pogorelshchina* appeared in *Novy mir*, July, 1987. Some of his letters and documents appeared in *Novy mir*, 1988, no. 8.
4. The "Oberyuty" were a Dada-like group of poets in the 1920s; Velimir Khlebnikov (1885–1922) was famous for his linguistic inventiveness and his "transrational" language; Varlam Shalamov (1907–82) wrote, in addition to poetry, a large number of short narratives about the seventeen years he spent in Kolyma; until recently they were available only in samizdat and in editions published outside the Soviet Union. —*Tr.*
5. Boris Slutsky, a talented poet and one-time supporter of Stalin, published pseudonymously in 1960 what may be considered the first samizdat poems. For Russian and English texts as well as a commentary, see "Poems from the Underground" and "The Conscience of a Generation—A Commentary," by A. Zr., in A. Brumberg, ed., *Russia under Khrushchev* (New York: Praeger, 1962), pp. 408–40. —*Tr.*
6. Vladimir Kornilov, *Muzyka dlya sebya* (Moscow: 1988), p. 4.
7. Kornilov, *Nadezhda* (Moscow: 1988), p. 15.
8. "Svoboda" in Kornilov, *Muzyka*, pp. 18–19.
9. "Trofeiny film" in Kornilov, *Nadezhda*, p. 6.

10. Captured films with one of Hitler's favorite actresses, Marika Rokk, were shown after the end of the war. At that time the pogrom-like anti-Semitic campaign against "cosmopolitans" and the "Doctors' Plot" were going on in the Soviet Union.

11. L. Timofeyev, "Fenomen Voznesenskovo," *Novy mir*, 1989, no. 2. (Belinkov was a literary critic who spent several years in the GULAG and emigrated to the West in the early 1970s. —*Tr.*)

12. Boris Chichibabin, "Sklonyonnykh nebes tishina," *Druzhba narodov*, 1988, no. 4, p. 197.

13. Chichibabin, "Pamyati Tvardovskovo," *Druzhba narodov*, 1988, no. 4, p. 198.

14. Chichibabin, "Zashchita poeta," *Druzhba narodov*, 1988, no. 4, p. 199.

15. Chichibabin, "Stikhi o russkoi slovesnosti," *Druzhba narodov*, 1988, no. 4, p. 200.

16. Its editor, Vasili Aksyonov, also resigned from the Writers' Union after two of the *Metropol*'s contributors were expelled; the "Metropol Affair" was one of the reasons Aksyonov left the USSR in 1980. —*Tr.*

17. Inna Lisnyanskaya, "V gospitale litsevovo ranenia," *Druzhba narodov*, 1987, no. 1.

18. Valentin Rasputin is one of the "village prose" writers whose theme is the disappearance—from human as well as natural causes—of rural Russian life. In recent years Rasputin became prominently identified with the russophile and anti-Semitic notions of organizations such as Pamyat. —*Tr.*

19. Aleksandr Ostrovsky (1823–86) was one of the most popular playwrights of the late nineteenth century; his most famous play is *The Storm*. —*Tr.*

20. Lisnyanskaya, *Druzhba narodov*, 1989, no. 2, p. 108.

21. Lisnyanskaya, *Druzhba narodov*, 1988, no. 4.

22. Oleg Chukhontsev, *Druzhba narodov*, 1989, no. 1, p. 51.

23. Butyrki is a famous Moscow prison. The house Chukhontsev lived in at the time is not far from there.

24. Stalin called the prisoners "camp dust."

25. A large number of those repressed under Stalin were charged under various sections of Article 58, dealing with "counterrevolutionary" offenses. —*Tr.*

26. Solovki, a former monastery on an island in the White Sea, was a notorious place of detention for political prisoners; Magadan, equally notorious, was the capital and administrative center of the eastern Siberian part of the GULAG, five hundred kilometers north of the northernmost point of Sakhalin on the Sea of Okhotsk. —*Tr.*

27. Aleksandr Kushner, *Zhivaia izgorod* (Leningrad: 1988), p. 9.

28. Ibid., p. 13.

29. *Moscow News* is the name of one of the boldest newspapers and has become a symbol to readers of the changes taking place in the country.

30. Kushner, *Zhivaya izgorod*, p. 36.

31. Until recently, perestroika and glasnost were accurately seen as "a revolution from above" and "freedom granted from above." See N. Eidelman's analysis of analogous historical processes, " 'Revoliutsia sverkhu v Rossii," *Nauka i zhizn*, 1988, nos. 10–12. (Also see note 1 to the introduction of this volume. —*Ed.*)

32. Nonna Slepakova in *Novy mir*, 1988, no. 7, p. 28.

★

CONTRIBUTORS

☆

Abraham Brumberg is former editor of the bimonthly journal *Problems of Communism*. He has also edited *Poland: Genesis of a Revolution* (1983), *In Quest of Justice: Protest and Dissent in the Soviet Union Today* (1970) and *Russia Under Khrushchev* (1962). He frequently writes on Soviet and East European issues for *Foreign Affairs, Dissent,* the *New York Review of Books,* the *Economist,* and other American and British publications.

Leonid Batkin—historian, contributor to the monthlies *Nauka i zhizn* and *Vek XX i mir,* the weekly *Moscow News,* and other Soviet publications.

Julian Bromlei—for many years head of the Soviet Ethnographic Institute of the USSR Academy of Sciences, author of numerous works on ethnography and Soviet nationality policies.

Archie Brown—professor of politics at Oxford University and fellow of St. Antony's College, Oxford; author, editor, or co-author of nine volumes, the latest being *Political Leadership in the Soviet Union.*

William E. Butler—professor of Comparative Law of the University of London; director, Centre for the Study of Socialist Legal Systems, University College London; Dean of the Faculty of Laws, University of London; author of *Soviet Law* and other volumes; and special counsel to Leonid Abalkin, first deputy chairman, USSR Council of Ministers.

Yuri Davydov—specialist on Soviet foreign policy, member of the USA and Canada Institute, USSR Academy of Sciences.

Vera S. Dunham—emerita professor of Russian literature, Wayne State University and CUNY, associate of Columbia University's Harriman Institute, author of *In Stalin's Time* and other publications.

David Holloway—professor of political science at Stanford University. Author of *The Soviet Union and the Arms Race* (1983) and other works on Soviet policy and US-Soviet relations.

Natalya Ivanova—literary critic; poetry editor of the monthly *Druzhba narodov.*

Boris Kurashvili—professor of political science; corresponding member of the Institute of State and Law, USSR Academy of Sciences.

Otto Latsis—economist; deputy editor of the monthly *Kommunist.*

Roy Medvedev—historian; author of *Let History Judge, On Socialist Democracy,* and many other volumes; member of the Supreme Soviet of the USSR.

Sergo Mikoyan—expert on Latin America; editor of the monthly *Latinskaya Amerika.*

Alec Nove—emeritus professor of economics, University of Glasgow; author of *The Soviet Economy, Economic History of the USSR, Stalinism and After, Glasnost in Action,* and other volumes.

Gavriil Popov—economist and political scientist; editor of the monthly *Voprosy ekonomiki;* member of Congress of People's Deputies.

Jutta Scherrer—professor of Russian history at the École des Hautes Études en Sciences Sociales, Paris, and visiting professor at the Harriman Institute at Columbia University, New York.

S. Frederick Starr—president of Oberlin College; founding secretary of the Kennan Institute for Advanced Russian Studies.

Ronald Grigor Suny—Alex Manoogian Professor of Modern Armenian History, University of Michigan; author of *The Baku Commune, 1917–1918*, *Armenia in the Twentieth Century*, *The Making of the Georgian Nation*, editor of *Transcaucasia, Nationalism and Social Change*, and other works.

Aleksandr Vaksberg—legal correspondent of the weekly *Literaturnaya gazeta*; author and playwright.

INDEX